Folk Culture of

The Misings of Assam

– Tradition and Change –

In memoriam of my father

Late Radha Sarma

Folk Culture of

The Misings of Assam

– Tradition and Change –

Ashok Sarma

Decent Books
New Delhi

Cataloging in Publication Data — DK
[Courtesy: D.K. Agencies (P) Ltd. <docinfo@dkagencies.com>]

Sarma, Ashok, 1960-
Folk culture of the Misings of Assam: tradition and change / Ashok Sarma.
p. 25 cm.
Includes bibliographical references (p.)
Includes index.
ISBN 8186921273

1. Miri (Indic people) — India — Assam — Folklore. 2. Miri (Indic people) — India — Assam — Social life and customs. I. Title.

DDC 398.095 416 2 21

ISBN 81-86921-27-3
First Published in India in 2004

Published and printed by:
Decent Books
D-36/A-1, Mohan Garden
Najafgarh Road
New Delhi - 110 059
Ph. (011) 2535-3435

Distributed by:
D.K. Printworld (P) Ltd.
Regd. office : *'Sri Kunj,'* F-52, Bali Nagar
New Delhi - 110 015
Phones : (011) 2545-3975, 2546-6019; *Fax* : (011) 2546-5926
E-mail : dkprintworld@vsnl.net
Web : www.dkprintworld.com

Preface

EVERY ethnic group of Assam is culturally rich and the cultural items of each group are quite distinct. The Mising, a well-known community of Mongoloid stock linguistically belonging to the Indo-Tebeto-Burman language family is an important ethnic group of Assam. The Misings are riverine people and their culture, particularly folklore is distict and colourful.

I am fascinated to take up a cultural study of the Mising tribe of Assam as I have been closely associated with them since my childhood. In the rapidly changing world their culture, however, rigorous and colourful, gradually gives away before the impact of modernity.

In this research work, I have tried my best to give a true picture of the folk culture of the Misings which are still existing in the area of my study. The purpose of the study is to focus the artistic skills of the tribal folk, their love for the traditions and the trend of change in the society.

I express my profound sense of gratitude to my reverend teacher Dr. N.C. Sarma, Retd. Head of Dept. of Folklore Research Gauhati University for giving me a chance to work in this field of study. His parent-like guidance and constant encourangement in preparation of this research has enabled me to overcome many difficulties.

In the course of investigation and collection of information for this work, I got the opportunity to visit a number of Mising villages of upper Assam. The people of these villages were kind enough to furnish the required information. I express my deep sense of gratitute to them.

I am thankful to the staff of K.K. Handique Library of Gauhati University; the District Library of Jorhat and the Assam Institute of Research for S.C. and S.T.

Khanapara for their co-operation in consulting various relevant books in their libraries.

I wish to express my gratitude to all those scholars whose works have been a source of inspiration to me.

I shall be happy if I could make a small contribution to the knowledge of the existing folk culture of the area which has been neglected despite its growing importance and relevance in national integration.

I sincerely believe that the study will definitely help folklorists, anthropologists, administrators, planners and general readers.

14 April, 2004 **Ashok Sarma**

Contents

List of Plates, Figures, Maps and Tables

Plates

Figures

Maps

Tables

Abbreviations

IORTSC	:	Institute of Research for Tribals and Scheduled Caste
MAK	:	*Mising Agom Kebang*
MSA	:	*Mising Sanskritir Alekhya*
MTHC	:	*Misings, their History and culture*

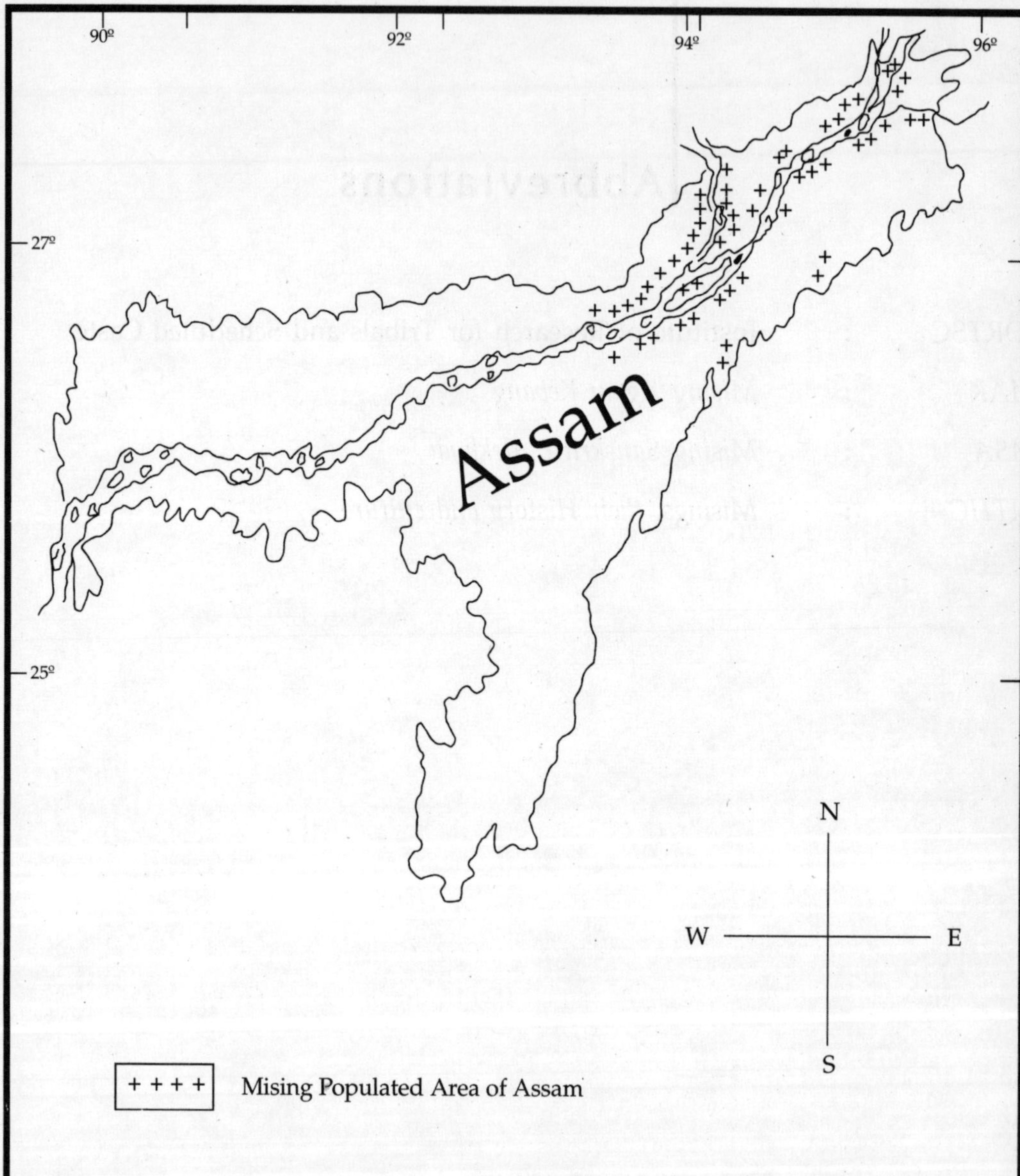

***Map.* 1. Mising populated areas of Assam**

Chapter 1

Introduction

Land and the People of the Study

ASSAM is one of the States of Indian sub-continent and is located in the north-east corner of the country. It extends from 24° N to 28° N latitude and 49.8° E to 96° E longitude. Assam is bounded by Bhutan and Arunachal Pradesh on the north; Meghalaya, Tripura, Mizoram on the south; Manipur, Nagaland in the east and West Bengal, Meghalaya and Bangladesh on the west. Topographically it can be divided into three distinct zones, namely: the Brahamputra Valley in the north; the Karbi-Anglong and North Cachar Hills in the middle and the Barak Valley in the south. The long and narrow Brahamputra Valley stretches across the state from east to west. The plain zone is starting from the Tinsukia and Dhamaji districts in the east to the Goalpara in the west covering the vast area of 56194 km^2.

The Barak Valley lies on the southern side and it is fertiled by the river Barak and its tributaries. It covers an area of 6922 km^2.

In between the two valleys, there lies the Karbi plateau and the North Cachar Hills. The average height of this plateau is 300 to 400 m. The highest peak is known as Singhasana which is about 1360 m. This two hill districts covering an area of 15322 km^2. The soil of the two valleys is alluvial and the hill areas are red and acidic. The total area of the State is 78,438 km^2.

Mineral Resources

Petroleum, natural gas, coal and lime stone are the important mineral resources of the state. Assam possesses valuable deposites of coal and iron and smelting of these ores has been an important industry. Earth quakes are also of frequent occurrence of this region.

Climate

Assam has a tropical climate. The monsoon starts here generally from mid-May and continues up to September. The winter season begins from the mid-October and continues up to the month of March. The summer days are quite hot while the winter days are sufficiently cool. Humidity is high in summer season than the winter. Annual rainfall is from 40" to 60" (100-50 cm). Most of the rainfalls pours down during the four months from June to September and the rain during April to May is rather low. Strong winds blow from the south-west during February and March.

Flora and Fauna

Assam is known for her rich forest wealth with varieties of flora and fauna. Sub-tropical evergreen forests are found in the whole region. The total area under forest in Assam was 21.52 lakh Ha. at the end of March, 1994, out of which area under reserved forests was 17.58 lakh Ha. Thus the area under reserve forest constitute about 22.40 per cent of the total geographical area of Assam.[1] In the early decades of the twentieth century, there was much denudation of forests. In these forest zones grows enormous number of vegetation species. Timber, bamboo, cane, grass, gum, lac and medicinal herbs are such forest products. The soil of the state is suitable for growing cotton, silk, coffee, sugar cane and tea. Like the flora, the deeply wooded terrains of Assam are no less rich in fauna. One of the most attractive feature of the State's forest sector is its colourful wildlife comprising variety of animals, birds and fishes. Some of the species found in the State are either exclusive to her or are rarely to be seen in any other part of the country. In this connection mention may be made of species like the hoolock gibbon, the stump-tailed macaque, the golden langur monkeys, the pigmy hog, the clouded leopard, the golden cat, the white-winged wood-duck, etc. Among the greatest varieties of wildlife, one horned rhinoceros, tiger, wild elephant, sambur, bear, barking deer, leopard, wild elephant, smbur, bear, barking deer, leopard, wild buffalo, musk deer, wild goat etc., are common. During the winter season, the region also receives visits by migratory birds from the Northern Asia.

People of the Study

Assam has a very ancient civilization. Situated in "one of the great migration routes of mankind" the region of north-east India, ones forming the greatest State

1. Director of Economic and Statistics, *Assam — Economic Survey*, Assam, 1996-97, p. 24.

of Assam, forms a museum of races. People of different races and cultures have come to this part of the country and contributed to the formation and enrichment of the local culture throughout the centuries.[2] Assam is a meeting point of colourful tribes consisting tribes consisting of both hills and plains tribes having different ethnic and linguistic background. Among the plain tribes of the region, the Misings occupied a significant position, being the second largest group with a population of 259,551 as recorded in 1971 census. In remote past, eastern part of the sub-Himālayan range of mountainous region especially the Siang Valley of present Arunachal Pradesh was the homeland of the Misings. The Misings were formerly referred to as Miri in religious scriptures, ethnographies. Ahom chronicles and government records till very recent times. They have been living mostly along the banks of the river Brahmaputra and its tributaries for which they are called riverine people. They now spread over wide range of the plains of Assam and are found in the districts of north Lakhimpur, Dhemaji, Jorhat, Sibsagar, Golaghat, Dibrugarh, Sonitpur and Tinsukia. These districts are situated on the eastern part of Assam bounded by Arunachal Pradesh and Nagaland.

The Misings belong to the Tibeto-Burman language speaking group of the great Mongoloids. They present very attractive varieties of material culture, such as spinning, weaving, basketry, cane and wood works which have been known to the tribe for quite a long time. The Mising people of the region have an excellent taste in colour and remarkable skill in diverging patterns. Their handiworks show high standard of technical perfection. They are self-sufficient for centuries with their home products. It is seen that the Mising folk is gradually assimilating themselves with other indigenous people of the plains of Assam and their culture.

Aim of the Study

The Misings of the plains of Assam carried some distinctive artistic skills in making their useful articles, art, craft, costumes, cookery and architecture. But no systematic study or research has been done on this topic.

The aim of the present study is to collect elaborate data on the material culture of the Mising society. Moreover, the present study attempts to analyse the changes in the field of material culture due to various factors.

Scope of the Study

The present study is confined only to the systematic study of the material culture

2. D. Nath,"The Misings in the History of Assam" in the *MTHC*, ed. J.J Kuli, p. 1.

of the Mising people of Assam. This study includes various aspects of material culture of the Misings, such as folk art, folk craft, folk architecture and folk cookery. The study has tried to show that the Mising people are expert in both folk craft and folk art. Besides they give more emphasis on the pleasure giving aspects in the context of folk art. The Mising weavers can web artistic ideas in their various designs of clothes. The women folk may show their distinctiveness in this respect. Furthermore the building process and style of various houses founded in the field seemed to be significant since such types of houses are rare among other tribes of Assam.

The various dimensions of the material culture of the Mising including their raw materials, making processes, style of those artefacts, their domestic utility and their aesthetic appeal have fully been discussed keeping in view the historical and comparative aspects of the topic. As such the study is based on the historical and comparative methods.

Emphasis has been given to the changes that have taken place in various aspects of material culture of the villager's life.

Objectives and significance of the Study

The importance of the study of material culture of the Misings of Assam is great from the point of view of both Assam and India. Such study will reveal truth and provide historic continuity, cultural progress, skill and needs of the folk. The Mising folk culture is a part and parcel of the Mongoloid culture which has influenced to some extent the indo-Aryan culture and vice versa. So the folklore studies may helps to strengthen a cultural relationship between the tribal and non-tribal forms of the region. Thus the scientific study and analysis will also pave the way for national development and emotional integration in our independent India.

There is also potential dynamism in folklore. The tradional life and folk culture are being eroded day by day due to the advancement of modernity and urbanization. Folklorists have always been warning that folklore items are disappearing without leaving any trace behind. This warning is relevant to material culture of the Misings also. A scientific study of the cultural heritage and socio-economic conditions is and imperative necessity with a view to formulating plans and programmes for the future development of the community.

Methodology of the Study

INTERVIEW METHOD

I have met a number of representatives of the villages belonging to the area under investigation. The purpose of this interview is two-fold: (i) Securing certain information on the subjects under study, and (ii) to obtain in picture of present position, appreciation and transition of folk material culture.

PARTICIPATION METHOD

During my field survey, I have met some of the folk artisans personally for first hand knowledge of the subject.

I hope the oral introduction of the village folk. Photographs of the specimens, observation of the working process of the folk artisans have certainely helped me in studying their material culture.

LITERARY WORKS

I have essentially applied the method of descriptive analysis which is elaborately exemplified in a good number of books written by the folklorists and social scientists.

I also take the help of a number of selected published journals, gazetteers, census reports, bulletins and a good number of research papers on different aspects of folk culture.

INFORMATION FROM THE INFORMANTS

I have kept constant connection with my chief informants.

I have tried my best to present a true and authentic description of the folk material culture of the Misings of Assam with my available equipments in the light of the knowledge gathered from fieldworks as well as theoretical training. As there is no written history of the Misings and their culture therefore most of the information is taken from the widely prevalent oral history.

The designs on craft works, housing, cooking ánd artistic works are described here with personal observations during the field study.

Fieldwork

With a view to getting an indepth insight in the material culture at micro level, field study has been carried out in twelve Mising villages located in five different districts of Assam. The following villages are chosen for intensive survey.

Sl. No.	Name of the village	District	Total families
1.	Bahphala village	Jorhat	120
2.	Gondhia Mising Gaon	Jorhat	72
3.	Bodoti Dohghoria Gaon	Lakhimpur	40
4.	Bokakhat Bohikhowa	Golaghat	65
5.	Jengrai Mukh	Jorhat (Majuli)	
6.	Ratanpur	Jorhat (Majuli)	65
7.	Kamalabari Dhopak Gaon	Jorhat (Majuli)	47
8.	Dikhowmukh Jan Missing Borgaon	Sibsagar	35
9.	Jonai	Dhemaji	100
10.	Gogamukh	Dhemaji	100
11.	Vekuri Chapori (Dehing Mukh)	Sibsagar	60
12.	Disangmukh	Sibsagar	55

CASE STUDIES

Some case studies are taken to provide concrete examples in suitable fields that are practised in contemporary Mising society.

Apart from these techniques a camera was used during the fieldwork to illustrate the specimens.

Organization of the Study

The study is divided into ten chapters.

In the introductory chapter a short description of geography, land and people, their history, aim, scope and methodology of the study is given.

The second chapter deals with an introduction of the Mising tribe of Assam-their origin, migration, clans, religion and festivals, marriage, birth and death rites, laws of inheritance, dialect, folk literature and economic profile.

The third chapter deals with a general study of material culture and its classification. It is a general discussion of physical folklore (material culture).

The fourth, fifth, sixth, seventh and eighth chapters discuss the folk art, folk architecture, folk cookery and folk costumes of the Misings of Assam respectively.

Chapter 9 is related to the trends of change in various fields of material culture of the Mising folk in recent years. This chapter envisages the recent changes taking place due to the impact of urbanization and modernization on the Mising society of Assam.

The conclusion drawn on the study has been presented in chapter 10.

Chapter 2

The Misings of Assam
An Introductory Survey

THE Mising are the second largest tribe in the plains of Assam. As per 1971 census report the total population of the Mising in Assam was 259551 and they constitude the 1.77 per cent of the total State population and 16.31 per cent of the total plains and hills tribe population and 19.31 per cent of the total scheduled tribe population (plains) of Assam.

Habitat and Geographical Distribution

At present, the Mising people are distributed throughout all the districts of upper Assam. The riverine areas of the northern and southern banks of the Brahamputra stretching from Sodia in the east, down to the Jia Bhoroli in the west lying approximately between 93° E and 97° E longitude and 27° N and 28° N latitude may be regarded as the areas of habitation of the Misings.

The Misings are originally a hill tribe who inhabited the Abor, Miri and Mishimi hills in Arunachal Pradesh. Arunachal Pradesh, formerly known as NEFA (North-East Froniter Agency) cover an area of roughly 33,000 square miles of wild mountains.

> This area is the home of at least 25 distinct tribes, who have an extraordinary divergence of culture, language, dress and customs. These tribes have similarity in some cases like agricultural techniques, housing, practice of human care, lack of indigenous script, tendency to remain isolated and seek security in clan tribal compositions.[1]

1. P. Chaliha, *The Outlook on NEFA*, pp. 1-2.

The Mising of Assam have much similarity in respect of language, customs, dress, and physical status with the Adi of Abor tribes of Arunachal Pradesh. According to Mackenzie "the Abors and Miris belong to the same habitat and they are still alike in all material aspects."[2]

Origin of the word "Miri" and Mising

The Misings are called Miri by the plains men of Assam. The origin of the word "Miri" is shrouded in mystery. There are a lot of opinions among the scholars about the origin of the word Miri.

"The Abors of Arunachal Pradesh called their Priest Miri or Mirin. It is probably the non-tribal people of Assam who called the tribe as Miri after they came into contact with the Priest."[3] Some writers observe that the word Miri is derived from the term "Mienrient" which is a part of Abor hills. The plains people being unable to follow the correct pronunciation simplified it to Miri.[4]

According to E.W. Gait, the word "Miri" means "middle man" or "go between". They work as middle man between hills and plains and carry out the business.[5]

Gunaviram Boruah in his "Asom Buranji" mentions that the word "Miri" is derived from "Mikir," "Sakhamig," or Mokott.

In Arunachal Pradesh there is another tribe known as Hill Miri or Porbotia Miri, but they have no cultural similarity with the Misings of the plains of Assam. Probably, observing the similar behaviours and lifestyle with the Misings, the plain people of Assam called them Hill Miri.

We can conclude therefore that the word Miri has been derived from the Mising word Miro which stands for Priest of the tribe. Throughout the Assamese literature and historical records (Buronjis) we find the use of the word Miri.

The word Miri is also used in the devotional songs of Sri Sankardeva, the great Vaishnava scholar of the fifteenth century in Assam. Thus Horibuli tore Miri, Ahom, Kochari.[6]

---

2. A. Mackenzie, *The History of North-East Fronitier of Bengal*, pp. 33, 36.
3. J. Mipun, *The Misings of Assam, Development of a New Lifestyle*, p. 17.
4. G.C. Thakur Sarma, *The Plain Tribes of Lakhimpur, Sibsagar and Nagoan*, p. 2.
5. E.W. Gait, *A History of Assam*, p. 373.
6. N. Pegu, *The Misings of Brahmaputra Valley*, p. 19.

R.P. Srivastava observed that before coming down to the plains of Assam, the Miris or the Misings called themselves Ami or Tani meaning "man."[7]

The tribe called themselves Mising which means "good people". *Mi* (man), *yashing* (bright or good) which means "we are good or bright people". In other words *mi* (man), *ansing* (calm or peace loving). Srivastava observes that the word Miri derives from Mirien, which means "man like real god". All these imply that they are peace loving people. They call the other people Mipag which means people who are not included in their community.

Migration

The Misings have no written history. As such we have to depend on the oral traditions current among them to know their origin and migration. The origin of the tribe has been discussed by many writers, but it has not yet been satisfactorily answered. No definite account can be made about the migration of the Misings to the plains. History of their migration to the plains still remains obscure.

The earliest migration of the Misings started in different batches of migration and they brought certain traits of culture from their ancient abode in the east.

British Officer Col. F. Jenkins mentions in his letter to A.J.M. Mill, dated the 4 June, 1853, about the tribes of Assam. Which goes thus —

> Miris and Abors are kindred tribes and more or less intermixed in the hills extending from Luckimpoor (Lakhimpur) to Dibing. The Abor generally occupy a jurisdiction over the latter, whether in the hills or on the plains. From the Persecution of the Abors arising throughout Upper and Central Assam is small clans in the midst of jungle, mostly along the banks of the great rivers and their tributaries. The Miris near Lakhimpur are not mixed with the Abors, and the Abors beyond the Dibang and up to the Dibong are with the former exchanging the products of the plains for canoes and large timbers.[8]

W.W. Hunter observed that the Misings are semi-barbarous people whose original home appears to be the low hills north of Lakhimpur, whence they spread in large number through upper Assam. Their language is similar to that of the Adis

7. R.P. Srivastava, *Impact of Community Development and Cultural Change Among The Mising of Assam* (Project Report, Dibrugarh Univeristy, 1972), Introduction.
8. A.J.M. Mill, *Report on the Province of Assam*, p. 215.

and they are supposed to be an offshoot of that tribe. Indeed, the Adis look upon the Misings as their dependants, and used to demand a heavy tribute from them, to escape which, the Misings migrated to the plains of Assam.[9]

LEGENDS RELATED TO MIGRATION

There exist some legends among the Misings which are transmitted through generations. We can accept them as folk history which are related to migration of the tribe from hills to the Brahmaputra Valley. Some clue regarding their migration can determine from careful analysis of such popular stories. Some of such stories are mentioned below.

How the Miri came to the Valley?

Myong, an old widow had two sons named Eyekong and Kobba. They were expert craftsmen having different types of weapons. The people of other clans were jealous and they planned to kill the two brothers. One night a group of wicked people attacked them. Myong was a brave woman. she mixed some chilli powder with water and threw at the eyes of the enemies and fled away from the village with her two sons. They finally came down to the plains of Assam.[10]

Another such myth states that there was a Miri village called Damro in which a beautiful and expert weaver Turi lived. Turi's father, at her marriagable age declared that he wanted an expert in athletic events as his son-in-law. Hearing his declaration a young athlete of Miyong village name Moyoung came to visit the Damro village and defeated all the youths of the village in athletic events.

The father of Turi was pleased with this young man and fixed the marriage with him. This was an insult for the young men of the Damro village and they made a wicked plan to kill Moyoung. They arranged a feast on the very day when the young couple visited their village. They threw Moyoung into a river binding his hands and feet. Turi also jump into the river with her husband.

The villagers of Miyoung became angry with Damro hearing the incident. They tried to take action against the members of the Damro village. One day the villagers of Miyoung arranged a great feast and invited all the members of the Damro village. The youths of the Damro village suspected conspiracy and they did not attend the feast except a few. The participants of the feast were murdered

9. W.W. Hunter, *A Statistical Accounts of Assam*, p. 239.

10. T.C. Pamegum, *Mising Sadhu*, pp. 28-29.

by the people on the spot. One man escaped and he informed his villagers. The villagers of Miyoung were comparatively smaller in number than that of the Damro village. So they fled towards the plains and finally they settled in plains of Assam.

It is worth mentioning that the Misings migrated to the plains due to increasing fragmentation of land holding, ecological crisis caused by intense cultivation and chronic deficit in food production in the hill areas. The geographical situation of hill areas also made the livelihood of the Misings very difficult and intolerable by unfriendly topography interated by mountainous passes and rivers.[11]

They perhaps migrated towards the plains due to pressure of population. They converted the wasteland of the Brahmaputra Valley and small forests in some places into agricultural lands.

Thus the Mising people belonging to one of the earliest groups of races migrated of the Brahmaputra Valley and their migration started before the advent of the Ahoms. E.W. Gait observed that the Misings had their first contact with the Ahom king Pratap Singha in 1615.

Now they have been maintaining close relation with the other tribes and non-tribes of Assam and made substantial contribution to the evolution of culture of this land. Their culture is influenced to some extent by their natural envionment and neighbouring plains men of Assam.

Clans and Sub-Clans (Opin)

The Mising belongs to the Tibeto-Burman family of the Mongoloid group. It is found that the Misings are divided into two exclusive sections which are known as Barogum and Dahgum. According to an oral account the tribe had migrated to the plains in two different groups. One under twelve chieftains and the other under ten chieftains. Accordingly they were called Barogum and Dahgum.

Barogum has a number of clans, such as Doley, Kutum, Kuli, Patir, Basar and Pasar. Similary Dahgum has the clans like Taye, Pamegum, Bori, Pawo, Panging, Noro, Koma, Maying, etc.[12]

Another source gives the sub-divisions of the tribe in as a different way. Here the whole Mising tribe is divided into three gotras. Such as — (i) Sobo

11. J. Doley, *The Misings* — In retrospect (Souvenir, MAK-1999), p. 47.
12. B. Das, *Goalpara Jila Samaj Aru Sanskriti* (As.) p. 27 (Janajatir Vivah).

(Doley), (ii) Kander (Pegu) and (iii) Bomi.[13] The Sobo or Doley *gotra* has four sub divisions like Lasum, Lodong, Gajara and Patir. The Kander *gotra* has also four sections such as *Gupit, Godong, Kari,* and *Lagasu.*

Likewise the Bomi *gotra* has five sub-sections which are Pama, Mili, Kaman, Payun, Payang. Depending upon the place of dwelling, the Misings are divided into eight *khels* such as — Shayangia, Mayingia, Dolu, Pagor, Dambuk, Samoguria and Tamar.

It is said that different groups were migrated at different times and they frequently changed their dwelling places in the plains. The groups who once migrated up to the river Bhorolee and later came back to the Sovensiri Valley were called Salat (means come back). Hence they were called Shayangia. The groups who settled on the southern bank of the river Brahmaputra were known as Dola (means south). The section of the tribe who settled in a narrow place of Moying were called Moyingia.[14]

According to one of my very experienced informant Sree Sowana Pegu (76) the Dahgum section are called Mayangia and the Barogum section is called Pegroo. A few clans are found to be created due to the contact with the Ahoms, Chutia and Bhuyan community in the past.

Some writers are of the opinion that the Misings who came down through the Chutia Kingdom of Sodia were known as Sodial Miri or Chutia Miri.[15]

The Ahom Kings selected some eligible Mising members and offered them administrative posts like Miri Borua, Miri Handique etc. The Barua Pegu of Dhemaji, Samuas of Namsai and Patgris of Lohitmukh areas have similar historical past and maintains their titles offered by the Ahom kings with much pride.[16] The Mising clans are derived from the names of their forefathers. Generally, they used the surnames of their paternal side after their given names. Hence surname is regarded as clan name among the Misings.

Customs Relating to clan organization

The family members accept the name of the forefather or an imaginary deity as

13. T.C. Pamegum, *Miri ba Mising;* in (*MSA*), pp. 40-41.
14. *Ibid.*
15. L. Devi, *Ahom Tribal Relation,* p. 157.
16. N. Pegu, *The Misings of Brahmaputra Valley,* p. 56.

clan. The boys belong to their father's clan whereas the daughters after marriage accept the clans of their husbands. No person is allowed to perform death ritual of his parents or any other important ritual who dwells in other's clan except his own. It is believed that if a person accepts any other clan he cannot prosper and his family cannot increase. Such a person loses the right to his father's property.

If a child is born in the house of other clan except his own, the child is to be purified socially. Marriage relationship with the same clan is prohibited.

If a Mising girl marries a man whose clan is unidentified, both of them will be excommunicated from the Mising Society. A non-Mising can enter into a Mising clan through certain ritual of purification.

Society

Almost 90 per cent of the Mising villages are situated on the river banks. A village may consist of twenty to hundred or more houses built generally on two sides of the village road. Generally, it is seen that several families built their houses on the same countyard very closely. The village headman is called *gum* or *goanburah* who discussed and solved the problems of the villagers. *Gum* is an experienced elderly person who has enough knowledge on tribal lore. He is selected on the basis of qualities. The democratic village council common in each village is called *kabang* in which social problems are solved. It has jurisdiction over its own village at micro-level. The aged men and the heads of the families can join in the *kabang*, for discussion. Before the British rule, the *kabang* was of three stages, viz — (i) the smallest village council under the *gum* is called *kabang*: (ii) the aggregate of several *kabang*s is called *bana-kabang* and (iii) the aggregation of several *bana-kabang*s is called *bango-kabang*. These *kabang*s discuss and solve the local and regional conflicts and problems.

In bye-gone days, there were bachelor's dormitory separately for boys and girls. The young unmarried boys learn the art and craft in their respective dormitories. It was a place of training, learning and socialization. It was the duty of the youth in those days to protect the village from outsiders at night Bachelor's dormitory for boys is called *murong* amd for girls is called *resang*. In our times the *resang* has been abolished and the *murong* is active in the form of a youth club. The annual festivals like *Ali-ave-ligang, Porag,* etc., are performed in the *murong* of the village. In the pre-British period, the *kabang* was led by the elders like other traditional Indian societies. They were the exponents and custodians of the traditional laws and customs and in that capacity judged the activities of the members and directed the general affairs. The decisions of the *kabang* were not binding and enforced. But it is equally true that the society members showed obedience to the *kabang*'s order or decisions. The members of the *kabang* enjoyed a kind of status which was more psychological than material. *Gum* was the capable captain of the village wielding power, maintaining discipline and guiding to controlling and directing all other affairs. In the British period, the village community came gradually under the administrative control and the gumship became dependent on the British administration.

In traditional societies, most of the works are done on family basis or with hired assistance. There is however a tradition of co-operative labour within the community which cuts across the lines of kinship and clan. Such voluntary help is undertaken when someone announces that he needs help in carrying out a task. Co-operative labour is required in case of constructing a new house, agricultural works and on festive occasions. After the work has been completed the host serves some refreshments but no formal obligation to repay is incurred. Village properties like road, water supply, wells are repaired co-operatively when condition demands.

There is a benevolent organisation of the young men and women in a Mising village called *Mimbir Yama*. The members of the *Mimbir Yama* render helps to any villager in need.

FAMILY

The basic residential, social, religious and economic unit is the patriarchal extended family. No person thinks himself apart from the family. A Mising family consists of parents and children as the smallest unit. Joint family system under the same authority is common in Mising villages. It is found that 70 per cent of the families are living as a joint family system and 30 per cent are nuclear families. Properties like land, livestock, food staff, house and forest trees are held jointly by the family. Family is a close unit in which children respect their elders. Father exercises authority over the entire family. In the joint family system, the headman is the person in whom a family has absolute confidence for the discharge of managerial responsibility in all social functions. The wife of the eldest male is the head of the female components of the household in domestic matters. She becomes the titular head of the house hold upon her husband's death if there is no brother to take over, but generally a son acts in her stead.

The Mising folk constitute patrilineal society and the descent is traced from the father's side. The tasks of management of the family, chiefsmanship and priesthood are given to males. Women take part in agriculture and management of family equally with the male members. The main job of the women is to spin and weave clothes for the family. Nowadays educated ladies take part in government or semi-goverment services. All members share the family occupation and the products obtained. All eat from the same cooking hearth.

POSITION OF WOMEN IN SOCIO-ECONOMIC LIFE

The women among the Misings have a role in all economic and income generating activities as well as in social functions and ritual matters. But they have generally a lower status and only a few among them have decision-making powers.

The women-folk cook and take care of their children. Besides they carry water from nearby river or pond necessary for the entire members of the family as well as domestic animals and so forth. They brew rice beer, and do weaving at home. They collect fodder for animals, take part in weeding crops, harvesting and threshing. They are also expert in swimming and rowing. Thus the women are equal partners of their male counterparts in all outdoor activities. Women folk contributes to all the functions of the agricultural activity except ploughing. Otherwise, the family may not remian strong without the sincere co-operation of their women. She shares her husband's sorrows and troubles and as a mother, she gets immense respect from her sons and daughters-in-law.

Kinship

It is found that father's elder brothers and father's younger brothers are regarded as *babatta* or *baboi* or *apang*.

Similarly father's elder brother's wife and younger brother's wife are called *aoatta* and *nanoi* respectively. The elder sister of the father is regarded as *aben nyanyi* and her husband as *kake*. Father and mother are regarded as *abu* and *ane*.

The elder brother and his wife are called *abhinebero* and *memo*, similarly the younger brother and his wife are called *amenbero* and *yigne*. The elder sister and her husband are called *abinbirme* and *magbo*. The younger sister and her husband are called *amenbirme* and *vigo* respectively.

The term *yameng* is used for son's wife, elder brother's son's wife and younger brother's son's wife. Son and daughter are termed as *ao* and *ome*. Daughter's husband is termed as *dune magbo*. Son's son and daughter's son are termed as *ao* and *eo* respectively. The daughter of the son is called *ome*.

The table given below illustrates he kinship terms in the Mising language.

Table 2.1: Kinship of the Misings

Father's side		Mother's side and wife side	
Relation	Mising terms	Relation	Mising terms
Fa. Fa. Father	Taku tata	Mo. Fa. Fa.	Taku tata
Fa. Fa. Mother	Taku yayo	Mo. Fa. Mo.	Taku yayo
Fa. Father	Tako	Mo. Fa.	Tako
Fa. Mother	yayo	Mo. Mo.	Yayo
Father	Abu	Mother	Are
Fa. el. br.	Babotta	Mother's el. br.	Abine Kake
Fa. el. br. wife	Aoatta	Mo. el. br. wife	Nayanyi
Fa. el. sister	Aben Nayanki	Mo. el. sister	Oatta
Fa. el. si. hus	Kake	—	Kake
Fa. yo. sister	Amen Nyanyi	Mo. yr. sister	Owoi
Fa. yo. si. hus.	Kake	—	Kake
Fa. yo. brother	Baboi	Mo. yr. br.	Amen Kake
Fa. yo. br. wife	Nanoi	Mo. yr. br. wife	Nyanyi
Elder brother	Abine bero	W. el. brother	Magbo
El. br. wife	Mamo	W. el. br. wife	Birme
Younger br.	Amen bero	W. el. br.	Yigo
Yo. br. wife	Yigne/Yamang	W. y. br. wife	Yigne
Elder Sister	Abine birma	W. el. sister	Amo/Memo
El. si. hus.	Magbo	W. el. si. hus.	Alpoti
Yr. sister	Amen birme	W. yr. sister	Yigne
Yr. si. hus.	Yigo	W. yr. si. hus.	Yigo
Husband	Ego		
Wife	Neng/Egna		
Son	Ao		
Daughter	Ome		

Abbreviations:

Fa. - Father	Mo. - Mother	Br./br. - Brother	Si./si. - Sister
Hus/hus. - Husband	El./el. - Elder	Yr. - Younger	W. - Wife

OBLIGATION AND RESPECTS

In the Mising society, the family members show their respects to the family head and seniors. After the death of a senior they show their respect by death rituals and by other social activities.

Marriage

Marriage is the starting point of conjugal life. In the Mising society marriage could be performed after attaining the maturity of both the sexes. It is only after marriage that a Mising is considered to be a full-fledged member of the tribe. Marriages are held through the age-old customs even today. There exist two types of marriage system among the Misings. The formal marriage is called *midang* and the other is called *mogob-dugnem* or *dugalanam*. Child marriage is obsolete and widow remarriage exists. Marriage between boys and girls of same clan is prohibited. Marriage of one's mother's sister's son or daughter is retricted because they are like brothers and sisters. Similarly one cannot marry his or her uncle's son or daughter's on both father's and mother's side. Marriage with a non-Mising boy or girl is not allowed. Marriage within kinsmen of prohibitive degree is considered illegitimate. A married woman while her husband is alive cannot marry an other person. Polygamy is allowed but rare. In such case wives live in separate rooms in the same house. The first wife enjoys the highest position among others. Widow can re-marry the younger brother of her husband. In any case she cannot marry the father or elder brother or the uncle of her departed husband. If the widow returns to her father's house, she can marry astranger. In such a case she forfeits the ownership of property belonging to the former husband.

MARRIAGE PROCESS

As is already mentioned, the formal marriage is called *midang*, which means "taken away man" (*mi*-man; *dang*-taking away). Marriageable boys and girls select their life partners before their life partner before their marriage. There is ample freedom in choice of their life partners which is called *kaligosunom*. In such case, an elderly person, generally the father of the boy, goes to the parents of the girl or to her nearest relatives and submit a proposal for marriage. It is called *ymmotadnam*. Here the bride's side offers a bundle of *akum* containing betelenuts (areca) to the guardian of the groom. Then the girl's father or elder brother or mother (if father is dead) takes over the matter and if they agree, they accept the proposal and both the parties talk over the matter.[17]

---

17. D. Regon, *Mising Bibah Paddhati* (in *MSA*), pp. 281-82, 289.

According to the tradition, the boy has to work for some days at his father-in-law's house before marriage which is called *magob-duglum*. Nowadays, such practices are rare or obsolete. In final fixation of marriage the boys side has to pay *arooakum* which contain *poro apong* (rice beer) dried fish and areca to the grooms family. This event is called *tadpin*. The marriage is performed according to the Hindu form of marriage but no *homa* sacrifice is observed.

The women-folk singing folk songs called *midangnitiom* which express the sadness of the bride who leaves her own house and enters a new house of her life partner. The songs express the beauty of the bride and also contain various martiful expressions.[18] The villagers and the guests are dined and wined on the marriage day with meat and rice beer.

DUGLA-LANAM FORM OF MARRIAGE

The formal marriage process (as described above) is quite expensive. The poor boys and girls who cannot afford to meet the cost of a formal marriage follow the *dugla-lanam* form which seems to be most popular. It can be called *gandharba* form of marriage in which the interested boy who decides to get married takes away the girl with her support and the marriage would be formalized by the villagers in certain process. The elders or relatives of both the sides have no role before such abduction but they take important part in formalizing the marriage later.

On the third day of such abduction of the girl, massenger or relative from the boy's side is to be sent to the family of the girl who is abducted. He informs her parents and fixes a day for establishing a relation between the two families. Such event is called is *jagor vanga*. The boy's side offer bride price of *ara adum* or *ga-dhon* and the girl resigns from the membership of her village club by offering *manoni sorai*. All meet and celebrate the occasion with a feast.

After formalization of the marriage, the parents from both the sides meet in a feast caked *beyoni bhat* which tightens the relations of both the families.

On the eighth day after marriage in both the forms it is the tradition to celebrate *yaga chut lung* in which the newly married couple visit the bride's house and accept a feast there.

---

18. G. Pegu, *Mising Jana Sahitra*, p. 15.

SOCIO-ECONOMIC ROLE OF DUGLA-LANAM FORM OF MARRIAGE

As the *dugla-lanam* form of marriage is less expensive, hence it is most popular among the Misings. But there are some disadvantages which are suffered by the society involved.

(i) It is seen that before getting maturity of age, qualifications and without sound economic conditions or income capacity, the boys feel affection for the girls and they marry. This hampers their education, employment and causes problems in the future course of their lives.

(ii) Sometimes it so happens that before the marriage of the elder brothers or sisters in the family, the younger brother abducts his lover and family disputes ensue.

DOWRY AND BRIDE PRICE

There is no dowry system nor bride price in the Mising villages. Feast with wine (*apong*) and meat forms the major part of the marriage ceremony. Either party can give something as per capacity but no hard and fast rule prevails. In earlier days, a mithon or pig or its equivalent of rupees 100 or 50 was charged as bride price (*alige*) payable to the parents of the bride but latter the amount has come to many variations. Some families have totally abandoned the custom.

PRE-MARITAL RELATIONSHIP

Though the parents allow their sons and daughters to move freely, yet pre-marital sexual relationship is not encouraged. If one indulges in such affairs, one must marry the opposite and if pregnancy occurs before marriage then it requires a ritual of heavy cost along with worship of God.

People avoid pre-marital contacts and try to marry as prescribed by the customs.

Birth, Childhood and Puberty Customs

DURING PREGNANCY

Neither a pregnent Mising lady nor her husband is required to observe any particular taboo or restriction. In some places, of course, in the period of pregnancy both husband and wife abstain from killing any animal. The women have to follow some restrictions regarding their food during the pregnancy period. After birth, the umbilical cord is severed by the midwife with a knife. The baby is then bathed in tepid water. New clothes are given to the baby. If a child does not cry after its birth, it is their tradition to blow air to it with an *ugon* of it's father. If the child does not accept its mother's breasts, the oldest women of the family prays to certain spirit by offering a metal utensil, a ritual that has probable influence upon the child. The mother of the baby has to undergo ceremonial purification by taking a ceremonial bath. She is to be well fed with special dishes of curry, *apong* and meat. On the fifth day of birth the baby is taken to the sunlight outside of the house. The hair of the baby is then removed. The priest purifies the mother and father by traditional methods. The village women come with bottles of *apong* to the mother and offer new clothes to the newly born baby, the host offer feast to them with certain formalities. Without performing these formalities, the father is not allowed to go to a river, a forest and a paddy field.

At the termination of the anthropological birth on the fifth day after birth, a name is ceremonially selected for the child. In giving the name of the child they generally follow the procedure of keeping the last letter of the father's name. The midwife, who help in the child birth is presented with gifts on this occasion.

Tending Children

The journey from infancy to youth is not easy for the Mising child. Childhood is full of obstacles. The parents cannot leave agricultural and other activities to look after the children properly. The situation is somewhat easy where grand parents are staying with the family. Otherwise, the eldest children look after the younger brothers and sisters till the parents come back home in the evening.

In addition to child-care, another equally grave problem is of immunization against disease. In byegone days the survival of children depended upon nature. Herbal medicines and religious rituals were the only measure against disease. Today people of all nooks and corners accept the programmes offered by W.H.O., through the State Medical Departments.

Traditional Laws of Inheritance

Like other societies, the Misings also possess the laws of inheritance of property. Although there is no written forms of these laws conventions have been continued and followed from generation to generation.

Although, the Misings follow the Hindu forms of lifestyle, yet their laws of inheritance are based on their own distinctive customs.

(i) The male children should accept the title of his father in order to inherit his father's property.

(ii) Illegitimate child or child having no Mising title cannot inherit any property of the Mising family.

(iii) During the lifetime of his father no son can claim the parental property. It is after his father's death that he gets the right to inherit property.

(iv) No girl child has a claim to inherit her father's property. She has right over the *strīdhana* like ornaments, dress items which she gets as an offer.

(v) During the lifetime of the father, a Mising youth can marry and lives separately but he cannot claim the property of his father. After the death of his father only the son can claim the property. If a man has more than one son who all live separately, the property is to be divided equally among the sons after his death.

(vi) If a Mising dies without a son, the widow can inherit the property. If the widow remarries a man of other caste or clan, then she shall lose the right of property of her deceased husband. In such case the nearest relatives get the property. If the widow remarries person within the family in compliance with the prohibitory taboos then she shall not lose the right of the said property.

(vii) If a Mising dies leaving only minor son or sons, then the property will be on the custody of the brother of the deceased person. As soon as the minor son or sons mature, the property will be given to them.

(viii) Regarding any disputes over the partition of property, the village council (*kebang*) will decide and subside them.

Adoption

A sonless Mising may adopt a son belonging to the Mising tribe of any clan.

Right of the Minor

Minors are looked after by the nearest patrilineal relatives. After the death of the father, if the mother is married by the uncle, then the rearing of children does not create any problem. If the mother wants to marry a person other than the brother of her husband, she leaves behind the children with the nearest patrilineal relation. In case both parents are dead, the infants are looked after by the elder brother or an uncle. The share of property is given to them when they mature in age. The children who lose their parents and are reared up by matrilneal relations get their share of property from paternal uncles after maturity.[19]

Funeral Customs

When a Mising dies in a Mising village, everybody is to be informed by ringing the bell (*lenong*). The relatives and villagers come to the deceased's house to make arrangements for the burial.

DISPOSAL OF DEAD

The dead of the average Misings generally receive an earth burial. The families who accept *Vaiṣnava Dharma* and belong to the fold of *Śaṅkara Songha* also practise earth burial. No Mising cremates the dead body. The corpse is washed, oiled and newly clothed and its hair is combed with a wooden comb and then taken out from the house. The fire place (*moirum*) is removed from its place and is newly set up. The corpse is then wrapped in an *epoo* (*nogadhari*), and carried to the burial ground on a pier made of bamboo. In a procession of relatives and villagers, the body is taken by few persons to the *ago-gulang* located generally outside the village and away from the river side. In the case of burial, the corpse is placed into the grave with head to the north and face to the east, in some place the face turned upwards. The eldest son throws a clod of earth into the grave. Everyone present in the burial place offers a handfull of soil into the grave and says, "we do not kill you, go to your own place, give your back to us". All the clothes, utensils of the deceased, are buried along with the corpse. The burial place is circularly fenced off with bamboo sticks. A symbolic house is built and a white sheet of cloth is erected over it.

FUNERAL RITES FOR WOMEN DYING IN CHILD BIRTH

A special funeral ceremony is observed in the case of woman dying during pregnancy or in child birth. She is buried with the child. No *lenong* is beating and no fencing is arrange on the tomb. It is believed that the soul (*yal*) of such untimely dead is very furious towards the family and the villagers. After burial of the dead, the husband of the deceased woman runs on the village road and several villagers follow him. All the villagers beat a metal plate to drive away the spirit of the untimely dead woman. The custom is called as *pakang megnum.* Accidental deaths, suiside cases, death occurring due to cholera, small pox and other abnormal deaths are given simple burial. If such death occurs outside the house, the corpse in not entered into the house and is directly taken to the burial ground.

---

19. N. Padun, *Mising Sampatir Adhikar* (in *MSA*), pp. 257-59.

PURIFICATION OF THE FAMILY

When the burial or cremation is finished, all who attend it purify themselves by a bath and go to the house of the deceased with their wet clothes on. The family members abstain from all kinds of work till the purification ceremony known as *ochi* is over. The death pollution and taboos due to death of an adult observable by the relatives last for ten days. Members of the deceased's family may not, during the period of pollution, rub oil on bodies, eat fish or flesh, shave or pair their nails. On the tenth day, all the male members get themselves shaved. All anoint themselves with oil and turmeric and take a bath. After purification, the sons put on new clothes. A funeral feast is offered to the relatives and villagers. It is known as *dodgang*.

Religious Beliefs and Festivals

The Misings follow their traditional tribal religion. They worship spirits and deities and sacrifice birds and animals. They believe that there is an Almighty God above us Who has created the universe and all the creatures of the world. They worship nature not by making any image or *idol*. They do not worship trees or animals. They only worship the spirits which are responsible for disease and troubles to mankind. *Mibu* — the priest — establishes connection with the so-called *doue bhot* or *urom* by their traditional hymns. Thus *mibu* is the respected person who performs the religious functions by means of their traditional lore.

The Misings regard the sun and the moon (*donyee, polo*) as their ancestors. They regard the moon as their father and the sun as their mother. In any ritual performance they first recite the name of *ane donyee* (means mother sun) and *abu polo* (means father moon).

The Mising does not believe in re-birth and "law of *karma*". In their belief the earth is the only playground of mankind. One had neither come to this world perior to this birth nor will come after death in the form of a man or any other creature. But they believe that the soul is immortal. The soul of the deceased moves around the human habitat and in jungle. The soul of the unnaturally dead are thought to be very angry and harmful to mankind. They pray the spirits (*uroms*) to provide prosperity and protect from evils.

Long before the arrival of the Christian missionaries, the Misings became Hinduized. They had continuous contact with the Hindus of plains through trade relations.

Recently, they followed Vaiṣṇavism founded by Śrī Śaṅkardeva. This religion among them is known as *kewalia* or *kalhanghati*. A small section of them have now accepted Christainity. Although they entered the fold of new religions, they celebrate a good number of traditional religious festivals.

Traditional religious observations are mentioned below:

(i) *Sarag Puza*: It is the worship of the sun and the moon (*donyee-polo*) which is observed in five years interval.

(ii) *Urom Apin*: It is the annual worship of the spirits of departed forefathers.

(iii) *Asi Eue or Jalkhai Puza*: It is the worship of the water goddess.

(iv) *Tallu Eue*: It is the worship of the God who is the creator of thunder, storm, disease like leprosy, etc.

(v) *Bor Seva*: It is the worship of lord Śiva.

(vi) *Doboru Puza*: It is the worship of mother earth performed in forest to protect the villagers and their domestic animals from evil spirits. It is also observed to increase the fertility of the cultivated land. In some places it is called *chang bihu*, in which the men-folk associated wih this *puza* beats the household structures (platforms, walls, etc.), with a stick to drive away the evil spirits that are thought to be the causes of any disease in the village. In such *puza* occasions, the villager observes *gaṇa* for five days. No outsiders are allowed to enter the village.

Depending upon the purpose of the observance, the *Doboru puza* can be divided into following types[20] —

(a) *Mopun doboru or Motto doboru*: It is observed in paddy fields to protect the cultivated crops.

(b) *Raban doboru*: It is observed to protect the people from evil spirits.

(c) *Buttow doboru*: It is observed to protect villagers from magical activities of unknown devils.

(d) *Kosson doboru*: This type of *puza* is observed by the hunters who are engaged in hunting in the jungle.

---

20. N. Padun, *Doboru Puja* in *MSA*, pp. 415-17.

ALI AYE LIGANG

The *Ali-aye-Ligang* festival appears to be agricultural in colour and tone. The term *Ali-aye-Ligang* means the first day of sowing seeds. It is observed on the first Wednesday of the month of the *Phagun* in the Assamese calendar. The farmers started to show the seeds of *ahu* paddy and some other varieties of crops of the season. The festival is started with the worship of the souls of the deceased persons of the family which is known as *urom apin*. The elder men of the family performs the rites and pray for well-being of the community and also for best production of crops during the year. The heads of the families sows a handfuls of seeds of their respective fields reciting the prayers to the mother earth. After that, they sprinkle a few drops of *apong* over the four corners of the fire place in their respective households. Community feasts with pork, *apong* dried fish and *purang* (boiled packed rice) are associated with the celebrations.

Music is a part of the life of the people of the north-east. There is no festive occasion, where music is not considered as an essential part of the celebrations. *Ligang* is an occasion of great merry making. With the beat of the drum sounds like *gumrug-gumrug,* the youths start vigorous dances in accompaniment of matching songs. It is called l*igang soman*. Like the *bihu* festivals, the *soman* party also dance in every house of the village and appeals to God to bless for the prosperity of the family throughout the year. The themes of the songs have a wide range of varieties. They may glorify a tradition related to a love story or narrate an important event of the past.

The dancing is always in a group. Both man and woman join in the dancing making a circle or any other geometric formation. The folk dance basically copies the action of hunting, fishing, rowing, weaving etc., in rhythmic way. The beauty of the dance is heightened by the colourful costumes.

People believe that divine power is bestowed upon them for rich harvest. They generally observe five days holidays following the *Ali-aye-Ligang* festivals, when they obstain from all sorts of work.

PO-RAG

Po-rag is the harvest festival of the Misings which is "grand re-union festival". It is celebrated at every three, four or five year's interval at the end of a good harvest usually in the month of August, September or December or January and it continues for three days.

It is celebrated with feast and prayers. *Po-rag* festival is observed in the m*urang* of the village. Before celebration of the festival a strong management committee of village youths is formed which is known as *Member-Yame.*

The preparation for the festival starts with the collection of cash and kind which is known as d*oglik*. One person from each household joins in the collection of foodgrains, construction of *murong* and clearing the area for the festival. Portfolios like *dekabora* to control the workers of boys staff and *tiribor* for female staff are selected by the public. Similarly *migom bora* and *bor puwari* manage the religious sides of the festival.

The starting of the construction of the *murong* is called *Esang* which means establishment.

Migom bora and *bor puwari* march to the establishment ground with traditional dance called *gumrug*. The function starts with the prayers of the creators *shedi melo, donyee polo*, etc. No feast is arranged on this day.

The members from the neighbouring villages and the married girls of the village, who have gone to their husband's house of distant villagers are also invited. The expert traditional dancer (*nasoni*) and drumbeater (*dholiā*) are invited to perform their arts and provide merryment in the festival. Besides these, the preparation of *apong*, sacrifice of pigs, feast are intergal part of the festival.

As the festival is observed mainly with a feast for the youths, so it is sometime called *yame munbir donam* meaning the feast of harmony. The *po-rag* runs for three days and is concluded with a prayer dance — *ponu nunam*.

Besides these religious practices, the Mising family, like other Hindu Assamese people practice the worship of *Aie Sakam, Dangoria-Sakam* and *Gorokhia-Sakam*.

FESTIVAL CYCLE

Ritual observations and religious ceremonies are observed in a public place of the village but life-cycle ceremonies like marriage, birth and death rites of the members are performed in the household. An account of month-wise festivals of the Misings is given in the following calendar.

Table 2.2: Festivals round the year

English Calendar months	Indian Calendar Months	Festivals
January-February	*Māgh*	*Māgh Bihu*
February-March	*Phālgun*	*Ali-aye-Ligang*
April	*Baiśākha*	*Bohag Bihu*
May-June	*Jeṭh*	—
June-July	*Āsāḍh*	*Chang Kubuwa Bihu*
August	*Śravan*	—
September	*Bhādon*	—
September-October	*Kārttik*	*Katibihu*
November-December	*Aghon*	*Porag*

Folk Literature and Performing Art of the Misings

Mising oral literature is considerably rich in terms of both quality and quantity. Much of the material is made up of various kinds of narratives, songs, rhythmes and other rhythmic compositions, proverbs and popular expressions habitually mouthed by the folk reflect the phenomenon of cultural synthesis.[21]

Although the Mising language is oral in nature yet it is rich with folk songs, oral narratives like myths, legends and tales, proverbs, riddles and charms.

These verbal arts are mainly composed of words of their own dialect and also local Assamese words. The folk songs are called *nitom* and can be classified into the following catagories.

SONGS ASSOCIATED WITH WORSHIP (AONG BANG)

It is of two types — *mibu* and *miro*. The priest (*mibu*) sings and dances through which acts he satisfies the spirits and establishes a connection with the spirits and advises the villagers the ways to solve any problem that creates misfortune to the village.[22]

SONG CONNECTED WITH A STORY (KABAN)

Kaban is just like an English ballad. They express their sorrows of the past and present through *kaban* songs. It consists of unhappy events, misfortunes and loss of lover, etc.

21. B. Dutta, N.C. Sarma, *A Hand Book of Material Culture, of North East India*, p. 83.
22. G. Pegu, *Mising Jana Sahitra*, p. 6.

SONGS OF LOVE AND YEARING (OI-NITAM)

Folk songs related to love and yearing are called *oi-nitom* which reflects the erotic feellings like the *bihu* songs of Assam in both form and content. Dr. B. Dutta writes

> Short and terse compositions of normally two (and occasionally three or four) lines, the *oi-nitams* are pieces outstanding for their natural lyricism, poetic sensitiveness and picturesque imagry.[23]

MARRIAGE SONGS (MIDANG)

Like other Indian society, the Mising girls and aged women sing together the marriage songs which are connected with the sorrows of childhood friends of the bride, expression of the beauty of the bride and groom, etc. The theme of such songs purports to remind the bride as to how she was born and brought up and how she spent her early life with her parents, brothers, relatives and friends from whom she was getting plenty of love and affection. Now she has been given away to the stranger's house for good to lead a new life. So, *midang* song is an expression of farewell wishes to the tearful bride.

LULLABIES AND NURSERY RHYMES (KONINUM / BI-NI-NINUM)

In order to please the child, the mother and grandmother sings some songs (rhymes) which are known as *koninum*. Such songs describe jocular events or simple tales which satisfy the crying babies.

CHILDREN'S GAME SONGS (MO-MA-NO-NAM / SONAA-NO-NAM)

Mising children play various games, many of which are linked up with the signing of songs or recitation of rhymes. The Mising term for such items is *mo-maanonitom*. Interestingly, some of these game-songs contain fragments of legends concerning the migration of particular Mising groups and also information about the origin of certain Mising customs of institutions.[24]

The junior boys while grazing cows in the field take delight in singing certain songs. Besides these songs, the Mising folklore is enriched with short tales (*doying*), jokes, proverbs, charms and prayers.

---

23. B. Dutta, N.C. Sarma, *op. cit.*, p. 85.
24. B. Dutta, N.C. Sarma, *op. cit.*, p. 87.

FOLK DANCE

The Mising folk dance is similar to the *bihu* dance of the non-Mising Assamese. Both boys and girls take part in dancing. In festive seasons they enjoy themselves with singing, dancing and playing by beating drums.

The group dances are associated with the festival like *Ali-aye-Ligang* in which hunting, fishing, rowing, weaving, harvesting, etc., are suggested through the actions of the dances. All age groups, men and women, young and old, married and unmarried take part in the dance performing in rows and circles.

The rituals dance of the Misings is performed by the priest (*mibu*). The *bihu* dance of the Misings has its distinctive style.

Economy of the Misings

The Misings are an agricultural community and hence their economy primarily depends upon agriculture. Their source of income fully depend upon paddy cultivation and some other *rabi* crops like potato, mustard seed, banana, etc.

Domestic animals also support some parts of expenditure of the family.

The women-folk are expert weavers and almost every family possesses traditional handlooms. They meet the need of clothes by themselves. Nowadays Mising women earn cash by selling their colourful costumes.

Agriculture is a family enterprise. All the members take part in the work and get good harvest. There are three annual crops and harvests which govern the works of villagers and influence the yearly cycle of all activities. These are — *lahi-sali* harvest in early winter (September-October); *rabi* crops harvest in December-January; and *abu* paddy harvest in mid-summer (in June-July). Growing of crops primarily for sale is relatively recent in the villages. The most important among such crops are potato, ginger, onion, sweet potato, and other vegetables.

ANIMAL HUSBANDRY

Second to crops in the economy of rural Assam is livestock. A man's first investment after land is in livestock. Most important of these animals are his bullocks which pull the plough and cart. Buffaloes are also tamed for the same purposes. They also provide milk and manure.

Milk is cash product and most of it is sold to the shopkeepers and hotels of urban areas where it is used in preparation of sweets. Relatively small amounts of milk are consumed in villages.

Animal manure is considered necessary for agriculture. Pigs and fowls are rare for meat and religious sacrifies. Horses are used as beast of burden and for human transportation. It is worth mentioning that livestock and land are determined as wealth of the family because these provide them with most of their livelihood.

A substantial number of Misings are engaged in various business or trade either retail or wholesale. A good number of Misings are engaged in service, especially in the various departments of government and semi-government offices and institutions. In addition to the business or trade many Misings are engaged in occupation like tailoring, carpentery and shopkeeping.

Fishing and fish-marketing is another important occupation among the Misings. All section of the tribe, rich or poor take delight in catching fish for their house consumption. Fishing is both a favourite sport and, for many, a part-time grainful occupation.

A small number of Mising craftsmen are currently engaged in the occupation of bamboo craft.

Contribution of the Misings to the Culture of Assam

In the socio-cultural and political activities of Assam, the Mising community is quite equal to that of other sections of the people of Assam. They have contributed to various nation-building affairs by engaging in different fields of activities.

In politics too, Misings are quite conscious and capable. Some of them have shouldered a political leadership and have discharged great responsibilities in the government of Assam. They have been involved in both regional and national party/parties and hold positions on national level.

A substantial number of educated persons have been engaged in the medical engineering and film industry.

The Misings have made very remarkable contributions towards strengthening the agricultural economy of the State.

So, it is evident that the Misings of Assam are an integral part of the contemporary Assamese socio-cultural life.

Chapter 3

Material Culture and its Classification

Material Culture

HUMAN kind established material relation with nature before the dawn of civilization. Man always materialized his action. Food and clothes are the primary needs of man since the beginning of creation. The satisfaction of hunger, to cover the nakedness and protect himself from the inclemencies of nature and to beautify himself are the various desires of a man's life. The making of cloth may hence be regarded as one of the earliest industries of the world.

Needing shelter and protection, man builds houses and wear clothes; finding it necessary to travel from one place to another, he developed rapid means of transportation. Man being an intelligent animal, sets about to meet his needs and adjust himself to his environment. Man makes countless objects by using folk techniques and from the raw materials collected locally. Such objects constitute folk material culture in folklore studies.

The artefacts made by the folk craftsmen or technicians adorn the community whose members profit by utilizing them in their day-to-day life.

This subject is also studied by anthropologist under the same disciplinary name which also brings light to the artefacts and technology of the early days, folklorist sometimes calls this subject "physical folklore".

In folklore studies, the object of material culture is to study the living and non-living methods, techniques and styles of hand-made items. The study of material culture is not limited to artefacts and technology of the folk, but it also studies how the traditionally oriented groups and tribes build their houses, their patterns of settlement, their cooking procedures, symbolic and religious arts, ornaments, hair styles, tattooing, etc. All these are objects of the study of material culture.

Thus the scope of the subject is to study the total physical culture of the community. The importance of material culture may be viewed in both acadamic and applied contexts. Sociologist and anthropologist study this subject form acadamic interest. Recently folklorists have given attention to this aspect for better study of the verbal art.

Interdisciplinary studies among the sociologist, anthropologist, art historian, archaeologist, linguists are felt necessary for fruitful progress in the field of material culture of various social groups in India. Social and cultural problems arise due to the technological change and industrialization which gives rise to unequal development in material life.

Rightly does B. Ghosh observe:

> In order to understand these problems, the scope of material culture will have to be extended from rural-peasant tribal base to urban industrial field also. At the same time the traditional material culture traits which are being replaced by new ones will have to be preserved in the interest of cultural history.[1]

Classification of Material Culture

Material culture includes various subjects which may be classified under following broad headings:

(i) Folk art.
(ii) Folk craft.
(iii) Folk costumes.
(iv) Folk cookery.
(v) Folk architecture.

FOLK ART

Folk art is a human skill in making something useful to mankind. Traditional art or folk art adheres to this fundamental truth. The primary aim of folk art is not only beauty but a thing useful to society. According to the *Kāmasūtra* of Vātsyāyana (composed between first and fourth century AD.), there are sixty-four arts (*Kalā*) prescribed for the learned. In material culture folk art means the hereditary

1. B. Ghose, *Traditional Art and Craft of West Bengal*, p. 2.

monopolistic decorative works of the artisans which reflect their skill and available resources of the geographical area. These artefacts give pleasure and serve some practical, social and economic ends.

Early people of the dim past began to ornament their person, then their artefacts of everyday use, later weapons and finally their surroundings. They decorated the rough walls of their huts, the floor on which they sat, ate and slept. Thus the tradition of folk art started from the remote past of human civilization and continued throughout the ages. Art products based on magic and witchcraft traditions of the pre-Chiristian era are found to this day in a deminished form in the superstitions and customs of the people. The religious forms of arts come out in the worship of nature and forces which form part of a cult. These forces are carried by the symbols of their masks or images which give birth to ritualistic art forms. What is beautiful and pleasing to one may not be pleasing to another. Therefore beauty has not been the chief content of the artist since the beginning of art.[2]

Folk artist or traditional craftsman did never worry about the likeness in making things with his skill. He learnt his skills form artisan father, the father from his grandfather and so on.

Many theories have been advanced to explain the appearance of the first art expression. Some believe that it sprang from a playful desire to emulate similar linear marks made on cave walls by the deer in sharpening their claws. Others believed that the beginning of art was purely accidental.

Anthropological studies confirm it that the beginning of art can be traced to the paleolithic age. Arts like pottery, weaving, metal craft developed from the Neolithic age onwards. With the advantage of agriculture, fixed settlement patterns, villages and towns were created. The folk art also developed from stage to stage. The development of a particular kind of art in a region is related to the historical continuities, religious cults, immigration of artisans from other places and contract of cultures. Every man-made objects, regardless of purpose or technique, entered the field of folk art because of its decoration. Folk art is a symbol of social life. The tradition and customs of a community are perfectly mirrored through the beauty, shape, colour of things used in its daily life.

Folk art is a kind of collective aspiration and expression of the people who generally live in rural areas. Pottery is an ancient folk art form found in almost all

2. P.C. Roy Choudhry, *Folklore of Bihar*, p. 167.

parts of the world. Wall-painting is seen in almost all parts of India drawn for occasions like marriage, festivals, etc. In marriage, for example, the room for the bride and bridegroom is very delicately decorated with different motifs. Indigenous colours are usually employed in such art forms. Says Roy Choudhry,

> Black is obtained from soot, yellow by mixing the juice of banana leaf and milk with lime, red from the juice of kusum flower, green from the leaves of creepers and trees.[3]

In the Bhojpuri speaking areas of Bihar, wall-painting is done by women-folk, but in tribal areas both men and women participate in such arts. Wall-painting is generally done by women in three places — the room for the deity of the family (*gosāī ghara*), the room for newly wedded couple and in carridor or covered space just outside the room.

In Bihar, the Santhal huts have colour-washed walls with crude printings of trees, cycles, cars, etc. In Mithilā, wall-painting is done by the women of the upper castes like Brāhmaṇa and Kāyastha.

Among the stylist folk art in India the *alpanā* is one of the best forms. *Alpanā* is the floor decorative art in which various objects like flowers, leaves, trees, fruits, peacocks, snakes, astral bodies, gods, goodesses are depicted. Some specific worships and festivals like Lakṣmī-pūjā, Dīwalī, etc., are the context of such arts. The ingredients used for such *alpanā* are rice powder and water sometime mixed with *sindūra*.

The woman layout a fairy carpet of geometrical patterns, flowers and birds on the entrance to the house and in the principal rooms. In certain regions of India, the outer walls of the village cottages are also decorated in this way. The young Hindu girls exercise her talents through *alpanā*.[4]

Folk art is the product of human will and action, from natural events to artificial.

S.K. Chetarji says:

> Painting, sculpture and architecture were considered by the ancient Hindus as science (*vidyā*) on the same footing as geometry, grammar or

3. P.C. Roy Choudhry, *Folklore of Bihar*, p. 167.
4. S.K. Chaterji, *Indian Culture*, p. 99.

logic. The term art (*kalā*) was reserved for the minor arts and handicrafts.[5]

Hindu society with its guild system, was planned so as to make the village a self-sufficent and independent unit. Each region of India produces everything it needs. That is why the products of local handicrafts travel so littte. Each region has its own forms of pottery, copper work and textiles, which preserve the traditional farms in great variety and wealth.

D.N. Pathy observes:

> In folk art nothing is accidental, experimental and freakish. Every detail has a meaning and every symbol has a significance though some of this may have been forgotten, much of it is ritualistic and religious. It is difficult to trace the original folk art but it can be guessed from the prevalent tradition that folk art or rural art in the development phase of primitive art in general.[6]

Thus, it is correct that folk art is the expression and communication of man's deepest instincts and emotions reconciled with his social experience and cultural heritage. This artistic impulse may change with the development of the society.

Art spans the bridge between human contrivance and aesthetic pleasure. Says Vidyarthi:

> The people of north-east India who live in hilly, forested and scenic habitat of rivers and valleys also reflect high accomplishment in the fields of art and crafts. The expression of art in tribal societies of north east India had a wider span and implications. The media of artistic expressions are varied and unique.[7]

FOLK CRAFT

Folk craft grows out of the necessity to meet the everyday needs of people. Folk craft is said to be more cohesive to human life than even language. Craft is an experience of the human spirit in material from which fulfilled the needs and gave delight to mankind. In the world of craft there is no hiatus between service ability and aesthetics. Handicraft of any region reflects and preserve the experience

5. *Ibid.*, p. 102.
6. D.N. Pathy, "Folk Art and Contemporary Art — A study in Relation," in *Folk Culture*, vol. 3, p. 164.
7. L.P. Vidyarthi, *Art and Culture of North-East India*, p. 95.

of man under varying circumstances. The forms and techniques remained the unchanged or unaffected over generations.

In folk craft study, the folklorists intend to study the making of basketry, pottery, wood carving, horn and ivory carving, metal works, weaving and dress designing, making of toys and tools for various works and also the sculptural arts.

It is seen that folk crafts are hereditary in nature and the craftsmen utilized their spare time which were also their occupation for living. The tools and implements which are essential parts for daily works are also the object of folk craft study, which include the hunting and fishing articles, agricultural tools, musical instruments, sacrificial implements, and tools for various craft activities. There are some castes and tribes in every parts of the world who are traditionally engaged in manufacture and trade of certain groups of craft items. Such craftsmen have been living in unchanged and traditional modes throughout the ages.

For example, in Assam the pottery and goldsmithy are important occupations of the *Hira* and *Bania* groups of people. The specialization in craft is hereditary. Some craft forms are concentrated in certain areas irrespective of castes and tribes. This is due to the availability of raw materials in abundant quantities and collective works of the people.

As described earlier, folk craft specimens mainly include utilitarian objects. Mention may be made of textile items, baskets, vassels for keeping domestic articles, oil and water containers, musical instruments, stools for sitting, fishing traps, smoking pipes, tabacco cases, footwears, hunting arrows and war weapons, etc. The decorative works mainly include jewellery and ornaments such as bangles, amulets, necklace, finger rings, ear rings, forehead ornaments, combs, neckbands earplugs, wristlets, anklets, headgears. Basketry is one of the earliest crafts that prevails all over the world. A greater variety of plants are used for basket making.

In 1902 a renowned botanists Fredrick V. Covillie identified 87 plants employed by North American Indians in making and colouring baskets. Some of the plants such as reeds, rushes and sedges, flourished in marsh areas in many parts of the world and have been widely used since early times. Indian basketing has taught us to appreciate the beauty of primitive weaving and furnishes, the most striking illustration of the wonderful patience, fertility of resource and intensive genious of the aboriginal women in using nature's materials, roots grasses, twigs, vines, rushes, plant-fibres, shells and feathers, shaping them into useful and beautiful forms.[8]

In the life of the Indians, baskets have filled every needed demand for cooking, burden carrying and storing of goods.

Making of the masks of human and animal figures are one of the popular craftsmen activities in rural areas of the globe. Such masks are still found in north east India, Himachal Pradesh, Madhya Pradesh, Orissa, Nagaland, Assam, Manipur, Tripura and Arunachal Pradesh. Some of the masks are woven like basketry, some are carved out of wood. Various materials like wood, bamboo, clothes, paper and straw are used by the village craftsmen in making masks. The popular masks-making crafts are related to socio-economic acts like drama, folk dance, etc. Several colours are also used to illustrate the masks. Fishing traps are also woven in similar way as that of baskets with certain shapes and techniques to enter the fishes and store inside it.

Music plays a very significant role in the socio-cultural life of the folk. The musical instruments mainly consist of wood, brass and iron strings. Flute, horns, drums, bells are the product of some simple craft activities of the music lovers.

Wood carving is one of the ancient folk crafts that prevails among mankind. Wood appears to have been the main material for house construction. In India, wood has been considered as a standard material for architecture and decorative art since ancient times. Cave, temple, pillars were decorated with various motifs and figures. Besides the archaeological evidence, we come across a number of reference to carpenter's work in literary texts belonging to ancient period. Memorial pillars of wood, metal or stone may represent the craft practised by the associated people. The Nāgās, for example, decorate their village dormitory (*morangs*) with big size figures of man, tiger, elephant carved on the pillars. Some of them are even life-size. The outline of the desire figure is first sketched with charcoal, and then cut away to leave in high relief. The carves are coloured with animal blood. The rural art and craft activities are also reflected in ornament designs. The technique followed in the manufacture of ornaments is adopted traditionally and the ornaments are the examples of stylish art forms of the folk.

> The world of craft is as valuable as the world of science, philosophy or ethics. Craft reflects the state of human society through the individual who has to him, in small or big portion, what mankind as a whole possess.

8. Navajo School of Indian Basketing, *Indian Basket Weaving*, New York, 1971, p. 7.

Craft treasures gives us a glimpse into the core of collective mind and societies through the mirror of the individual mind that creates them. As the crafts are the indigenous creation of ordinary people of villages and small towns, they reveal the innate artistic taste of masses and their desire to combine utility with beauty. The people's instinct for the beautiful has been expressed by the craftsmen in an infinite variety of traditional forms which remain unchanged or unaffected over generations.[9]

FOLK COSTUME

Dress is one of the basic needs of mankind which may lead men to weave textile. The woven textiles in varied forms and designs replace the use of animal skin and bark of trees as dress item which was a symbol of wandering man for a considerable period of time in the history of mankind. Today dress is a marked characteristic of any culture. Fashion in dress is as interesting as any other fact of human self-expression. The taste and tendencies of an age are clearly indicated by the type of clothes of that period.

Rightly does observe V. Elwin:

> Dress is something much more than a mere protection of body against the weather. It is a form of art on which some of the finest minds of all nations have lavished their attention. It is a symbol, whereby a man's social structure can be determined.[10]

The study of regional dress or dress of small tribes reveals the tendency towards creating a natural look. Custumes were not always uniform in style and colour, the maker and weaver often adding a bit of her own creativeness to their works. Though regional dress is worn in many lands modern machinery is slowly pushing it to aside.

The making of cloth may be regarded as one of the earliest household industries of the world. Indian traditional textile art is very old. Cotton weaving is a kind of special product of India and she is famous throughout the world for her fine cotton muslins.

Silk is a special product of the Chinese. Silk weave was known in India before the age of the epics. The Indians also turned this material into a highly specialized

9. M.K. Pal, *Craft and Craftsmen in Traditional India*, p. 320.

10. V. Elwin, *A Philosophy of NEFA*, pp. 32, 33.

craft and Indian silk products were praised greatly in other countries until recent times.

Cotton, wool, jute and such other substances have been used in India since ancient times. This tradition has been continued till recent time. New techniques are invented and new designs are added by displacing of colours and costly materials. Textile came to be associated with social and ritualistic event from the very early times. Now it plays a pivotal role in the social and economic life of the Indian. Ornaments must have originated from man's innate desire to decorate himself. It is the art of self-decoration. The love of beauty is inbred in man, people use ornaments for satisfying their thirst for adornment. Generally females are more conscious of physical beauty than males. Some ornaments are used as a symbol of status, rank, of the wearer and position and prosperity in the society.

Jewellery has been regarded as wealth and attract the notice of others. The planning and making of different styles of ornaments and wearing it indicates the supreme selection and inter beauty of mankind. The jewellery worn by different tribes and non-tribes of Assam have a unique place in India and is made of the purest and finest materials.

Among the ornaments used by the tribal people are amulets, animal-horn, teeth and bone, headdress of different colours and lengths. Headgears are made of cloth, wool, animal skin, paper and bamboo strips.

The history of Indian dress and ornament indicates that the dresses of kings and nobles differed from that of the commoners. Laymen used garments that were tabooed for persons belonging to religious orders.

Different religious orders prescribed different types of dresses for their members. People belonging to different regions dressed in different styles. People of torrid region, dressed in light and cool garments. Men coming from cold regions used warm and woollen shawls and blankets. Dress worn on festive occasions were chosen with meticulous care.

The dress history of India has a dynamic adaptability to the different conditions of life. The diversity of dress habits naturally pre suppose a developed knowledge of the art of weaving.

Kings also wore head jewels (*cūḍāmaṇi*) necklace made of gold *kuṇḍala*s, etc. Princes also were gold crowns.

The tradition of jewellery in India goes back to the Vedic Age.

The analysis of the style of costumes may focus light on the psychological aspects of the people of a particular culture. Costumes provide us a picture of way of life of a certain folk group.

Don Yoder writes :

> Folk costumes is the visible, outwards badge of folk group identity, worn consciously to express that identity. . . . In every case the costume is distinct and identifiable, it identifies the wearer to the outside world as well as to his own community, it is prescribed by the community and its form is dictated by the community tradition.[11]

The dress and ornaments take shape in accordance with the needs of circumstance like weather, religion, local products and choice of the weavers. Costumes of a particular area are not the same throughout the year. Geographical, climatic and racial factors may greatly influence the nature of costumes of the people of that area.

The weaving of cloth, the whitening of the cloth in water and drying it in the sun, the cutting out of the garments and sewing also the weaving process all are included in the study of costumes of the community. Besides these, tattooing on the body, use of cosmetics and perfumes, headdress are also included in the study of folk costumes of a community or people of a certain area.

FOLK COOKERY

Food habits are not only dominated by materialistic considerations but also the availability of food stuffs, climatic condition and religious and social pattern of life. Taboos, existing among different classes of people, also determined the diet.

In food-gathering stage of mankind food was consumed raw or roasted. Cooking came only when man invented pottery, that could stand heating.

Thus the introduction of cooked food brought a great change in diet. The evolution of methods for preserving food wiped out local differences in diet and in modern times the industrial production of food stuffs and propaganda have materially influenced man's diet. Form the time of acquistition of cultivated cereals, people prepared flat biscuits and alcoholic beverage and used them both as food and for fun. Meat and fish formed an important part of the diet, wild animals still contributed a large percentage to the meat supply.

---

11. D. Yoder, "Folk costume" in *Folklore and Folk life — An Introduction* ed. R.M. Dorson, p. 295.

Don Yoder has defined folk art of cooking and food habit as traditional domestic ways of cooking and consumption pattern and its associated beliefs and practices marked by regional variations. Since everyday family cooking is based on regional tradition it is obviously the opposite of the commercial, institutional and scientific-nutritional versions of cooking. Thus according to Don Yoder the scope of the study of folk art of cooking and food habits is wide which includes the food themselves, its morphology, preparation preservation and social and psychological functions, and their remification into all other aspects of folk culture.[12]

Food habit, like other biological supportive activities is an aspect of cultural behaviour. In no society people are permitted to eat everything, everywhere, with everyone and in all situations. As in other aspects of socio-cultural life, there is also diversity in food habits of the people of India.

An interesting regional variation of food habit is seen in India. In West Bengal, Bihar and Assam, people take rice as their staple food. South Indian depends on rice and wheat. In Rajasthan, Punjab, Uttar Pradesh and Madhya Pradesh people depend on wheat as their staple food.

FOLK ARCHITECTURE

Folk architecture is that branch of study deals with the size, form and functions of houses and settlements of the human race. When paleolithic man moved from his cave into the shelters, he constructed huts with leaves and branches. He was making the first step towards urbanization. Then the Neolithic man cultivated plants, domesticated animals and introduce agriculture. He created possessions in the forms of crops, animals and tools. They constructed friendly groups and formed villages in which the agrarian propulation enjoyed the advantages of mutual protection. The primitive peasant population had developed into a complex society which was dependent on a feudal lord. But gradually, when trade expanded and old landowning society changed into money -using society, it established towns. The towns in pre-madiaeval period (AD 1000 onwards) had walls around them for protection and defence, and were very crowded. The fields and pasture lands were outside the ramparts. Folk architecture deals with human settlements including types of settlements, selection of site, boundary of a village and separate households, arrangement of houses, structure of houses, material use in construction, shape and size of houses, and its different parts.

12. D. Yoder, "Folk Cookery" in *Folklore and Folklife — An Introduction*, p. 325.

The regional variation of houses in relation of wall, roof, method of construction, style, cost, placing of courtyard, verandah, female apartments, male apartments, fire place, etc., are the important aspects of consideration. The density of the houses, occupancy rate and demand and shortage of houses are also the subject-matter of such studies.

Three types of human settlements are observed among different races of mankind, they are permanent settlement, semi-permanent and temporary. Temporary settlement are still existing among certain nomadic groups. Settlement pattern also can be seen as several forms like compact, semi-compact, semi-sprinkled and sprinkled settlement. The boundary of a village is often defined in terms of its government revenue area. But there exist some geometric terms to describe the shape or size of a village like linear, square, rectangular or circular. Local terms regarding the shape of a village settlement and types of houses also exist.

In Assam the names of the villages or areas of settlement somehow originated from historical events, roads, trees or rivers. Thus some folk stories or events are associated with the names of the settlement areas.

In a traditional Indian villages the four *varṇa*s are assigned separate sides of the villages — the brāhmaṇa in the north, the kṣatriya in the east, the vaiśya in the south and the śūdra in the west.

Such historical villages do not exist now due to the fact that a village must depend on a neighbouring village in various ways in various fields of life and therefore inter-settlement and inter-market formation has come into existence in the villages. Ecological factors, wind direction, river position, road and communication, suitable agricultural and horticultural lands, land structure for construction are some of the factors of settlement geography.

Since settlement is the man-made habitat on the rural land scape, based on primary occuptions such as agriculture, foresting, fishing, hunting, etc., which flourished on local resources, hence, settlement studies are basically related to the use of natural rosources like soil, water, forest products, availability of food in the region, etc. The higher density of settlements has been found in the region of agricultural prosparity since ancient time.

With the development of agriculture and livestock breeding the technique of house construction seems to be developing rapidly. Not only was timber the solitary source of materials for housing but the sun-dried brick made from alluvials mud was also widely used.

In some places people plated their walls made of vegetable matters with mud layers while the floor was made of coloured clay layers. The study of development of architectural designs from earliest to the present time is nothing but the history of mankind. Each culture produced new versions of houses for shelter, prayer and for burial purposes. Hence their dwelling houses, religious houses and burial tombs can tell us about their past culture.

> Buildings that survive from the past are fossils of civilization. For certain early cultures that left no written records or whose records have not been desciphered, monumental remains are the principal sources of information.[13]

Man-made physical environment is the sum of a number of distinct and variable elements. Factors of environment over which man has bona fide control and interpretation of one factor with another help in settlement of a particular region.

Architecture is the mirror of history and social culture. A few definitions offered by artists are quoted below:

Tommaso Temanza writes:

> Architecture is diverse because the different customs and different religions of nations are such that what is suitable and proper in one province is not in another.

Vincenzo Lamberti maintained that:

> Architecture has been the keeper and refuge of man's repose, the principle of society, the division of populations, their pomp ceremony, the docorum of religion and the sustainer of human life.[14]

The houses and buildings generally show definite adaptations to physical conditions in different localities.

Climate has a pronounced effect upon various architectural designs and the climatic factors like rainfall, direction of wind and storm are important. The

---

13. T. Copplestone, *World Architecture — An Illustrated History*, p. 11.
14. Cited from *Encyclopedia of World Art*, vol. I, p. 629.

intensity of slopes of the roof depends upon the intensity of storms in summer season, atmospheric temperature and amount of rainfall.

In Assam, climate is the main reason why most of the inhabitants of the region built their houses facing east instead of the west. East facing houses are better ventilated, and the sun rays of the early morning are able to enter it while the west facing house is subject to getting afternoon sunlight. Houses can be classified according to physical factors, build and architecture, accommodation space, sanitation, occupancy rate, density of building, etc.

It is interesting to note that a good number of terms are used to describe different types of housing units and their component structures. Linguistically, a house is called *ghar* or *gr̥ha* in Assamese. *Barghar, saraghar, malghar* are the parts of a house used for different reasons. Rooms are called *koṭhā* and so on.

Houses built with bamboo walls plastered with mud are generally known as *kochaghar* while brick built structures are called *paccaghar*. Platform houses are called *changghar*.

Chapter 4

Folk Art of the Misings

Folk Art

MOVED by the charms of nature around him, man can express the appreciation of nature through various media and thus art is created. Man is used to expressing his feelings and ideas from his primitive stage. Art has had a softening influence on him. From the prehistoric times to the late medieval period Indian creative mind made considerable advance in the field of art and architecture. Ancient Indian art occupies a prominent place in the art history of the world. These rich and varied art forms were developed in the country during the long span of time.

Folk art is a spontaneous expression of the past experience of a community. There products are utilitarian in character which serves as need of the people. These may be works on wood or clay, metal or wool. The child of this folk artist carried the art traditionally. Indian folk artist could maintain the beautiful form of their artefact, as well as they were also very conscious of the aesthetic aspect of their artefacts.

Folk Art of the Misings

The mode of living and the expression of joys and sorrows of the Misings of Assam are practically the same as those of all the people of north-east India. The art and craft practised by the Misings are essentially the product of artistic skills and creative imagination of the tribal craftsman. Some kinds of arts are developed and confined within them, some forms of artistic activities are synthesis of all traditions which are found among other groups of people in Assam and north-eastern region of India. Folk art for them is a vocation, not a profession in the conventional sense. Mising ladies are fond of colours and their skillful hands create wonderful colours, forms and designs in clothes. Some of the Mising farmers are expert artists and they may curve out excellent figures both in plastic and in pictorial art. They are also master of architectural details. Folk art of the Misings can be discussed under two heads — (1) Decorative art and (2) Ritualistic art.

Decorative works are those which are related to drawings, paintings and embroideries on different dresses, the metallic ornaments, wood and ivory works. The ritualistic arts are related to religious festivals and ceremonies performed by them in their society round the year. In actual words, the Mising ritualistic arts cannot be called developed art form. These seem to be crude.

The decorative arts of the Misings are well-developed, which may fulfil the demands of both folk craft and folk art.

Decorative Folk Arts

The folk arts are rooted far back in the distant past. There are no records of pictorial folk art preserved in any form. It is due to the fact that the old artists express their feelings through the medium of colours which are temporary in nature. Moreover the pictorial art is done on animal skins or on wooden boards or on earth which all have no long life. The colour use for such arts was charcoal lime and juice of herbs. The pictorial arts can only be traced from the wooden bars and posts of the *Murong Ghor* in which the folk artists express their excellence. The decorative Mising folk art included — the art on ornaments; the art on dress items; decorative art on objects, walls and such other things.

ART IN ORNAMENTS

Ornaments are the expression of artistic mind of both the maker and wearer. The style of making the ornaments and the decoration on them are some of the artistic features in the history of Assamese folk art. The common use of similar type of ornaments among the women-folk of the Misings is the striking characteristic of their art. The names of the ornaments are usually taken from flowers or fruits. Some ornaments of the Mising community are often very finely crafted in many pleasing designs. They are elaborately decorated with stones. The golden ornaments are called *avn-attar* and the silver ornaments as *murkong-attar.*

The earring known as *thuria* or *turi* has its own distinctive feature in the form of a lotus having a heavy stem. It is made of gold and studded with uncut rubies on the both sides. This ear ornaments which were common in old generation still survive among the present generation also. The artistic minds of both the maker and wearer are reflected through such *thuria*.

Some earrings are made with tiny star at the top and a crescent below. It is studded with pearls or tiny precious stones. The wooden earring called *kentu* also bears some floral motifs.

The *dugdugy* which is worn as neck ornaments with *powalmoni* is like the shape of a leaf. Rubies of different shapes are studded on it. It is commonly made of gold but silver made *dugdugy* is also prevalent.

Imitating the figure of a fish, the folk artisan made a sophisticated U-shaped necklece called *mogordana* which was most popular in Assamese society along with the Mising ladies. It is a U-shaped metal piece without any joint whose two ends are like the mouth of two fishes and the surface is moulded like the body of a fish.

Dholbiri is another neck ornament like the shape of a drum. The whole surface of the *dholbiri* is studded with red and blue stones which attract the eyes of a person easily. Similarly another neck ornament of the ladies named as *cipatmoni* is the copy of a fruit called *kordoi*.

The bangles also have their own good artistic qualities. The *gam kharu* as it is called by the people is made of silver which carries the motifs of creepers, stars, flowers, etc. It is made of gold also.

Sometimes the artisans purposefully embossed floral or animal designs on their works. Such ornaments give stimula-tions and satisfaction to the folk. The ornaments of the Misings portray mythological influence of their religion and are superior in quality and craftsmanship.

The gold beads are not naturally solid, but hollow and are filled with rasin or wax. The jewellers produce an ornament from the smallest possible amount of the precious metal. The *dholbiri*, for example, is also a hollow cylindrical ornament filled with rasin. This makes it as light as pith. Very fine filigree work is performed on *gumkharu*, *necklace*, *dugdugy*, and on bracelets. The outer surface of a bracelet is of gold and the inner is of silver, elaborately ornamented with flowers, wreaths, etc.[1]

Ornaments are sometimes bossed with coloured stones. Necklace made of gold and red coral beads is also found in some houses. The coloured stones and occasionally animal's body parts like teeth and claws are artistically put together

1. Sketch of ornaments are given in *figs*. 35, 36, 37, 38 of chapter 8.

in an ornament. The techniques used were pierced work, engraved relief and filigree.

ART IN DRESS AND DECORATIVE CLOTH

The Mising weavers portray their dreams into reality on various dress items with coloured threads. The most attractive point of Mising art and embroideries is the combination of different colours. The weaving designs of the Mising folk are almost exclusively of an angular geometrical type and there occur formal arrangement of lines and bands to elaborate patterns of diamond or triangular decorations. Of other geometric patterns there is an almost inexhaustible variety. Some remarkable designers of *ribi* are illustrated on *Pls.* 1 to 8 showing their art forms. These contain the curves and wavy lines which may represent the hilly areas and rivers moving in zig-zag ways. These zig-zag designs are most common in all the borders of *gasang*, *ribi* and *galuk*.

In bags and baby carrying towels such alternate uprights and pendant triangles are common art forms. In certain regions like Ratanapur of Majuli sub-division and some other nearby Mising villages, the chevron patterns are found in the woollen garments of both the sex. Diamond patterns are found in horizontal rows and are linked with other V-shaped motifs run in the weaving products. These diamond motifs may represent leaves of trees.

In some artistic designs as illustrated in *Pls.* 2, 5, 7 it is seen that diamond within diamond are drawn by the skillful hands of the artists in their shawls, coats, bags, *mekhela-chador* and *pathlies*.

Similarly a continuous link of diamonds in rows is also observed. It is remarkable that in weaving such design same coloured threads are often used in the same rows but not in differing columns. This makes the clothes more attractive and express their love for colour combinations.

Triangles occur enclosed with diamond patterns but these can also be called incomplete diamonds. In case of *ghai*, only triangular and cross-patterns are seen as illustrated in *Pl.* 4.

In some border designs we see that alternately inverted triangular motifs with intervals are repeated. Cross-lines are popular in *mekhela*s and *chador*s which are also formed by dotted lines of coloured threads. Such designs are illustrated in *Pl.* 6.

If the border is arranged with cross-mark it is called as *kaci ghai* or *gai gamic*. If triangular motifs occur in the whole cloth it is called *tigur gamic*. The dotted straight lines parallel to the rows of the combinations of other motifs are called *konger*.

These are exceedingly beautifully-formed and are clustered around the border of their costumes in a highly artistic manner. The small star like motifs occurring on the upper part of *ribi* or *gasang* almost 2 to 4 cm, intervals are called *buta*. The flower like structure mixed with other forms of motifs are called *punjok*. The arrow-like figures appear in some items as shown in *Pl*. 7. Such motifs are projecting from the main designs.

The unwoven portion of a *gasang*, *pathali* or *damur* is called *paksung nang*. The next most striking feature of these styles of work may be said to be the use of coloured wool in the middle of a *pathali*. It is interesting to note the formation of art and embroidery design of a *pathali*. In a *pathali* the whole cloth is woven with cotton threads but at the middle portion wool is utilized to weave as weft for the artistic motifs. *Pls*. 9 and 10 show the construction and art on a *pathali*. This is something different from other dress items.

In some *ribis* (*mekhela*) we have observed butterfly (*Pl*. 18) with separate border lines. Each of them is different from other which makes the butterfly of several patterns. This is certainly a wonderful design of art in dress.

No traditional dress is worn by man except the *mibogaluk*. In a *mibogaluk* artistic work is simple but not less important in comparison to the female dresses. The back side of the *galuk* is attractive due to the artistic works. In my field visit to Jonai I saw many Mising people attending the meeting of the fourteenth *Mising Agom Kabang* wearing their traditional *galuk* containing the motifs of *tajmohol* at their back. This is certainly a symbolic of the love the weavers bore for their lovers. *Pl*. 8 illustrates such art forms on a *galuk*.

Floral and animal motifs on clothes are also seen, but such motifs are rare in dress items. These are observed in *damur*, towels; bed sheets, pillow covers, seat back, table and box covers and in hankerchiefs. All these art forms discussed above are done in the looms.

It is worth mentioning here that the influence of modern art like frabics, aplifs, machine embroidery, are seen among the young generation of the Misings. In *Pls*. 11, 12 & 14 we have observed that motifs of deer, flowers, trees and toys are done by the above-mentioned process. Hand embroidery and hand knitting patterns adopted by the present Mising artisans are an important reflection of the folk art in dress items. The tradition of art depicting the content of the wavy lines and diamond patterns are ancient. More than thirty varieties of motifs are seen in their dress items. The use of rolex (gold like thread) is now known to the Mising weavers. Such gold like threads are used as special weft along with silk. In Assamese language such cloth bear the name *kingkhop*.

In some decorative clothes and dress items the threads of the warp are of different colours. But the same spools in the shuttle contribute to the flower designs on the surface. In some clothes it is so found that both sides are exactly the same. There is no right or wrong side of use.

MIMANG OR CHANEKI FOR LOOM EMBROIDERY

The expert artisans (both male and female) construct a kind of draft copy for the floral, animal or such other motifs for the weavers. Such draft copy help the weavers to trace the motifs in their looms and finally produce the motifs in required colours. The Misings called it *mimang* or *gamic*. The Assamese word for it is *chaneki. Mimangs* are excellent examples of folk arts of the Misings. It has two division — (i) *appun gamic* and (ii) *alam gamic*. The *alam gamic* contains the graphics of angular bands. In some *mimangs* motifs of bird, butterfly and fish are observed. Such *mimangs* are called *moimangs*.[2] Generally no men figures are observed in art on clothes but "a man in rowing," "a fairy in dancing" are sometimes depicted in their folk art. The architectural monuments of Ahom period like *joidol, sivadol, kareng* are seen on decorative clothes.

DECORATIVE ART OTHER THAN DRESS ITEMS

All art traditions must have some gestures in the modes and medium of expression. Toy making was not observed in my field study. I met an artisan who made some decorative art with wool and bamboo strips. Her work is illustrated in *Pl.* 15. Here the artisan Mrs. Korobi Pau Mili of Jonai town (P.H.E.) has decorated a bamboo made circular rice sieve (*chaloni*) with coloured wool of different thickness drawn a pair of geese with a lotus at the top along with other floral motifs on the sides (*Pl.* 15). She also adds three pairs of garlands that hang from the circular bar. Such art modelling is still practised by the women and these are delicately decorated with different motifs. We find a form of decorative art, which is very

2. A. Doley, *Mising Loka Silpa Kala Aru Sanskritir Nidarsan*, p. 14.

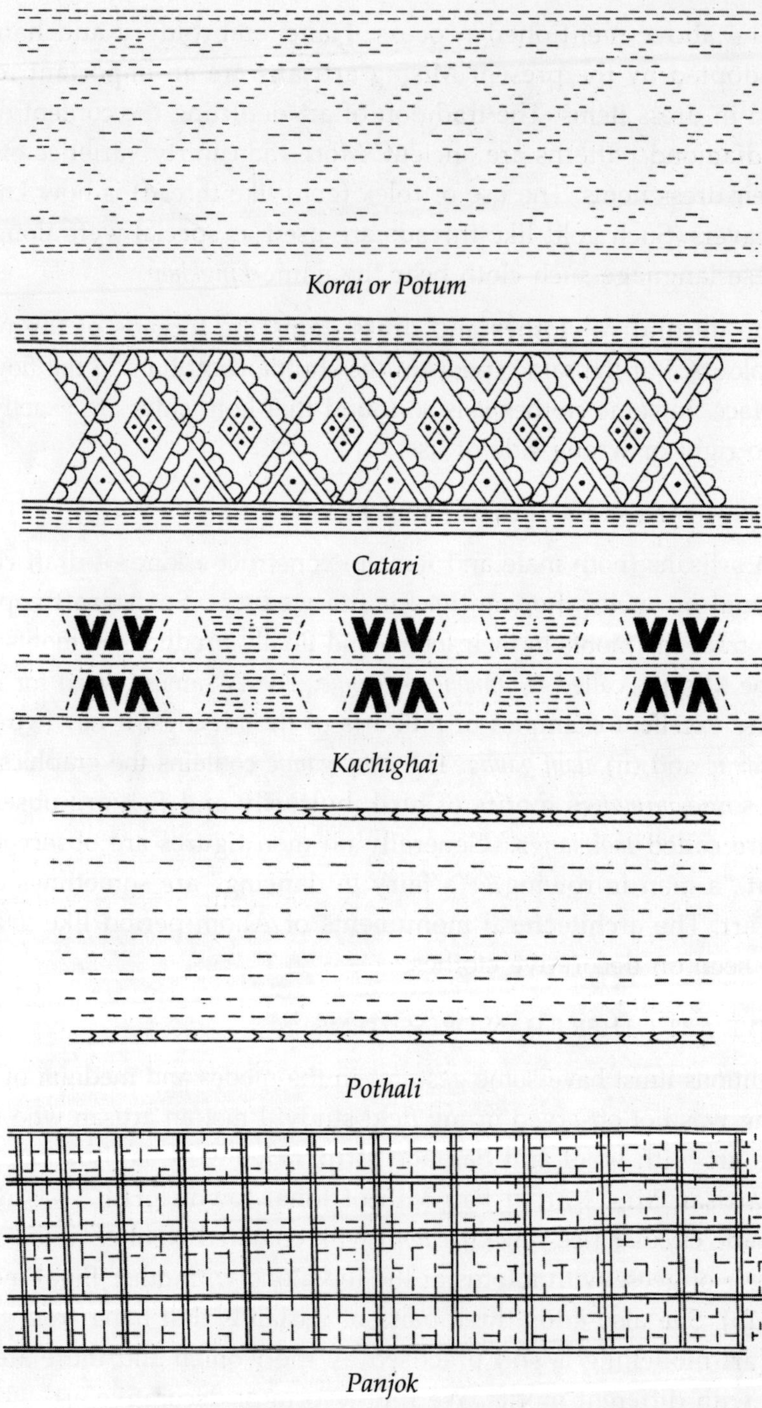

fig. **1. Art on clothes**

Tipan

Tigurgamic

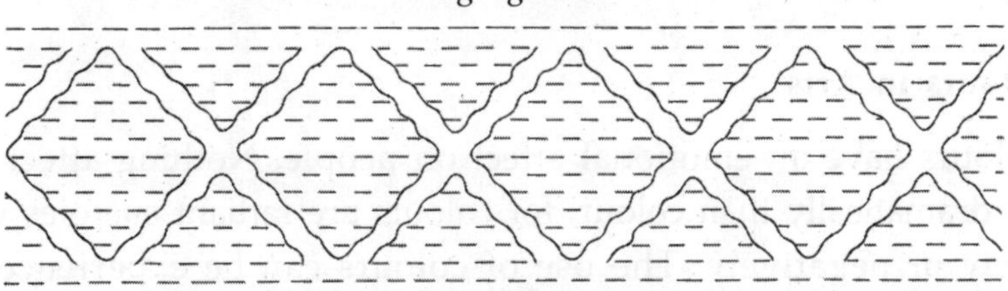

Lakagamic

Capsonmosang

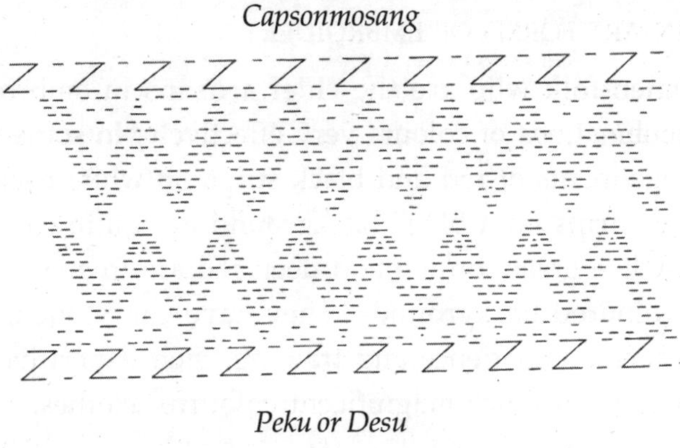

Peku or Desu

***fig.* 2. Art on clothes**

often influenced by all Indian styles — but these art forms are not dependent on raw materials. The tools and raw materials are those which are used in everyday life.

Decorative art on the pillars and wooden beams of the *murong*s are often seen in Mising villages. In Jonai town two figures of crocodiles are observed on the front beam of the *murong* which are drawn face to face with white paint on black surface.

In Ratanapur, the *murong* is decorated with bird motifs carved out of wood and fixed on the front beam.

Human and animal figures are rare. Stylized trees and geometric motifs are depicted on the pillars. Such long strips are hung vertically around the room. In the *murong*s these decorative arts are seen but in peasant's house there is no such use.

Use of Colours in Arts

Various colours have an emotional effect on people. Nothing affect the human mind more dramatically than colour, for colours are radiant energies which affect us positively or negatively. The use of colours can be experienced visually, psychologically and symbolically.

The symbolic use of colour is universal and has been used from the earliest time in rituals, in special rites and ceremonies which are closely associated with the day-to-day living. The colour may captivate the eye and produce a sense of beauty. One must have training to develop the beauty of colours.

COLOUR USED IN ART FORMS OF EMBROIDERY

The Mising women-folk who are the chief artisans in embroidery often make contrasts and combinations of colours very effectively. In some forms of garments we see the arrange-ments of red and black strips on white background. Similarly white and yellow strips on a black background are quite common and popular among the folk. Olive green, brown and deep red are frequently furnished on the white or other coloured backgrounds. They have comprehended the sensitivity to colour and by mere experience and training, their expert hands apply a range of suitable colours to produce magnificent colourful clothes.

Some floral designs on green or blue background probably indicate the lovely swamp full of lilies. It is also compared with the night sky full of stars. Many people have now forgotten the meanings if the designs or art on their clothes, but a few of the old men and women still had them in their minds. The interpretation of some designs vary from village to village.

Some of the symbolic meaning of the colours and designs on textiles are collected from some senior informants which are described below.

I was told that the simple triangles were regarded as mountains which are broad at the bottom and narrow at the top. It also represent the arrows or claws of hornbills.

The dotted designs with different colours represent either the marking on a snake or foot prints of the small birds on sandy river banks.

The interesting patterns of rows of very small pink triangles with a white filling represent the teeth visible when the lips are parted in a smile.

The very common diamond design is initiated with the marking on the cobra.

The circular designs are not common in dress. Such designs represent the moon and sometimes the human heads. Thus some geometric patterns may said to be cosmic symbols.

As described by some Mising artisans, the colours have some definite meanings. Such as the black stands for dark, blue for sky, red standing for blood of the enemies and so forth. The texture used in combination of *mekhela-chador* or *ribi-gasang* shows definite relation one to another. The pairs are harmonious and sometimes in common. A fathomless understanding of colour and design patterns seems to be an outstanding characteristic of the Mising clothes.

In byegone days the artists prepared the colours from indigineous materials. Now they use colours bought from the market. The coloured threads are also bought from the market.

The following are the important characteristic features in relation to the drawing and embroidery works of the weavers:

(i) In most of the weaving articles banded lines and V-shaped motifs are the dominant art forms with coloured threads.

(ii) These ups and downs lines represent the hilly tracks and small rivulets in hilly areas. It is more popularly called *paharia* which means hill areas.

(iii) It is surprising to say that most of the weavers take no help of any *gamick*. But the motifs display regular figures.

(iv) The weavers (or rightly saying the artisans) have a weakness for red and black colours along with violet.

(v) Figures of animal, floral and other geometric designs are common.

Art is often regarded as a matter of divine revelation or spontaneous inspiration of a man of genius. But art is not accidental achievement. The Mising folk artists (weavers) created works to meet their own needs as well as the needs of their own families. They therefore have a constant contact with their works. This led them to improve their works.

Decorative folk art has influenced various forms of emotions and feelings connected with religion, customs and their own experience.

R.K. Mukerjee observed on art as follows —

> Through the epochs of man's history art not only reveals man's intense emotional relations to the world, that he sees around him, but also supplies the formal symbols, patterns or designs for various activities that bind him to fellow man. . . . .
>
> Art is not only the ending glory of the individual and the imperishable record of culture, but it is also its principal impulsion.

He also said —

> All what humanity dreams, strives and suffers for stands behind art, giving man peace, peace with self, with society and with the universe.[3]

All these things are present in Mising folk art we find in Mising art the simplicity of style and felicity in expression. In conclusion, it can be said that there will be no decline in Mising folk art in costumes and ornaments.

It will enter a new and interesting period of development. The art on clothes by the Mising weavers bears the cultural heritage of the tribe throughout the ages. The old traditions relating to colouring the dress items are still resounding. The artistic vernacular of the Mising people are unparalleled and the range of colours and their use are widening. Despite the advantage of machine made clothes all the village women use clothes that are essentially woven in their handlooms. This is because the machine civilization cannot create duplicate of

3. R.K. Mukarjee, *The Social Function of Art*, p. xxi.

the hand-created art and embroidery. They are able to build a protective barrier around folk art. They carry their own undisturbed aesthetic approach for folk arts. Which are as yet preserved intact by the ladies and it has remained unpolluted.

The art creations of a particular time and place established certain norms which are known as art schools of those periods. With the influence of local environment the Mising weavers evolve individual designs for their costumes which have a range of multifarious colour combination and attractive design. The Mising folk art may certainly be regarded as a separate school of Indian folk art. Indian culture, in several times of her history gets contributions from several cultures for her development and growth. The Mising folk art is one of such valuable culture which contributes a lot to the country's age-old art tradition.

Ritualistic Art of the Misings

In India natural objects like mountains, hills, rivers, lakes, plants and trees are regarded as the abodes of deities.

Traditionally the Misings of Assam are nature worshipper. They followed some rituals relating to fertility of the earth for good hervest, protection from diseases and from the action of evil spirits.

The ritual art have their origin in rituals performed throughout the year in various occasions. It is a way through which man gets power and peace and satisfaction.

RITUAL ART RELATED TO ALI-AYE-LIGANG

It is discussed earlier that the *Ali-aye-Ligang* is the worship of departed souls. On the second Wednesday in the month of *Phalgun* they observe this festival. The head of the family with the help of a priest (*satola*) made an altar on which a number of pots made of banana leafs were arranged. A *mati chaki* with mustard oil was burning there during the festival. The head member of the family chanted *panoms* relating to the good wish to the departed soul and offered *apong* in the pots arranged on the altar. The whole arrangement symbolized religious art of the Misings.

ART RELATING TO CHANG BIHU

Chang bihu is a ritual function observed in the month of *Jeṭh* or *Āṣāḍh* or *Bhādra* of

Assamese calendar. To mark the occasion decorative sign posts of *khogoris* (a kind of reed) are pitched on all the ways to the village.

In the *pūjā* field, two idols of snake are prepared and from a kind of fern and splitted bamboo. The idols are placed on the altar and the altar is decorated with *mati chaki*, banana leafs with leafs of coconut and dates.

ART RELATED TO DOBORU PŪJĀ

In *mopung doboru* the people of the village cleaned a field in the midst of the village. A paddy plant is taken out and is bound with the leafs of a tree called *magala*. It is then put in a bamboo basket and hang in the midst of two posts. The priest offers *apong* and blood of pigs and cocks to the imaginary God.

In *kabankoson* types of *doboru pūjā*, five wooden posts of *magala* tree are planted with a cross-mark at their middle. Heads of cocks and pigs are hung on those posts in certain forms.

In *talo uee* seven cocks of different colour are offered to the God. In *urompidnum* three small huts are built with bark of banana tree for the imaginary gods of wind, water and land. Two tender plants are planted near the house for the rest of the gods. A bow and an arrow are also arranged there following some traditional beliefs. These explain the artistic minds of the community.[4]

All those ritual arrangements carried some folk art which are crude in form but have aesthetic values for the minds of the people who arrange those festivals.

4. T.C. Pamagum, "Mising Dharmo Bisar Aru Gana" in *MSA*, pp. 222-23.

Chapter 5

Folk Crafts of the Misings

CRAFT is the handiwork of man designed to achieve his ends. Handicraft has always been a basic activity of human society for craft is an integral part of our life. The Mising community has a proud heritage of handicraft which carries both decorative value and utility in daily life. Varieties of hand-made clothes using traditional techniques wove by the Mising weavers are fascinating and exquisite in character. Among the varieties of decorative art and craft, there are two distinguished styles which are enjoying monopoly among either sex.

The man's style is solely expressive in wood carving, basketry, metal work, horn and ivory carving and such other works. The woman's style finds expressions in weaving, embroidery, spinning and dyeing. In most of the Mising families the head member is a basket maker, his wife, the weaver for the members of the household; thus keeping every household self-sufficient.

The craft items produced by the craftsmen are basically utilitarian in which the efforts has been made to introduce aesthetic appeal. In the hands of an excellent craftsman the craft tends to be a highly decorative art.

M.K. Pal says:

> The arts and crafts as practised by the tribal people of India are essentially products of primitive artistic skills embroidering the creative imagination of the tribal craftsmen. Different types of utilitarian, decorative and ritual objects are still produced by them, which do not only serve the needs of the common people mostly in or around the centres of production, but also satisfy the artistic taste of the sophisticated community. The crafts examples have their age-old ways of production, their own designs, colour schemes and individual shapes. The tools needed by the craftsman though primitive in many cases, can produce unique examples of artefacts

impregnated with silent and subtle beauty.[1]

The folk craft is called *modvt monam* by the Misings which includes weaving or *sumnam panam;* cane and bamboo works or *jcingia ponam*.

For systematic analysis of the traditional folk crafts of the Misings, we can discuss it under the following heads:

(i) Cane and bamboo works.
(ii) Wood works.
(iii) Earth.
(iv) Metal works.
(v) Ivory and horn carving.
(vi) Spinning, weaving and embroidery.
(vii) Jute works.

Cane and Bamboo Works

RAW MATERIALS

Cane and bamboo are the raw materials used in basketry which are locally available in the hills and plains of Assam. Various species of bamboos and canes are found in these areas which are suitable for basket making and mat weaving purposes.

According to the forest division 51 different species of bamboo and three species of cane are available in the forests of Assam.[2]

Cane or *bat*, as it is called, is a kind of climbing plant having many joints stems. It can grow to an immense height, climbing over the highest trees to 500 or 600 ft. Cane is found in abundance throughout the state. It is observed that generally three species of cane are used in basket making. Those are *lejai* (*Calmus floribundus*), *tita* (*Calamuslapisadix*) and *jati* (*Calamustennis*). Some other canes like *sundi* (*Calamusgaruba*) and *raidang* (*Calamusflageihum*) are also found in the jungles of Assam. The stems are extraordinarily strong. Cane is largely utilized for works of various crafts. Picturesque cane crafts comprising bowl, mugs, containers and stools with different attractive designs are made from cane by the Mising craftsmen of Assam. Mats made of cane strings with fine texture and decorative styles are

1. M.K. Pal, *Crafts and Craftsmen in Traditional India*, p. 266.
2. J. Das, *Asamar Lok Kala*, p. 8.

also prepared by the Misings. Cane is also used for making durable and decorative furniture.

Bamboo lends itself to multifarious use. The use of cut bamboo tube as a water container is an ancient practice. The bamboo and cane are the two raw materials used by the people of north-eastern India for basketry, housing and other purposes. Bamboo is a versatile multi-purpose forest product which plays a vital role in domestic and individual economy. Bamboo has age-old connection with the material needs of the people of Assam where these are found in greatest abundance and varieties. The most commonly used bamboos belonging to the Poaceae family are *jati, mokal* (*Bambusa pallida*), *bojal* (*Pseudostachyum polymor phum*), *bhaluka, bijuli,* etc. Bamboo serves as pillars, beams for the house and provides materials for door and window, walls, basket making, agricultural implements, weaving accessories, bows and arrows and musical instruments. Bamboo is rightly called "Green gold."

Basket making is an ancient art done by knitting grass and interlacing leaves with minimum use of tools for domestic and ritual purposes. Assam and north-east India have a special tradition of basketry. It is observed that there is no particular caste or community in Assam who are exclusively connected with these traditional crafts. It is generally carried by all, particularly the peasants irrespective of caste, community or creed. Like other tribes of Assam, the Misings are also expert in the art of basket and mat making which are generally done by the men-folk.

TOOL AND IMPLEMENTS

In the sphere of bamboo and cane works simple and inexpensive tools are used by the craftsman. The most common tools used for manufacture of basket and other objects are — a long knife locally called *dao*, which is an iron blade sharp at one side and concave at one end while the other end is fixed with a wooden handle. The tool called *kotari* is smaller in size than a *dao*. The Mising term for *dao* is *yoksa* or *yakchik*.

WORK SHED

The manufacture of cane and bamboo products are mostly carried out outdoors and the craft does not require any housing arrangement. The *lotta* portion of a Mising house is commonly used for this craft.

PROCESS OF MANUFACTURE

In weaving baskets and mats various steps are to be followed which can be summarized as follows:

(i) Collection of raw materials from the forest.
(ii) Making of splints.
(iii) Colouring or smoking of splints, if necessary.
(iv) Weaving of baskets, mats, containers, etc.
(v) Giving the finishing touches.

It is already stated that the material needed for basketry are available in ample quantities in the region. The craftsmen collect the materials from their own woods or from public woods. They select the matured materials for suitable use in craft. Bamboos, which are above one year old, are more suitable for basketry. It is believed that these should be collected in autumn and winter as otherwise the spilt made out of them are harmed by insects.

After collecting these materials, it is essential to make required splints from it. In doing so, sometimes the knobs are not included in the splints. In some other cases of course, the knobs are also not excluded. The act of extracting bamboo splint is called *katituluwa*. The final splintting is done with a short knife. The splint is placed between the right arm and the side chest and the one end of the splint is held by the fingers of the right hand. The fingers of the left hand are also applied. The fingers of the right hand and the left hand pull the two corners of the splint in two opposite directions and make further splints. The uniformity and requisite thickness of the splint is maintained by the movement of the arms and the fingers of the operator. Splints are made sufficiently smooth and sundried and sometimes kept upon the fire place for smoking it. Such smoking increase the durability of the basket as the craftsman says.

Process of weaving of Basketry

The basketry technique that has been handed down from the earliest time is classified by O.T. Mason in the following ways:

(1) Hand woven or plaited basketry built on warp foundation.
(2) Sewed or warped basketry built on coiled foundation.

Again Mason has classified woven basketry into four different varieties, viz.,

(i) Checker work, (ii) Diagonal or twilled work, (iii) Wicker work, (iv) Twined or wattled work.[3]

He has classified the coiled basketry into six different techniques namely: (i) Single rod foundation, (ii) Two rod foundation, (iii) Rod-and-welt foundation, (iv) Three rod foundation, (v) Splint foundation and (vi) Grass foundation.

G.N. Crowfoot has classified various techniques of basketry as well as different matting technique. According to him there are six principal classes of basketry technique, e.g., (i) Coiled basketry, (ii) Twined work, (iii) Warped work, (iv) Matting work, (v) Plaited work, and (vi) Wicker work or stake frame basketry. Besides these six principal classes, he has further sub-divided coiled basketry, the twined work and the matting work into four, five and three different divisions respectively.[4]

Again from the viewpoints of techniques used the basket may rightly be divided into two distinct groups, i.e., (a) Plaited (woven) and (b) Coiled.

The methods employed by the Mising basket maskers with specimens and terms used to describe their works are discussed below.

CHECK OR PLAIN WEAVE

It is a simple and elementary combination of the two series of strips. The weft strip floats over the warp, on the other hand the warp floats over the weft. Thus the floating is equal in both the cases of weft and warp. They cross each other at right angles and no space between the overlapping strips is made while weaving for a basket.

TWILL METHOD

In the twill method of basket weaving, the floating of the warps over the wefts and wefts over the warps are equal in number. In general twill technique the weft passes over to consecutive warps and then it goes below two consecutives warps in the next series. It has a definite floating and sinking movement and hence it is called regular twill method.

The Mising term for twill method is *jawara mur* which means the method applied commonly in a fencing.

---

3. O.T. Mason, *The Origin of Invention*, p. 109.
4. G.N. Crowfoot, *Textile Basketry and Mats*, p. 418.

fig. **3. Check technique in bamboo works**

fig. **4. Twill technique in bamboo works**

IRREGULAR TWILL METHOD

In this method of weaving the weft and warp are not passed uniformly to the next series; it varies from one to another. In this method instead of definite floating and sinking move-ments an irregular sequence in the interlacement of strips is employed.

A particular sequence is again followed after an irregular interval. This type of twill may be called irregular twill technique.

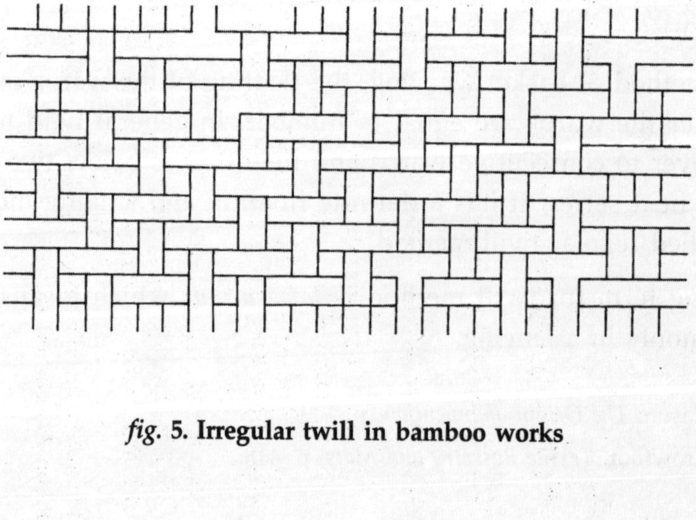

fig. **5. Irregular twill in bamboo works**

HEXAGONAL TECHNIQUE

In this method the wefts and warps are neither horizontal nor vertical, instead they cut each other at 45° forming hexagonal spaces. Two varieties namely "open hexagonal" and "close hexagonal" are found.

> Most of the tribes adopt open hexagonal technique for making basket for prolonged use. The hexagonal close technique is absent in basket making but is mostly adopted in the making of fans.[5]

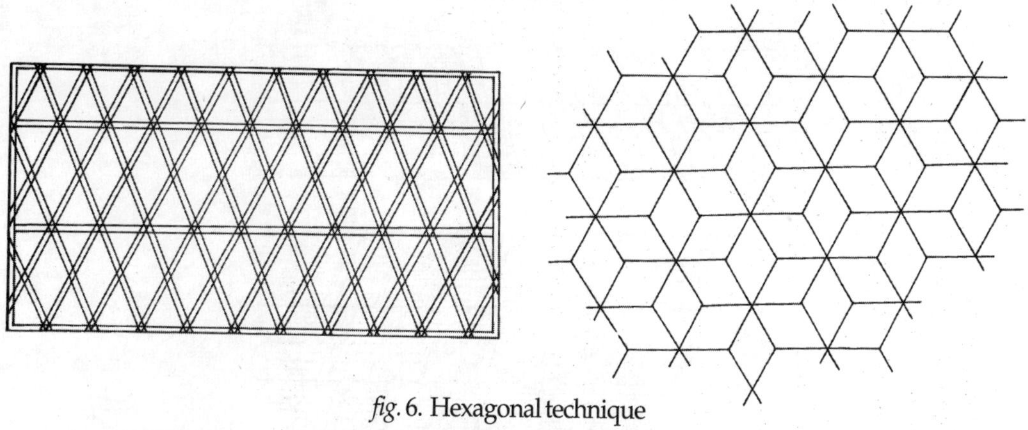

fig. 6. Hexagonal technique

Among the Adis of lower Siang the open hexagonal technique is known as *ponmik*. It is called *hopui* by the Apatanies, and the same is known as *abra* and *aguwang* among the *dafla* and the *sulang* respectively.[6]

It is observed that open hexagonal method of weaving is applied by the Mising craftsman while weaving minor works like container of paddy seeds for in the next year called *tum* and similar minor works of the protective mask for the bulls or buffalos while thrashing.

The close hexagonal texture is used along with the twill method in basket-making for keeping clothes.

Nets of fine bamboo strips woven in hexagonal method are utilized in celling and windows of the houses. The joint portion of a triangular *jakai* (*fig*. 14 (c)) is woven with hexagonal method.

---

5. N.C. Nath, "A Short Study of Basketry Techniques Amongs Selected Tribes of Assam." *Bulletine*, vol. I, 1994, Assam IORTSC, p. 35.

6. A.K Das, *op. cit.*, p. 36.

COILED WORK

Coiled work consists of sewing a spiral foundation of twigs, cane, grass or some other materials screwing in a flat or ascending coil. It is made up of a single element woven up in a spiral design. The work is done by stitching and coiling. The interlacement is done usually with help of an awl of metal or wood which makes a hole through which the coil or weft is passed. Two sets of elements are required in coil work, one of which is technically called core and the other coil. The core is thicker than the coil. The core and the coil may be of different materials.

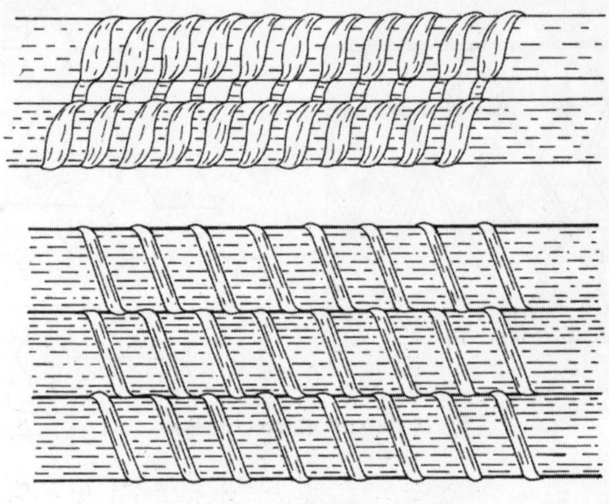

fig. **7. Coiled technique**

This technique is called *immam* by the Adis of lower Siang and is known as *puti* and *puwang* amongst the Apatanis and Salungs respectively.[7]

The Misings of Assam utilize this technique in making caps with sungrass and cane strips. It is observed in Majuli sub-division that the young school boys wear caps woven with sungrass which they utilized as headgears while playing folk games. It is a golden coloured lovely cap. This technique of coiled works is not observed in basketry but widely used in minor decorative works.

Depending upon the method of sewing two different varieties are found. These are (i) spiral coiling, and (ii) sewed coiling.

(i) *Spiral coiling* : In such coiling process, the single thread binds each of the preceding coil giving a diagonal twilled effect.

(ii) *Sewed coiling* : Sewing method rather than weaving technique is used for

7. A.K. Das, *op. cit.*, p. 37.

basketing with cane, grass or such other materials. An awl or needle is used to make the holes through which the warping is passed. The sewing passes up and over the new coil binding around it one or more times. The new coils are connected with each other by these sewing processes.

In some coiled baskets stitching materials are very fine. For large granary baskets the materials used are often half inch wide for stitching the coil together.

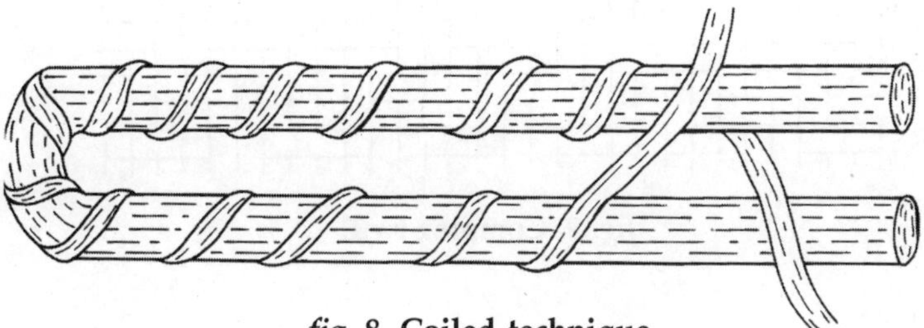

fig. **8. Coiled technique**

PROCESS OF WEAVING OF COILED BASKET

The reeds are coiled into convenient size, tying firmely for two or three times, leaving about ten inches uncoiled. In some cases the uncoiled portion is dipped into hot water for soften. The end of the reed is made like a needle with a sharp knife.

Holding the reed firmly in the left hand, it is drawn through the fingers of the right, shaping the end into a round coil. With the right hand, using the forefinger and thumb to fare the end of reed into a small possible coil. The weaving is really the stitching upon a continuous coil, and as the coil progresses, each stitch or weave is passed between a stitch of the coil beneath. The passing of the thread over and under the two reeds appears something like the following sketch.

In commencing to use a new reed or weft the old and new are wound closely and the ends are cut and thus continues weaving.

Angular Pattern

The angular design of basket weaving is the outcome of complex twilling. Sometimes varying degrees of prepond-erance of the warp and weft and sometimes the equal number of floating of the warp and the weft are seen. The structural pattern of the form is like the letter "V". Floating of the warps and weft strips in this pattern of weaving is appended below.

fig. **9. Complex twill**

TWINED METHOD

This is perhaps the most primitive method of weaving found among many Indian tribes. The Mising of Assam commonly utilized this method while weaving fishing traps like *ban, juluki, pollo, cepa, uvoti,* etc. Here the bamboo strips are woven with the help of two cane strings as shown below.

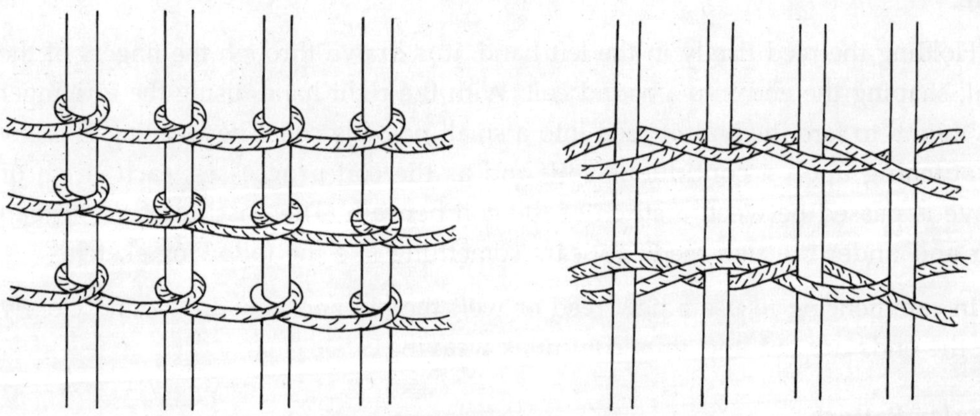

fig. **10. Twined technique**

Design

Nearly all the Mising basketry can be divided in geometrical divisions. Circular, semi-circular, hyperbolic, elliptical, conical, double convex, plano convex, square and rectangular shapes are found in baskets as these are suitable to a particular work or many works.

It seems difficult to produce these designs but the craftsman easily accomplishes and surprises us for giving the shapes by following the method of weaving as mentioned earlier. It is optional with the worker as to the shape and size of the basket. After the worker has woven the desired size for the bottoms, he begins shaping the basket by placing the reed over the last woven coil according to the shape desired.

The oval or conical-shaped baskets are shaped in different ways. These shapes are more difficult to manipulate than the round basket. The types of strips used in basketry vary in width and length depending upon the nature of material used and types of weaving technique. It is observed that if the strips are smooth and the materials (bamboo, cane, etc.), are matured the product will be attractive and durable.

Finishing Steps

After the last row of weaving it is beautifully finished. The unnecessary warps in some cases are cut-off and are sometimes bent and act as weft and are then fastened with it.

In some baskets (for example, *dolla, kula, chalani*, etc.), when the required size has been woven, it is finished by weaving a double row of two *kathi*s or reeds around the top.

In some cases a pair of rims called *baau* are fastened with the finishing steps by stitching it with cane strips. This strengthens the basket and increase its durability. In addition to *dao* and knife another implement called *bindhona* (a spike of iron or bone of animals) is used to tighten the rim. Often the operator uses his teeth for this purpose.

Cane Baskets

The manufacture of cane basket is very rare. It is not commercially viable. So the uses of such cane basket are also very few in the state. The baskets are used mainly for carrying goods, storing grains and keeping valuables. Some families use such cane baskets for keeping clothes and ornaments with locking arrangements. Cane baskets are generally prepared by coil method. The warp is arranged by cane of sufficient length. Such cane is soaked in water for sometime before weaving to give it a flexible character.

CANE FURNITURE

In a Mising house cane made furniture are rare. Only a kind of stool called *murha* found which are made of bamboo and cane. Some people nowadays buy some cane products from the market. These are manufactured by the craftsman from Cachar district.

Study of Some Specimens

The people of the plains and hills of Assam have there own bamboo and cane products with distinctive features and typical designs. The product of various types in hills or plains differ from one another in shape, design and uses.

Some specimens of baskets of the Mising craftmen are studied from the field. The specimens are selected from the following villages:

(i) Sham Mising Gaon (Teok) of Jorhat District.
(ii) Bah-phola Gaon of Jorhat Districts.
(iii) Dhonsiri Mukh of Golaghat District.
(iv) Dohgharia (Bor doti) of North Lakhinmpur District.

Mising name of the specimen : Cbong

English equivalent name : Headgear;

Assamese name: *Japi*;

Material used: Bamboo, leaves of *Tokow*.

Technique employed in weaving: Hexagonal net weaving.

Size of the weft: Length of wefts varies from centre to border is 2 mm.

Size of the basket: 65-70 cm diameter.

Size of he warp: Breadth 2 mm. length is equal to the diameter of the object.

Purpose: Protection from rain and sun specially in the field.

Description: It is a headgear used instead of an umbrella. Two similar nets of hexagonal weaving are woven having a "V" pattern in the centre which is equal in size of a men's head. In the midst of these two nets leaves of *tokow* (a kind of palm) after drying under sunlight are placed smoothly. A jute string is provided at the inner side of the V-shaped portion which helps the man to bind with his neck.

Name of the specimen: Duli/Gampa

English equivalent: Storage basket.

Assamese name: *Duli*.

Material used: Bamboo strips.

Technique applied: Check (one up one down).

Size of the warp: 1.5 cm.

Size of the weft: 1.5 cm.

Purpose of use: Storing paddy, mustard seeds, etc.

Description: It is a U-shaped basket but its diameter in the mouth portion is greater than the bottom. Gampa is longer and wider than any other baskets.

Name of the specimen : Epo

English equivalent: Winnowing fan.

Assamese equivalent: *Kula*.

Material used: Bamboo for weaving and cane strips for binding the boundary bars.

Technique applied: Twilled.

Size: Approximate length 63 to 65 cm, breadth 30 to 56 cm.

Shape: Semi-circular/hyperbola.

Purpose of use: For cleaning the corn, paddy, etc.

Description: It is a hyperabolic structure of bamboo made plates used to clean the corn and paddy. The boundary of such epo is tightly bound by bamboo bars suitably made and tied with strings of cane. The interior end of the fan is flat and the rims of the two sides gradually become higher, reaching the maximum height at the back.

Name of the specimen: Challoni

English equivalent: Sieve.

Material used: Bamboo.

Technique applied: Twill.

Shape: Circular.

Size: Diameter is approximately 40 cm.

Purpose of use: Used for separating smaller gains from corn, etc.

Description: It is woven with fine bamboo splits. Small holes are made between two warps and wefts woven by twill technique. In middle portion two pairs of warps and wefts are used which create four quardants in the *chaloni*. These are named as *ghai* which are wider than other splints. It is used for sieving paddy, rice and pulses and also for washing fish.

Name of the specimen: Dolla

English equivalent: Winnowing fan or bamboo tray.

Material used: Bamboo.

Technique applied: Twill.

Shape: Circular.

Purpose of user: For drying corns under sunlight or like that of a *kula*.

Description: *Dola* is a circular bamboo disc with thin strips and strong boundary rods tied with cane strings.

Name of the specimen: Passi/Gampa

English equivalent: Storing and carrying basket.

Material used: Bamboo.

Technique applied: Two rod foundation, checker work.

Shape: Circular.

Purpose of use: Use as storage of paddy or other corns.

Description: Foundation is started with twill technique with two pairs of *ghai* both as warp and weft.

Name of the specimen : Khorahi

English equivalent: Small basket.

Material used: Bamboo.

Technique applied: Irregular twill method.

Shape: Circular.

Size: Varies from 40 cm, in the outer diameter.

Size of the warp and weft: 3 mm (approx.).

Description: It is also a U-shaped basket like a *pasi* but its strips are smaller in width than the *pasi*. Generally it is used to clean any corn, rice with water the water pass through the smaller holes but the corn could not passed through it. It has also rod bars binding it at its boundary. The *khorahi* is woven in plain and square form buit is gradually bent in a round form at the time of final stitching by flexible cane strips.

Name of the specimen : Jopa/Cdum

English equivalent: Container with cover.

Material used: Bamboo.

Size of the warp: 0.5 cm.

Size of the weft: 0.5 cm.

Description: *Jopa* is a useful container with a lid and a handle. It is almost conical in size. It has various utilities such as storing of clothes and necessary goods.

The basket can hang on its handle. Another kind of *jopa* or *cdum* is woven in screw coil method using cane strings. Such *cdum* has a beautiful shape and most commonly used in storing valuable dress items. Small and very fine cane splints are used to weave it. Triangular and square designs are produced with the splints. The upper portion is folded.

Carrying Baskets

The carrying baskets are conical in shape. The basket is woven very closely in twill pattern with small fine bamboo splints. After the basket has been woven, several supporting bamboo strips are tied in regular intervals so that their ends join at the conical apex of the basket. Those strips are tied to the basket with cane. For carrying such basket a thin but strong rope made of jute is fitted at the middle of the basket. Small size carrying baskets commonly found in a Mising house are mentioned below.

PAPA

It is a bamboo basket weaven in hexagonal forms. *Papa* is used to carry lighter things or to store some valuable equipments. A special type of *papa* is necessary in *doboru pūjā*.

RASA

Rasa is also a carrying basket having two strings and can be carried like a school bag. It is woven in hexagonal forms.

POTUM

It is also a kind of storage basket made of flexible cane or bamboo.

FISHING TRAPS OF BAMBOO AND CANE

The Misings living by the river side are expert in rowing and fishing. They adopt various methods in fishing operations. The people do not use many baskets for fishing. A few valve traps like *sepa, uvoti, khoka* are woven with bamboo splints with a valve fitted to it and place on the flowing of water of low depths. The traps like *pollo, juluki* and *jakoi* are observed in group fishing.

Description of construction of these traps are given below:

Name of the trap: Jakoi

Size and shape: Triangular conical shaped bamboo device. Sides are 2 ft.

Technique applied: Twill in the three sides but the joining portion is hexagonal weave.

Size of warp and weft: 2 mm.

Description: The *jakoi* is used by the women-folk in community fishing in shallow pools or river sides. The trape is triangular at its front or mouth and conical at the ends. Small holes are kepting in it so that water passes through it. To produce these holes the warps and wefts are arranged at least 1 mm, distances while weaving it. A handle and a string are provided with the trap to pull it in water. The joining portion, i.e., the upper side of the trap which can be called diagonal of the triangle is woven with hexagonal method of weaving creating comparatively bigger holes.

Name of the trap: Juluky

Description: Bamboo strips are split first into 3 ft, long and 1 inch wide and that half of its length is again split into small stricks. One such piece contains three or four small sticks which are hared by rubbing with a sharp knife. These are then woven with cane strings following the twined method. It is then formed like a hollow cylinder whose lower diameter is 3 times greater than the upper part. A ring of bamboo and cane ropes are fixed at its upper mouth to facilitate it smoothly. *Juluki* is used for fishing in shallow water.

Name of the trap : Pollo

Description: *Pollo* is a fishing trap made of bamboo and cane used in group fishing in river or pools. In marking the strips of a *pollo* only the green portion which is harder than the other is utilized. Hexagonal twin method of weaving is applied. A number of circular rims of different diameter from top to bottom are applied which act as weft of the traps. The shape of the *pollo* resembles that of a dome with short stem of about 6 inches diameter open at the top. Diameter of the bottom varies from 3 ft to 3.5 ft, and the height varies from 3 ft.-3.5 ft.

Name of the trap : Chepa

Description : The *chepa* is made of bamboo strips and fine cane strings in a roundish fashion. The strips are weaven in twin fashion. The two ends of the *chepa* are kept close but one end can be open when required. In the middle portion two holes are kept and they are provided with two valves called *kol*. The small fishes can enter into the device but cannot come out of it.

Ovoti, Khoka, Pawa are similar fishing traps.

Besides the above baskets many other baskets of twilled and checker pattern are made to store dried meat, fish and salt. The work is always done in the household and produced mainly for one's own family. There is no household with basketry as a primary source of livelihood. Thus basketry is generally practised only for domestic consumption. Some old skilled craftsmen who are unable to work in the field, devote their full-time to basketry work. The articles produced by such men are sold in local market.

Dyeing of Baskets

To beautify the containers, baskets of soft uses, fans and caps coloured strips are used and these can be categorized as decorative art.

The process of making colour solution is an elaborate affairs. For different colours they collect bark and leaves of certain plants which after being boiled in water produces the desired colour solution. The bamboo or cane splints are then dipped for a day or more into the solution thus produced. In some cases the craftsman prepared the bamboo strips and kept them up on the fire place for smoking which gives a black coating to it. According to the craftsman such smoking increased the durability of the basket. In some cases such strips are buried in mud for several days. It is to be noted here that dyed cane or bamboo strips are very rare in the context of woven baskets among the Misings. There are many people who prefer the natural colour of reeds and do not care for the dull unfinished appearance of the bamboo strips. "The tribes of Arunachal Pradesh used bamboo and cane strips which were dyed for making their headgear, waistband, headband, armlet, etc."[9] But the Mising tribes in plains do not use such articles nowadays. It is due to the influence of non-tribal Assamese, that they leave such articles. Besides these they made beautiful scabbards from wood, bamboo and cane strips to keep the dáos or swords which have fine ropes to hang on the shoulder.

The dyeing by indigenous process increases the durability, protects the devices from insects and fungi.

The Mising people of Assam prefer the natural colour of the bamboo or cane that occurs due to fine polishing of it. The working baskets which are used frequently are not coloured.

Basketry in Social Spheres

Basketry is a part and percel of the total cultural spheres of a particular area. It is related to ritualistic associations, domestic and social spheres in various ways. The objects may not be always beautiful and fine.

The basket makers of Assam including the Misings have never formed a separate occupational group like the potter or blacksmith. Each and every workman of the village folk possesses the working knowledge of basketry. There are however expert basket markers who take the craft for livelihood. The basket makers are generally cutlivators with agriculture as primary occupation and they try to utilize their leasure in basketry. Only the menfolk seem to engage in this craft. So it can be said that the basketry is exclusively the man's affair.

Handloom, Weaving and Embroidery

Weaving in Assam is characterized by its distinctiveness, and most of the products are of purely utilitarian purposes. Some of those products are of durable quality, exquisite, beauty and delightful colours. Handloom industry has occupied an important place in every Assamese household. M.K. Gandhi said that the Assamese women can draw their dreams on their looms. During the Ahom period the weavers had a good reputation. The process is best known to the Misings of Assam who manufacture excellent fabrics of various designs even today.

9. A.K. Das, *op. cit.*, p. 87.

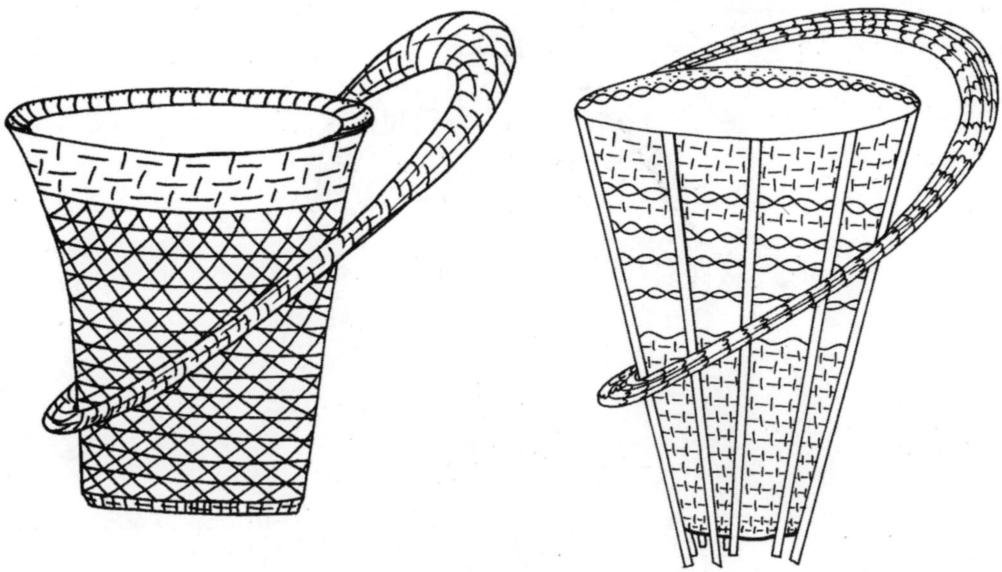

fig. **11. Carrying baskets**

fig. **12. Carrying basket**

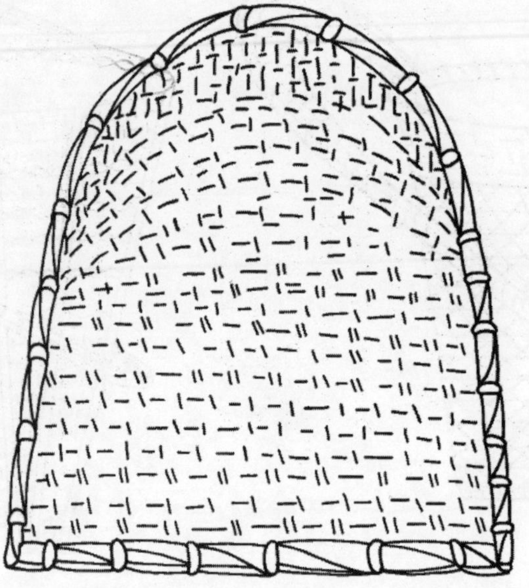

Winnowing Fan

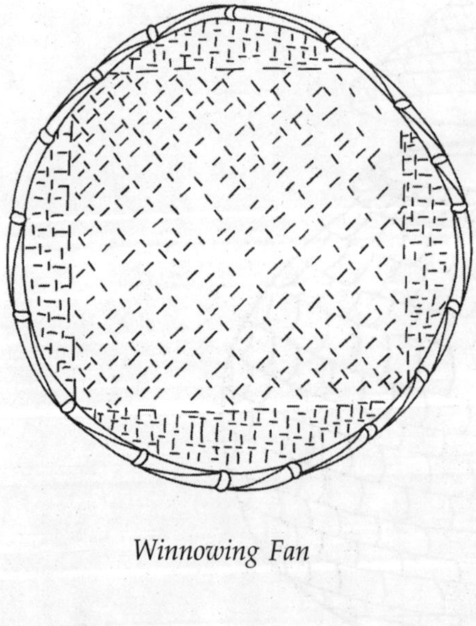

Winnowing Fan

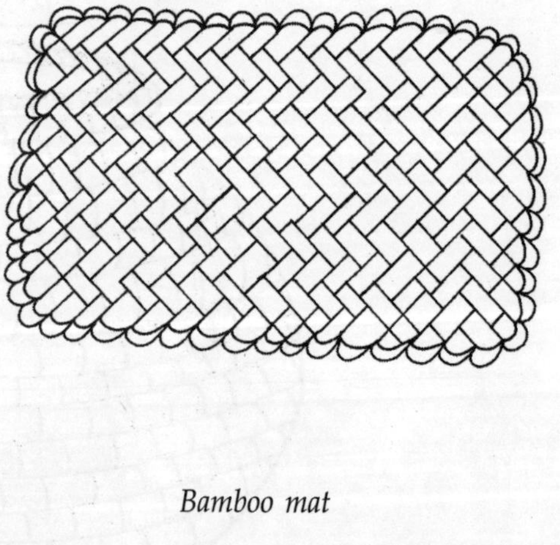

Bamboo mat

***fig.* 13. Winnowing fan and mats**

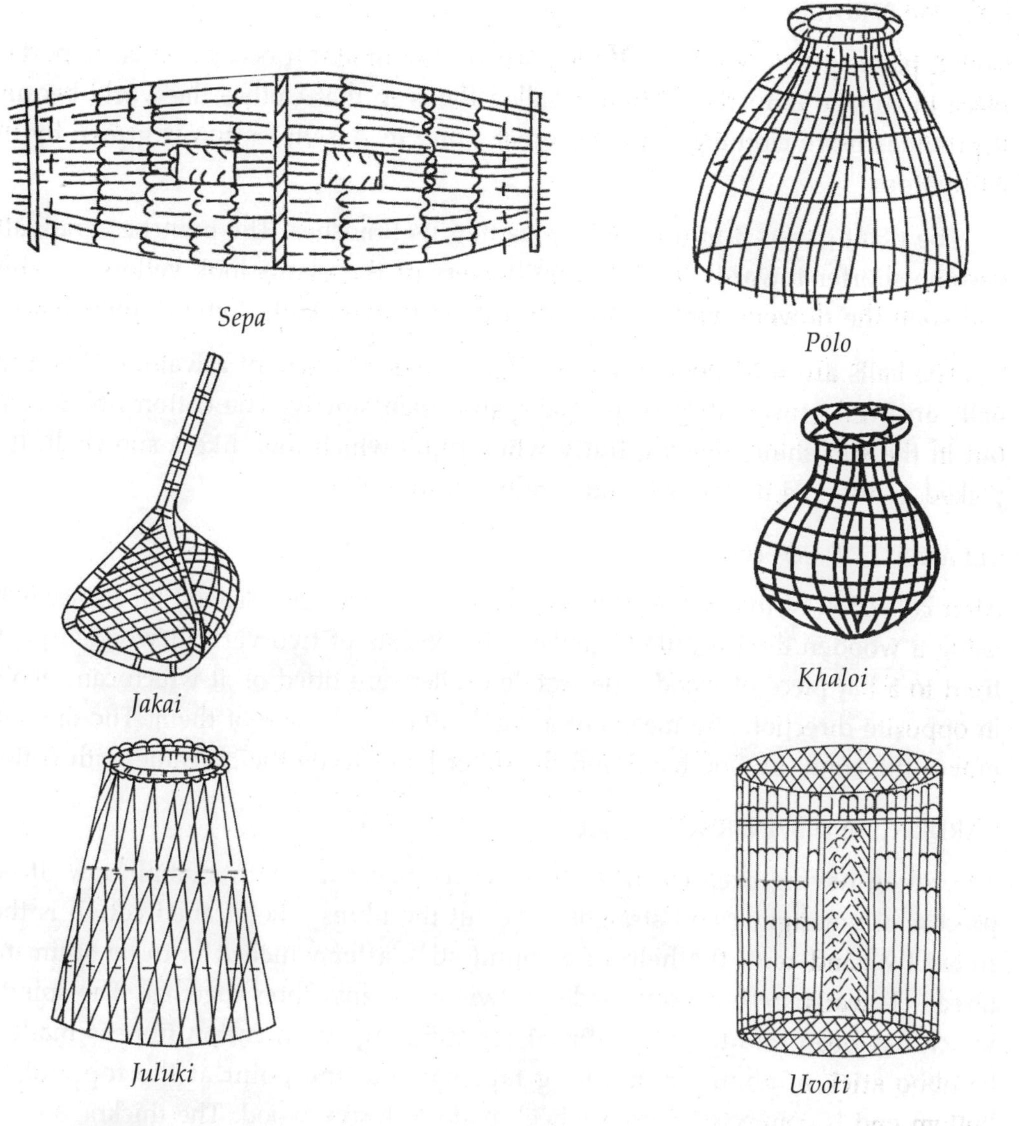

***fig.* 14. Fishing traps**

RAW MATERIALS

Cotton plants grow in almost all the parts of Assam and it occupying an important place in cottage industry. Cotton is called the crop that clothes the world because it provides more clothing than any other fibre. In Assam, cotton is grown by the cultivators.

The plant grows 5 to 6 ft high spreading its branches. The branches gradually become shorter towards the top. The flowers of the plants look yellow or white and soon the flowers wither and drop off, and green balls come in their places.

The balls are seed pods of cotton and become the size of a walnut. When the balls are well grown, they turn brown and open slowly. The cotton fibres come out in the sun shine, making fluffy white puffs which look like a snowball. It is picked as soon as it ripens because rain can injure it.

CLEANING OF COTTON

After collection of the cotton from the field, it is dried and cleaned off its seeds by using a wooden device called *newthoni*. It consists of two vertical wooden posts, fixed to a flat piece of wood. The wooden rollers are fitted on it which can revolve in opposite directions by means of a crank attached to one of them. The operator moves the crank by one hand and the other hand feeds the machine with cotton.

CARDING AND SPINNING

The cotton having been cleaned off its seeds, is carded with a small bow. It is a process of untangling and straightening out the fibres. The cleaned cotton is then rolled by hand with the help of a round stick after which it is to be spun into thread. Threads are fine cord made by twisting many fibres together. The spindle, which has been traditionally utilized for spinning from cotton fibre is made of bamboo stick of about 25 cm, long tapring to a fine point at the top and the bottom end is connected with a wheel made of heavy wood. The thickness of the stick is similar to a pencil but the bottom end is thicker than the top. It is called *takuri* in Assamese. To spin with this spindle, one has to sit on ground and rotate the lower part of the spindle in clockwise direction and with one's left hand one turns small thread from the cotton. When a foot has been spun, it is then wounded just above the wheel. The spindle is then worked as before. To make the spindle slippery for the operator, a sort of white powder from a kind of watermelon is applied on it at the beginning and at intervals. This makes the rotation easy. The wounded yarn, attain a conical shape on the spindle, which is replace by winding off on to a bamboo frame called *ugha*.

For starching the yarn, the threads are dropped into hot rice water or boiled with some rice grains, dried under the sunlight on smooth bamboo rods. It is then again rounded on *ugha*s, after which it is ready for the loom.

Cotton threads are strong and have some life and elasticity, takes dye readily and are good for the weaver to handle.

The age-old cottage industry of the Misings plays vital role in their economy. the tradition of spinning and weaving being handed down from mother to daughter, a young Mising girl has to know weaving before her marriage. Her eyes are focused and learn the contours of the comforting face of the mother. The infants lies in his or her mother's lap and observes the sounds of the humming spinning wheel. The spinning and weaving are carried on with the help of the other members of the family. The female members of the Mising family generally engage in such works. They usefully utilize their leasure in creative crafts.

TYPES OF LOOMS

Weaving consists in the regular interlacing of two sets of threads crossing each other at right angles. The Mising weavers weave in the "plain weave method" by lifting half of the warp thread at the same time for an opening to passing the weft by a shuttle. A loom is the framework across which threads are stretched in parallel order and tension for weaving of cloth.

There are many kinds of looms but the principle is the same in all of them. The common types of looms used by the Mising weavers are as follows:

(i) Throw-shuttle loin loom.

(ii) Throw-shuttle loom staying in four posts.

(iii) Fly-shuttle loom.

The first two types are commonly used by the tribal weavers of Assam and the third is also adopted by them.

(i) Throw-shuttle loin weaving method is common in the Mising villages of the state. It is woven with a bamboo tube. One end of the warp is fastened to the wall of the house and the other end is fastened the waist of the weaver with a cotton or leather belt. At each end of the belt is tied a string of cane which is attached to a bar made of wood. From this bar, the warps about 3 m in length and 40 cm in width, run to the beam which is fixed firmly either to the wall of the house or to a post fixed in the ground. Only hands can operate this loom. No reed is utilized here. A smooth and flat wooden sword is used to beat the weft (*fig.* 15).

There is arranged a long flat stick passed over and under the warp threads. If we look closely, we will see that the flat stick passed under all odd numbers of threads 1, 3, 5, 7 and so on and in next step another such stick passed under all even numbers of threads. To put a weaving thread through it the weaver simply turn the flat stick on edge. The opening thus made is called a "shed" which passes the first row of weft and is then beaten down with the sword or stick. Now the weaving thread is ready to come back across the opposite of the first row. This time the weaver moves the shed-stick which was pass through the even number of threads to edge and passed the weft through the opening and beat again. Thus in the second row the weft thread has passed through 2, 4, 6, 8. . . of the warps. By utilizing this type of looms, the Mising weavers weave their *gadu* or *mirsim* clothes, *mibu galuk, gapa* and bags.

A common loin loom consists of the following parts:

(a) A front bar which is a circular wooden bar about 45 inch long and of 1.5 inch diameter. It is fixed with the wall of the house.

(b) *Beast bar* : It is also a circular wooden bar 40 inches long and of 1 inch diameter on which the warp is fixed. The two ends of this bar are fastened with rope.

(c) *Sword* : It is a flat wooden piece.

(d) *Lease rode* : It is a wooden bar 54.2 inches long.

(e) *Back strap* : It is made of either leather or clothes having a length of 21 inches and breadth of 4.5 inches.

Names and dimensions of various parts used in a loom

The parts of a loom and their dimensions, local names, equivalent Mising names and materials used for making such parts are listed in Table 5.1. A complete loom on four posts measures 14" in width 22" in length and 3.5" in height.

(ii) Throw-shuttle looms based on four posts are most common in all the villages of Assam. Here the loom is fitted on four bamboo or wooden posts fixed in

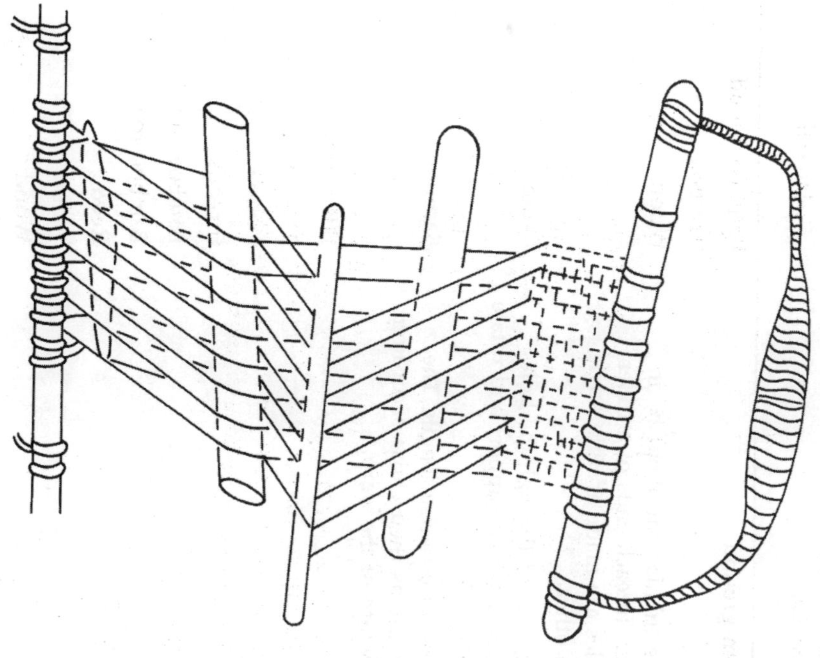

fig. **15. A typical loin loom**

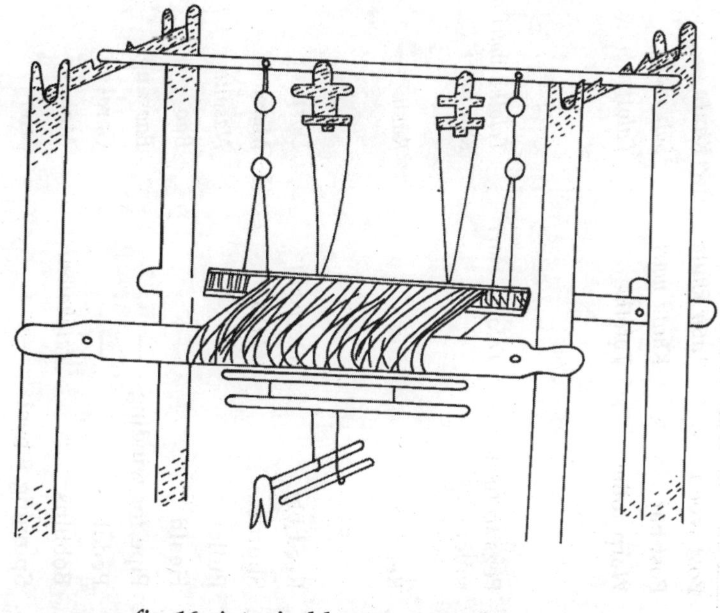

fig. **16. A typical loom rest on four posts**

Table 5.1: Weaving implements

	English used Name	*Mising Name*	*Equivalent Assamese Name*	*Dimension*	*Material*
1.	Post wood	*Tator khuta*	*Khuta*	3½" from ground	Bamboo/wood
2.	Post bar	*Khuta mari*	*Sali mari*	14"	Bamboo
3.	Warp roller	*Tolotha*	*Tolotha*	15" long tubular bar about ¼" in diameter. In each ends of a roller two holes are made at right angle to each other.	Wood
4.	Pegs to turn roller	*Tolotha mari*	*Tolotha mari* or *Kan mari*	3" long, passed through the holes of the roller which support and rotate the roller.	Bamboo
5.	Reed	*Rus*	*Rash*	Reeds are of different length. The weaver use as their chose according to the width of the warp.	Bamboo
6.	Reed bar	*Dorpody*	*Dorpody*	—	Wood or
7.	Shuttle	*Maku*	*Maku*	—	bamboo
8.	Pulley	—	*Nasoni*	—	Cotton
9.	Heald	—	*Bao*	—	threads
10.	Pipe for winding	—	*Baosunga*	—	Bamboo tube
11.	Pedal	—	*Goroka*	—	Bamboo rod
12.	Bobbins	*Jalahaloni*	*Muhura*	—	Reed
13.	Spinning wheel	—	*Jator*	—	Wood
14.	Spindle	—	*Takuri*	—	Wood
15.	Brush	*Popy sampuk*	*Brush*		Straw

the ground. Both the hands and feets are essential to operate the loom. The shedding (opening of the warps) is produced by a set of holds operated by the feet. The shuttle is thrown across the shed by one hand from one side and caught by the other at the opposite side of the cloth. The beating up of the weft is done by a reed commonly made of bamboo fitted to a wooden frame which is given a to-and-fro motion by the hands.

iii. *Fly-shuttle loom*: The loom is made of wood in such a manner that it can be fitted up and dismantled easily. It is an improved type of loom in which the shuttle is driven accros the shed by a string pulling by the hand. The making of the shed and beating of the weft are almost same as in throw-shuttle loom.

Technique of Production in a Loom

There are several different steps to be performed before starting the weaving in a loom.

(a) Warping.
(b) Beaming.
(c) Looming.
(d) Preparation of weft.

WARPING

The Mising weavers with the help of two expert women prepare the warp in an open space generally in front of their houses on a sunny day. Such operations are commonly called *tattbati*. The threads for the warps are previously wounded in different *ugha*s which are placed vertically on a line at equal interval of space on the open courtyard. The length is measured on the courtyard and a post is placed at the other end.

The ends of each thread from the *ugha*s are taken together by a workman and she moves toward the post and gives a turn of the threads at the post. She then moves to the *ugha*s and such operations are done until the required number of warps have been drawn from the *ugha*s. If coloured strips are desired, the colour threads are wound on similar *ugha*s and are placed at the two ends of the line.

The warping is accomplished on a framework by winding the yarn back and forth between the pegs arranged on the framework. The warping device is a cylindrical wooden log called *tolotha*. To prevent the tanglings and keep the thread parallel lease rods are passed through the cross. Before setting up the loom the whole length of warps is wound on a *tolotha*.

INSERTING A REED

The reed is a bamboo device having separate openings or dents like the teeth of a comb. The warp threads are passed through these openings of the reed. The reed is commonly called *rash* which acts as a beater of the weft threads. Threading the warp through the reed is done by a hook-like metal device called *ras-bhoruwa*. This helps passing the warp through the dents of the reed. The reed in a loom can move back and forth to pack the weft rows. The reed is inserted in a vertical wooden frame hanging from the top of the loom.

CENTERING THE WARP IN THE REED

The weaver can make his cloth equal to the full width of the reed or any width less than this. The warp should always be threaded as near to the centre of the reed as possible. To centre the warp threads one should count the number of dents of the reed at first and the threads of the warp. By this simple calculation the weaver starts to insert the warp into the dents of the reed so that equal portion both in left and right of the weaver is left unused if the width the warp is less than the reed.

ARRAÑGEMENT OF "BOO" (LOOPS OF ALTERNATED THREAD)

To make the opening to pass the weft through the alternate warps, an arrangement is made by the weavers during the preparatory process which is locally called *boo tula*.

After inserting the reed the next step of preparing the loom is to bind all the even numbers of warps by a string heavier than the warps with a cylindrical tube to form the loops of *boo*.

Two such rows are constructed one up and the other on the bottom of the warps. They help to create an opening to pass the shuttle by lifting up half of the warp threads at the same time by means of a stick-rope arrangement which is op- erated by the two legs of the weaver.

PREPARING THE WEFT

In simple weaving similar pattern of weft threads are used as the warp. In case of tabby weft or colouring weaves, the weft threads may be of little heavier colour. Threads for the weft may be taken from large spools or from balls and skins. The weft threads from spool or ball is wound on a bobbin with the help of a bobbin winder called *jatar*.

USE OF BOBBIN WINDER

To wind the small spools or bobbins it is necessary to use a bobbin winder (*jatar*) made of wooden crank and a thread is attached to the crank which revolves the stick at the other end of the winder. The tube like bobbins are commonly cut from a wild grass called *ekora*. The bobbin is filled tightly on the end rod during its winding. The operator by the right hand rotates the crank in clockwise direction and with the left hand controls the thread that is to go on winding on the bobbin.

To insert a bobbin in the shuttle the small pin is taken out and again inserted in the same position with the bobbin. The bobbin can rotate freely inside the shuttle taking the pin as axis of rotation. The thread of the bobbin comes out through the nozzle of the spindle.

LOOMING

A four posts loom frame is always ready outside a Mising house. The wooden warpers (*tolotha*) are bound on the four posts. Two sub-posts to hold the *tolotha*s at the weaver's end are also fixed with the loom frame. To rotate the *tolotha*, holes are created at its two ends. The warps run parallel to the ground and are kept about 2.5 ft above the ground. Two bamboo made pedals are arranged in ground which are attached to the *boo*. These pedals are called *gorokamari*. Each pair of posts supports a horizontal bar upon which another bar called *salimari* rests to support the whole loom and its parts.

WEAVING TO A RHYTHM

The weaver sits on a bench or a comfortable chair while weaving. The height from which to weave depends on her choice, but in general the loom should slant slightly downward from the elbows, so that one can throw and catch the shuttle with ease, and the knee should be a little below the level of the loom plane. The winding bobbins are made ready and kept in a small basket generally hanging in the upper bar. To start weaving she pushes the pedal with her left (say) foot to create the shed and her right hand pushed the shuttle by moving the wrist to the left, and sends it through the opening of the other side. Catching the shuttle by the other hand she forward the beater (reed) and changes the shed by releasing the left pedal and pushing the right. Thus shuttle is transferred rapidly from hand to hand without interruption. The repeated throwing and catching of the shuttle row after row, with the recurring thump of the beater, produces a rhythm in the weaving. To acquire this rhythm is a delightful experience. It increases bodily activity; and increases the quality and speed of weaving. An expert Mising woman can weave 10 to 12 ft per day. Some weavers sing songs at loom. There are sufficient folk songs, proverbs, beliefs and taboos relating to a loom.

Silk Works

The silk fabrics of Assam produce out of *eri, muga* and *pat* yarn are durable and attractive. The art of sericulture and rearing of cocoons for the manufacture of various silk clothes are known to the Mising weavers. It is a traditional and age-old domestic industry extensively practised in Assam. Sericulture is an off time occupation of the female members of the Mising families. The rearing is conducted in the dwelling houses of the rearers and sometimes in the open compound of their hutments during fair weather. The tools and imple-ments required for this industry are very few and simple. Most of the appliances are prepared by the family members. The varieties of silk produced in Assam are *eri* (Atpacusricini); *muga* (Antheroeaassmoea) and *pat* (Patta). The rearing of *eri* cocoons takes a long time before they provide silk for spinning. They are fed with the leaves of (1) castor plants (ricinis-communis) (2) *kaseru* (Acterepanaxfragons) and (3) Tapioca. The life of the *eri* worm undergoes four moultings. At its last stage the cocoons are formed. To make the cocoons ready for spinning, the chrysalis still alive inside the cocoon should be destroyed by exposing it to the sun or by boiling the cocoons in water. The spinning is done by a *takuri* or *poppy*. The *pat* and *muga* are generally not spun but reeled. For this purpose, the cocoons are boiled in a vessel for about an hour in an alkaline solution and allowed to cool. Generally two persons perform the reeling process. While reeling the fabrics come from the cocoons formed the thread. The reeled thread is wound on a bamboo *chariki*. The spinning of *pat* is also done by similar process. Some amount of Potass is added to the cocoons while it is boiling to make the thread white.

WEAVING SILK CLOTHES

The silk weaving is almost the same as that of cotton weaving. The art of silk weaving requires a high degree of skill and dexterity on the part of the weavers. Common *eri* products are *eri borkapor, eri shawl* and *mekhela*. The common *pat* and *muga* products are *mekhela, chaddar, riha* and *cheleng*. The *eri* products are warm, durable and easily washable. These silk clothes are used in winter. The *muga* fabric appear to be yellowish with a tinge of gold. It is lighter and attractive. The *pat* is finer and whiter than both *eri* and *muga* fabrics. It is very soft and durable and is the costliest amongst the three varieties. Silk manufacture at one time attained a high state of proficiency among the Misings. Nowadays a few Mising villages have a local reputation for their silk goods or mixed silk and cotton goods. The silk manufacturing families have fall on the victims to the modern cheapening process and the facility of supply from outside the state. So the silk rearing and production is declining rather than advancing.

Weaving of Colourful Designs

The craft of weaving with colourful designs developed and attained perfection in the Mising villages, which they weave by using good proportion of colour strips, either in warp or in weft or in both ways. Making designs with coloured threads in the loom is an interesting project for the weavers. The weavers sometimes used a *mimang* or draft copy of designs by counting the warp threads up and down and by inserting a small bamboo strip in it. The desired colourd threads are then passed as weft and beaten by the reed. For weaving a certain motif of design it takes time and a tedious but interesting work for the weavers. The count of the warp takes time and attention.

The pleasing texture, with the weft showing zig-zag lines, diamonds and stars form in the long standing rows of colour and design. Some of the popular patterns woven by variations of threading found in my field study are discuseed below.

THE RAIN DROPS PATTERNS (FUTUKI)

It is a simple and soft texture. The weavers utilized this pattern in the woollen scarfs, baby blankets, ribs of *mekhela*, ribs of *galuk*, etc. It is a favourite colour combinations woven with different coloured weft threads at regular intervals. The weft threads are simply heavier than the warp. This design is often described by the Misings as *futuki*.

THE ZIG-ZAG PATTERN OR V-SHAPED PATTERN (PAHARIA)

The charming and widely popular pattern of repeating V-shaped zig-zag pattern are woven on the border (ribs) of a *mekhela* and *chaddor*. A few of such patterns are shown in the *Pls.* no. 1 and 2.

The common names for such patterns are *pahria* and *tipem.*

THE DIAMOND PATTERN

Little diamond patterns are found in both rugs, shawls, *galuk*, *gasor* and *nesag* and even in *mekhela* and *chaddor* of the women-folk. In some forms of this pattern it is observed that there always exist a cross-mark and four diamonds woven at its four angles.

In some diamond patterns it is observed that dotted lines create the whole motifs and alternate coloured dots come one after another where one dot occupies the central place (*Pl.* 5). There are many varieties of diamond patterns and an expert weaver can create hundreds of motifs by changing her choice.

The number of weft rows necessary to make each block square depends on the number of threads in the block at this point and on the thickness of the thread used. The weaver may make her own adjustment to her particular material. They always took help of the draft to count the number of warp threads up or down while progressing from right to left.

WEAVING OF DIAMOND PATTERN WITH TWILL FASHION

Diamond patterns are also observed in simple twill fashion, without reversing their order. In such case miniature patterns occupying very small space result. They form most attractive tiny motifs and are useful for all kinds of small hand-woven items.

THE HONEY SUCKLE PATTERN

It is a charming, useful and popular pattern of short repeating motifs. It consisted of oval-shaped figures alternating with a cross. Generally this pattern is mixed with other patterns. The common term used for such patterns is *tigur gamic*.

COMBINATION OF ALL THE PATTERNS

In some weavings it can be observed that all the texture are present in one cloth in miniature patterns in which the blocks extend for a very short space.

The weavers who are experts in all these patterns can design miniature patterns by altering regular wefts according to their own choice. The traditional Mising textiles are remarkable for their fineness in texture, harmonious colours and flawless execution of patterns.

Salient Features of the Mising Textiles

1. The products are mainly cotton, *eri* silk and *muga* silk.
2. The weaving is done by traditional looms.

3. Dyeing of threads is common but dyeing after weaving a cloth is not common.
4. Print craft is unknown. All the motifs on clothes are designed either on the loom or by needle works with colourful combination of yarns.
5. A loud display of colours in female dresses produces a distinctiveness of their traditional art forms which gives a perfection to their culture.

Shawls Weaving

Of all the Indian textiles none excelled the beauty of colour, texture and design of the richly patterned shawls of Kashmir. Shawl weaving is common in the north-eastern part of India too. The shawl is basically woven from the under fleece of a species of sheep. These are imported from the Himālayan regions to the north-eastern states. Besides the woollen shawls, the Misings as well as the tribal people of the state weaven silk made shawls from *eri*. In some varieties of shawls, the yarn for the warp is woollen and that of weft is a specially prepared silk.

In the process of loom weaving, the patterns are worked out as loom tapestries in which an additional needle is used. The stitch employed in embroidery is invariably a form of parallel weaving, where the thread is allowed only to hip up the loops. The warps are occasionally penetrated in the texture.

The Mising shawls exhibit a few forms of patterns, (i) alternate parallel lines of different colours, (ii) plain with the two ends are woven with zig-zag motifs. Similar to an *ega*, and small floral or star like motifs in the two ends or on the whole shawls and (iii) cone patterns following curves and minute dipetalous flowers.

Generally bottle-green, rosy colours are favourite in a shawl. In these types of shawls, the same motif is used like a *mekhela* or *ribi* — *gasang* with limited space. No use of brocade by the weavers is observed. The colours are chosen to harmonize with the ground so that the finer examples of this work look like printings. The *pari* or border is disposed along the whole length, and the *phul* is the decorative part of the field or ground. The *buthas* are the generic terms for flowers which are specifically applied alone. The flower pattern commonly found on the Mising shawls is identical with the flower pattern of the *adis* of Arunachal Pradesh.

The blankets called *gadu* is a heavy homespun cotton rug woven in two ways: slender and thick. The slender weaving is performed through portable looms while the thicker is weaven in four posts looms.

Embroidery

In the field of ornamentation embroidery alone can match jewellery. Embroidery has a hoary past in Assam. There are local variations of embroidery and innovations in each part of the state.

Though certain basic embroidery stitches are common, each area has its own special style. It is a purely domestic art, dependent on the social customs of the people. Through embroidery brilliantly coloured flowers, creepers, stars, birds and animals are portrayed. The ground material is cotton and the patterns are worked out with silk threads in double satin stitch, so that they appear to be identical on both the sides. Embrodiery is done by the women-folk on cotton, silk and wool both in loom and with needle.

The use of embroidery stitches widely prevalent among the Mising weavers can be studied under three heads — (i) *kurusa* embroidery, (ii) frame embroidery and (iii) loom embroidery. These methods of embroidery have a long traditional background.

KURUSA EMBROIDERY

Kurusa is a steel hook by which the threads are sets into net with different designs. The embroidery net is later added in dresses by stitching with needle.

FRAME EMBROIDERY

A wooden circular frame is used by the artisans which tightening the cloth on which the motifs of birds, flowers, leaves are drawn with gradual introduction of coloured threads by means of one or more fine needles. Before such work the figures are carefully drawn with a black pencil so that the needle work is easier to the worker. Richly embroi-dered *rūmāla*s (handkerchiefs), pillow covers are done in such process.

LOOM EMBROIDERY

While weaving a dress item in a loom, the weavers arrange some embroidery works in the loom with the help of needle, fine bamboo rods and additional shuttles. In this process, artistic treatment is given subsequent to the weaving while it is in loom. After embroidery work is over starch is applied on the reverse of the piece so that the stitches are held tightly together. The richness and delicacy of the textile patterns are highly commended and are a class by themselves.

The decoration thus forms an integral part of the process of manufacture. It is sometimes impossible to say how much is a product a loom work and how much is it the work of the embroder. The highest achievement of the Mising folk artist is embroidery on loom's cloth. Following these processes, the patterns are so charmingly executed that it appears like fine printing. The weavers performs such intricate patterns either by warp threads or by weft or by adding extra threads in the warp and weft.

The designs used in all the above methods generally consist of small spots, circular and zig-zag strips. It is observed that the same process is repeated for every shade of colours that is desired.[10]

The man's shirt *mibu galuk* is embroidered a bit round the neck and the front sides. The women's blouses are fantastically embroidered at the sleeves and the halves that are opened at the breasts.

STRINGS AND KNITTING WORKS

Knitting is a special skill fulness that goes close to weaving and embroidery. The women-folk knit hats, socks, some smaller covers for the pillows and *saraidhaka.*

The Mising people both (man and woman) makes strings out of jute, silk, etc. They knit fishing nets and bags out of those strings. In knitting the fishing nets they utilized silk and nylon. The name of the common fishing nets are *tangijal, khowalijal, osap* or *ghatjal* and *langhi jal.*

DYEING OR COLOURING

Dyeing is connected with weaving and it can be regarded as an important subordinate craft under weaving. The north-east region provide the raw materials needed for producing a great variety of colours. Vegetable dyes have been the chief materials of dyer's art in this region. It is said that in the olden days something like 300 tints of vegetables extraction were used for folk dyeing processes. The cloth used for dyeing is thick and coarse. The process takes place stage by stage.

The vegetables, leaf, bark or root used for making colours are at first boiled in water. Next the cloth is dipped in boiling water for several hours. After proper dyeing the cloth is squeezed and sun dried.

---

10. Description, classification and name of the types of embroidery are based on personal observations

In the next stage it is dipped in the solution twice. After the last treatment the cloth is bundled in wet condition and allowed to remain so over night. Next day, it is washed in cold water and dried. It is then ready for use.

It is said by the Mising weavers that they mostly dyed the yarn used for colourful weaving and not the cloth after weaving. This is becuase they prefer several colours in dress item.

Printing on the other hand is not observed in the Mising villages. Probably they were unaware of this art or the expert painter were very few and hence the art may have vanished from the villages. The dyeing of the threads and cloth after weaving are skillful jobs done by expert women in the village. The new weavers take the help and advice of the elders while dyeing their clothes. There are many words (terms) in the process of dyeing. In byegone days the weavers of the state did not prefer to purchase imported yarn from the market, but locally dye their yarn. But now the majority of the weavers have to depend for their requirements on commercial dyeing industries. Unfortunately the skill of the dyer may have been in a state of decline due to the import of foreign synthetic dyes.

Wood Carving

The trees were the man's earliest friends which provided shelter and food products and out of the body he must have structured his first home. By sharping his skills and learning new methods of satisfying the going needs of the community. During all ages wood has played an important and friendly part in the development of mankind. Today timber has multifarious use.

The forests of Assam are full of valuable trees. Hence, timber is abundantly available throughout the state. Making of wooden article is a common craft which is considered as a subsidiary occupation by the carpenters. Generally a carpenter earns his living by building houses, manufactures carts, ploughs, looms, furniture, icons and boats. He occasionally repairs doors, windows and constructs bridge.

The art of carving wood is confined among particular carpenters of the Mising folk. Their working tools are of primitive type consisting of a *dao*, the axes, adge and chisel.

Wood is widely used as pillar in house construction, platform construction and household furniture. Wood was employed to make useful articles long before man knew how to use any other material. Timbers are cut into longs and sawed into planks or boards.

WOOD WORKING TOOLS

Wood workers need a number of articles to perform their activities. The simple but most important and useful articles that are traditionally used can be include in general classi-fication of hand tools. Every workman is familiar with the tools he uses. He knows how they are sharpened and kept in good condition. A brief description of the most commonly used hand tools are given below.

A solid bench

To provide a good working place the wood workers make their own benches of required height which is rigid and stationary and is always attached to the floor. This work bench is made in different shape and size. Some wood workers make drawers to store tools in his working bench.

Saws

Saws are of different types, shapes and sizes. Moreover each type of saws has its owns specific and certains jobs in wood working.

Crossent saw

It is used to cut across the gains of the wood. The saw teeth are set alternately to the right and left. Saws of this type are made of various sizes.

Rip saw

Rip saw has different size. It is so made that each tooth is sharpened perpendicular at the front and sharpened to the even edge at the cutting point. When it is used, those teeth bite into the wood like chisels.

Coping saw

Coping saw are used for cuting curves, roundings and special shapes. The saw is feeted on a rigid frame.

Hack saw

Hack saw is fixed on a iron frame to cut small and sophisticated works.

Compas saw

Compas saw is a type of small-size saw pointed at one end and operated by the handle of the other end.

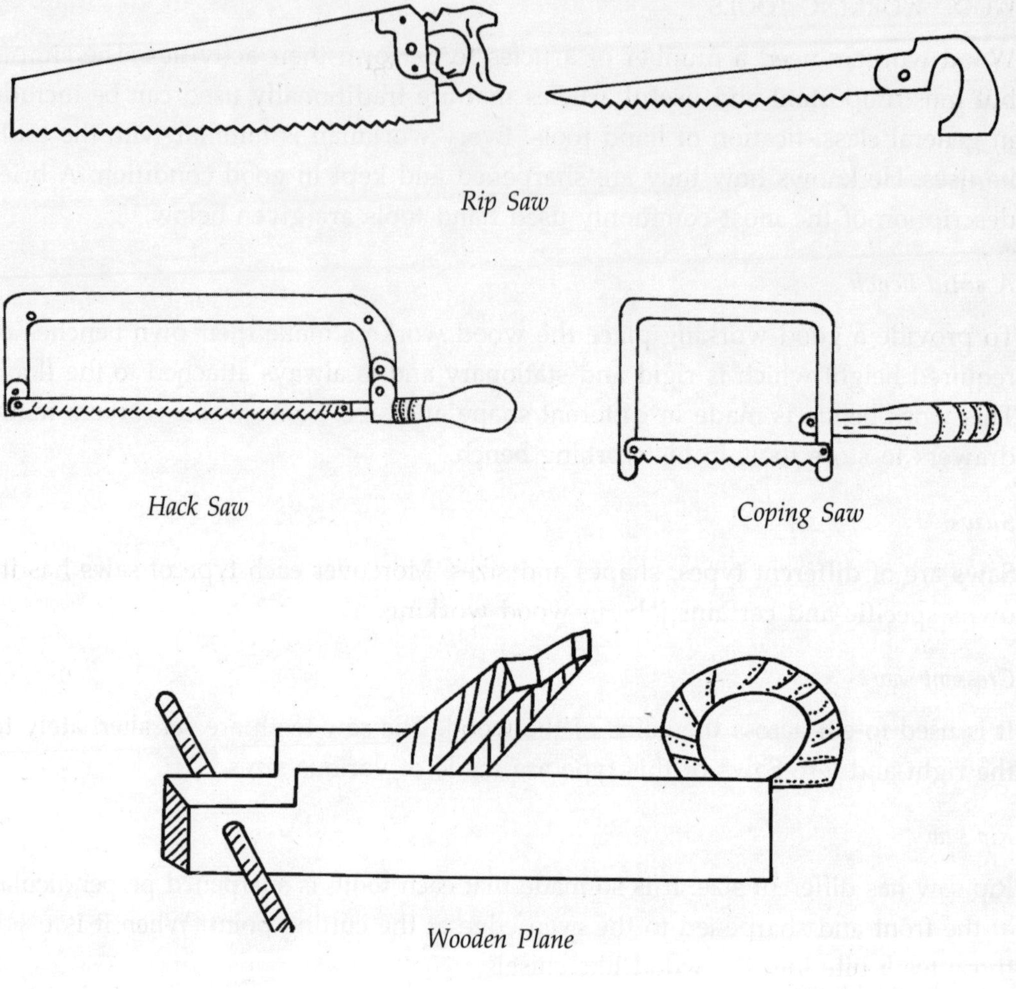

fig. **17. Wood working tools**

Sawing operations

In sawing, the wood worker take the saw handle lightly with four fingers extended along the side. The cuting movement depends upon muscles of the arm to give it movement and directions. With the back and forth movements of the saw without much pressure on the teeth give the best result in cutting and shaping the woods. Before the cutting is started, a line is marked on the wood with a pencil to serve as a guide. At times the saw may tend to run off the line, in which case the blade should be twisted gently, so as to change the course to the proper.

Plane (Randa)

To make a wood sufficiently smooth planes are used. Wood workers use various sizes of planes. A plane has different parts such as a cutting blade, the adjusting nuts, the adjusting levers, etc. All are fixed in a wooden frame.

Boring tools

Screw type hand drill device is used for making holes of specific required size.

Chisels

Chisels are one of the most necessary tools in wood working. Those are made of iron blades with wooden handles. A chisel, in connection with other tools is indispensable in the cons-truction of most joints. It is indeed one of the most important and most useful working tools. Two types of chisels are observed in general. (i) having a strong plain blade, and (ii) having a cylindcrical blade.

Hammer

The hammer generally used by the wood workers, has two parts the head and the handle. The end of the head used for striking nails is known as face, the other end of the hammer is bent and shaped so that it can be used for pulling nails.

The axe and the adze

Both the axe and adge have long handle operated with two hands. The axe is used to cut a tree and also for splinting log section. The adze is used for squaring logs.

Carpenter's pincers, vise, screw drivers are also some of the hand tools used for wood working.

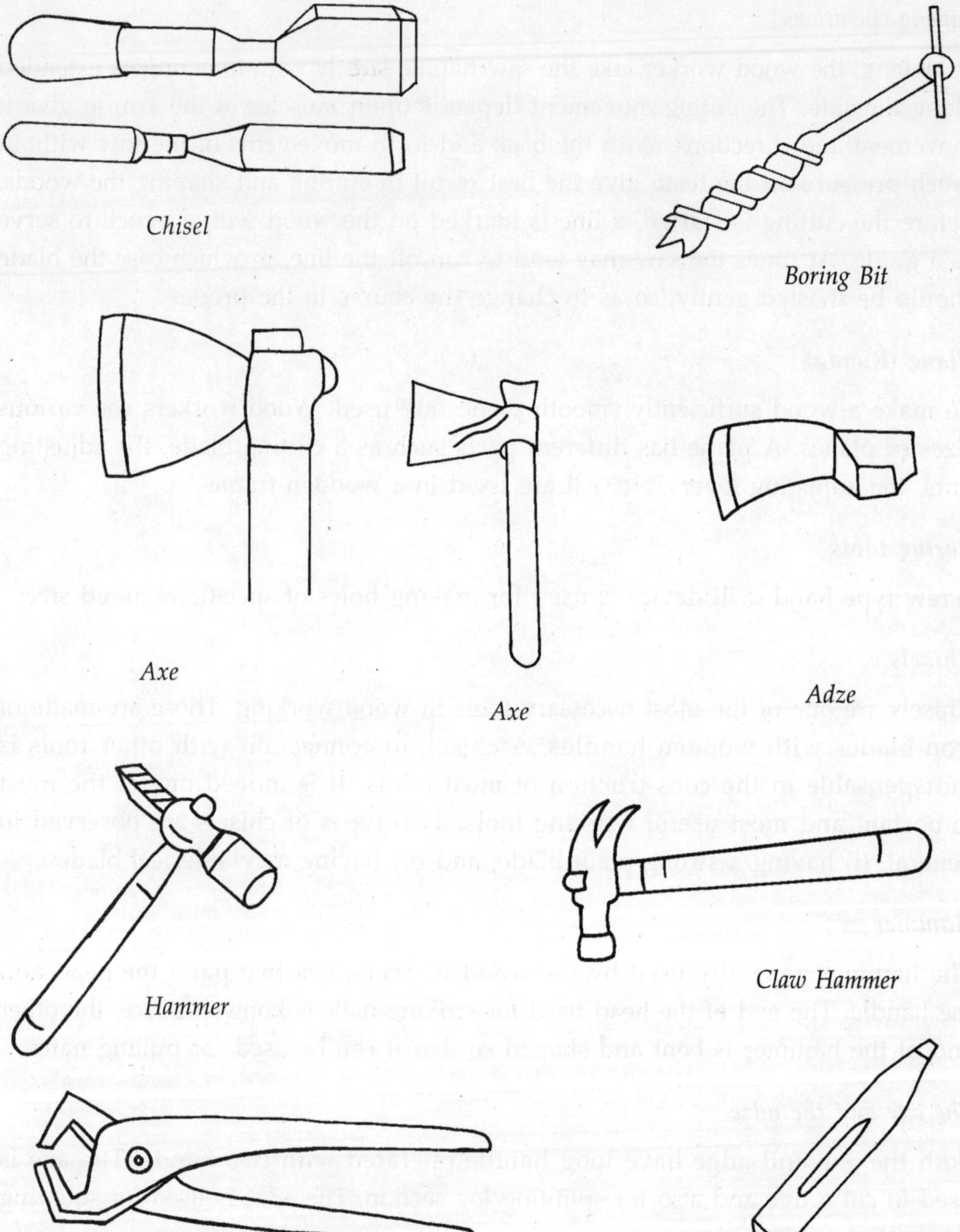

fig. **18. Wood working tools**

SHARPENING OF TOOLS

Sharpening the tools properly is the first requisite of a wood worker. The teeth of a saw can be sharpened by running a file over the teeth. The file is handled at the right angles to the saw blade and pushed slightly across the teeth.

Sharpening a blunt iron blade

It is necessary to grind a blunt blade or chisel on a grind stone to give it the required sharpness. The iron blade is moved back and forth across the face of the stone while grinding. Plenty of water is to be used to prevent burning.

TECHNIQUE OF PRODUCTION

Though less in number the carpenters living in the Mising villages carry their industries as a subsidiary occupation. Due to the lack of improved technical knowledge they cannot utilize their trade to much attractive dividends. In rural areas there is no work shed for carrying on the jobs of wood works and the artisans generally do the jobs in some open space near their dwelling houses. Many of the establishment are very small and carry on their business without adequate tools.

The process of manufacture is started with the accurate measurement of the raw materials. It is observed that most of the rural carpenters are accustomed to using only a foot rule and a wooden made gauge for the purpose of marking and measuring. The craftsman of young generation of course uses up to date measuring implements like mortes gause, try squares, steel squares, templates, bevels, spirit level, etc.

After the process of marking and measuring a timber for a particular job is over, the carpenter is to use his saw for cutting the timber as per measurement. The saw is pulled backward and then pushed forward with steady motions. Next to sawing comes the operation of planing. For this purpose a plane called *randa* is used. The purpose of planing is to remove the rough surface of the wood, to make it flat, smooth and straight and also to reduce the wood to exact dimension. For planing wood properly high degree of skill and experience is essential. The process of planing wood surface is continued till the wood is reduced to exact dimension. The next stage of operation is to make the join. This can be performed with a saw and a chisel. There are several types of joints that are worked out by the carpenters. A few joints are known as *bull* joints, dowelled joints, devital joints, etc. Different pieces are then fastened together to make the work complete. It is generally performed with nails, screws, hinges, nuts and bolts as the case may be. Nails are the most common type of wood fastener. Hinges are used for attracting doors and levers.

PAINTING AND VARNISHING

The carved objects are generally painted with different matching colours. Paints are purchased from the local market. In case of varnishing of wooden furniture the artisan prepares a solution out of the following ingredients:

(i) Resin.
(ii) Methylated spirit.
(iii) *Garuka mati* (red soil).

After the painting and varnishing operation is over, the products are kept in the sunlight or in open space for drying. When varnishing and painting is completely dried up and the colour becomes bright the objects are ready to use.

Some Wood Works of the Folk Carpenters

MAKING OF BOATS

One of the most outstanding characteristic of the settlements of the Mising population is their location near the river. Water bodies are important in the daily living of the people serving both resources and communications. The small boat is a typical feature of the cultural landscape of the Misings of Assam. These traditional boats are still essential in trapping, fishing and swamp economies. These are the means of communication in the rainy season when flood damages the roads of the villages.

Folk boats are constructed in two different ways. Most of the boat makers collect the raw materials from drift wood carried by the river during floods. The old method of making a boat is to cut a log of 10 ft to 12 ft length. The middle portion of the log is cut out and the two ends are made into some uprights. These two upright ends are called *tings* of a boat.

The second type of boat is made joining wooden planks by means of nailing or metal lock system. Boat making is an old profession of the Mising craftman living on a river side. To row a boat a wooden flat bar called *botha* is employed as pedal. The process of production such as sawing, shaping, joining and colouring are carried on outdoors.

CART MAKING

Cart making is another wooden work common in the rural village for transportation. The main job of the cart making is the manufacturing of the wheels. The carpenter with his age-old tools brings the shape of a cart wheel along with some blacksmithy works for it.

DOOR MAKING

Wooden doors commonly utilized in architecture are manu-factured by the professional carpenters. Two types of designs are observed in door making.

(i) Z-type and (ii) Panel type.

Wood made implements in agricultural processes are *nangal* (plough), *ural* (grinding device), etc.

Wooden articles used in a loom are *tolotha, rush bar, jotar, nasoni*, etc.

Wooden made seats like *pira, tul,* bench and chair are common in a Mising household.

Modern easy chair, sofa, bed, almirah, cupboard, wooden box are also now common in well-to-do families.

Wooden dishes was also common in bygone days which are now replaced by silver and steel made dishes. Wooden dishes are carved by the old craftsman for useful purposes. Such wooden dishes are of two types, one is shallow and circular without any stand while the other is a little deeper and has stands to support at a height of about 20 cm from the ground.

A piece of wood is first roughly given a round shape by a *dao*; next the cavity is scooped out by a small chisel. Finally the article is polished with a very fine knife or chisel.

Wood carvings depicting lions, horses, man, birds, tigers, etc., are common in the *murongs* of the villages. It is not uncommon to witness a few carvings on the beams and cross beams of a public house like *murong* which are generally covered with figures of flowers and creepers.

The finer sense of artistic beauty among the wood workers can also be traced from the manufacture of minor weaving implements like *makoo, durpoti, nasoni*, etc., which are generally ornamented with the carving of parrots, peacocks, fishes and floral designs.

Pottery — The Craft of Clay

Clay craft is probably the earliest of man's creation by which he expresses his creative spirit. Making of earthen vessels and hardening it by fire gives birth to the terracotta art. The potter's wheel seems to be the first machine by which power of motion was utilized for productive purposes. It was the women who work on clay, shape the vessels using wheel for softening and giving it the required shape. The potter of today still creates forms which were made five thousand years ago. The Misings use several types of earthen pots for their domestic and ritual purposes. Today we find no potters among the Mising folk but once pottery was practised by some craftsman of the tribe. Of course this craft is not widely practised now and as a result it is tabooed. In Assam it is seen that pottery has been made by the *hira* and *kumar* groups of people. Those groups of people are commonly living near the Mising villages. So the Misings collect pottery from the *kumars*.

MANUFACTURING TECHNIQUES

There are certain methods of manufacturing the earthen vessels. A short description of such methods is given below.

Composition and preparation of the clay

The clay used for pottery is called as potter's clay. It is available in all the districts of Assam. The clay is collected from the wells and allowed to decompose by the action of sun, rain and frost.

Shaping the clay

The earthenware bodies are extremely plastic and can be set by many methods. Generally a revolving wheel is utilized to give the required shape.

Drying and firing

Newly shaped articles are allowed to dry slowly in the atmosphere. A sundried vessel is not absolutely suitable for keeping liquids because it absorbs liquid and becomes soft. Such sundried vessels are then fired up to 500 degrees celcius.

Decoration

The potters draw some lines, motifs of flowers and fruits on the dried vessel, which makes the articles attractive.

fig. **19. Earthen pots**

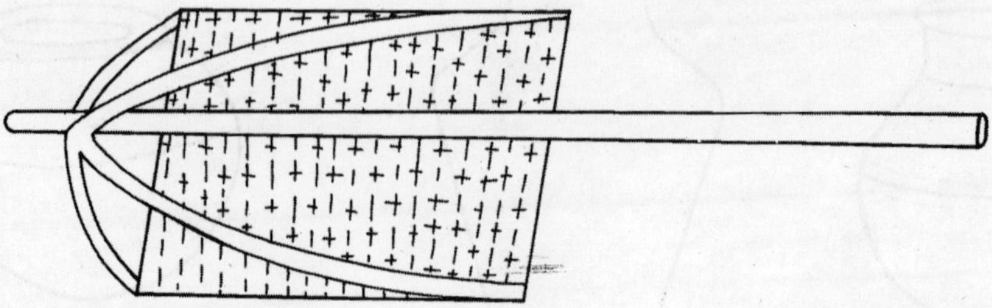

Tangi Jal

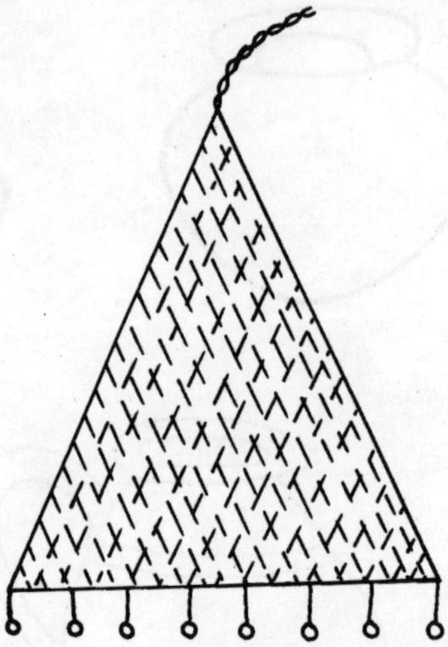

Khawali

Langi

***fig.* 20. Fishing nets**

***fig.* 21. Common wooden articles**

Earthen vessels and pots commonly found in a Mising household are as follows:

1. *Kilong* (*big size earthen pot*): It is used to store rice beer (*apong*) for fermentation.
2. *Lysur/ Ghot*: It is a small earthen pitcher used to keep milk.
3. *Lvtung*: Earthen pitcher without the neck portion.
4. *Gule/Borkoloh L.V. Tung*: It is used to store rice, potatoes and such other substances. It is widely used to store drinking water. Some families use it to carry water from river.
5. *Molla*: It is used as a dish.
6. *Religious uses*: *Dunori, mati chaki*.
7. *Smoking pipe*: *Silim*, etc.

Metal Works

The art of working metal is known almost all over the region. Blacksmithy is restricted within the *komar* and *lohar* groups of people. The bronze works are confined among the *kohar* groups and manufacture of ornaments on gold, silver and bronze are confined traditionally among the *sonari* and *bonia* groups of people. In hill districts of Assam and Arunachal the craft of blacksmithy is carried on by anyone choosing to learn the work. The decorative objects used by the people mainly consist of a number of jewellery and ornaments made of silver, brass, glass, copper, bell metal, alloy of zink, tin, etc. The technique followed in the manufacture of ornaments is same as in most of the other tribal crafts of India. The names of metal ornaments and their designs are described in chapter 8. No metal images of gods and goddesses are found among the Misings. Some of the old expert craftsman of the tribe practise these metal crafts using imported raw materials. Of course the sand of the Suvensiri river once contained gold dust extraction of gold was an important practice of this region.

The principal articles made of iron are the agricultural tools like dao, axe, hoe, scraper, sickle and weapons like spearheads, arrowheads, masket, knives, etc.

The blacksmiths by sheer experience of many years known that if a piece of iron in its high temperature is rapidly cooled by dipping into water it will acquire the properties of hard steel and there by the article may be made more durable. Blacksmith generally sets fire by charcoal, the iron piece is heated up to red-hot,

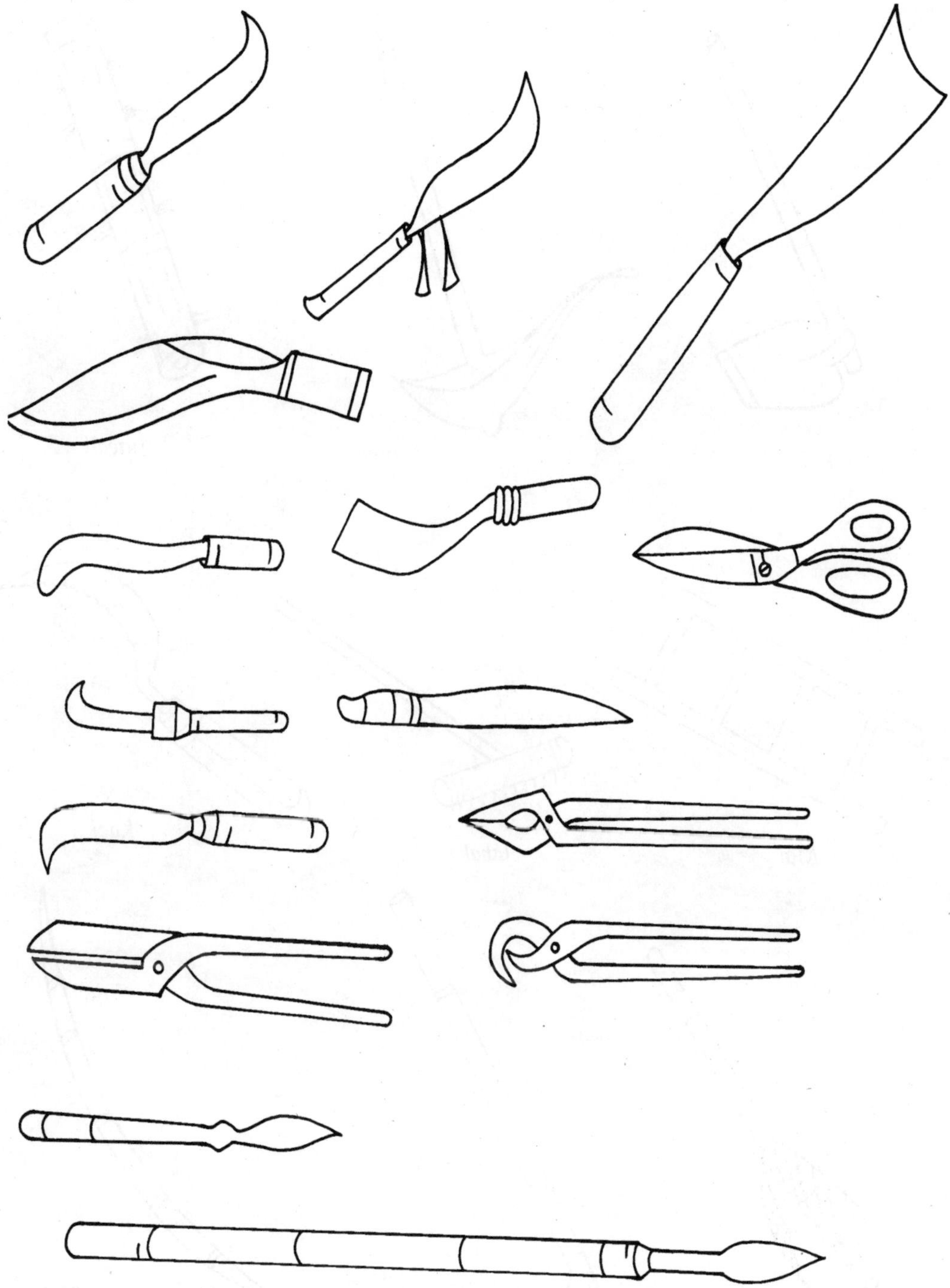

fig. **22. Iron implements**

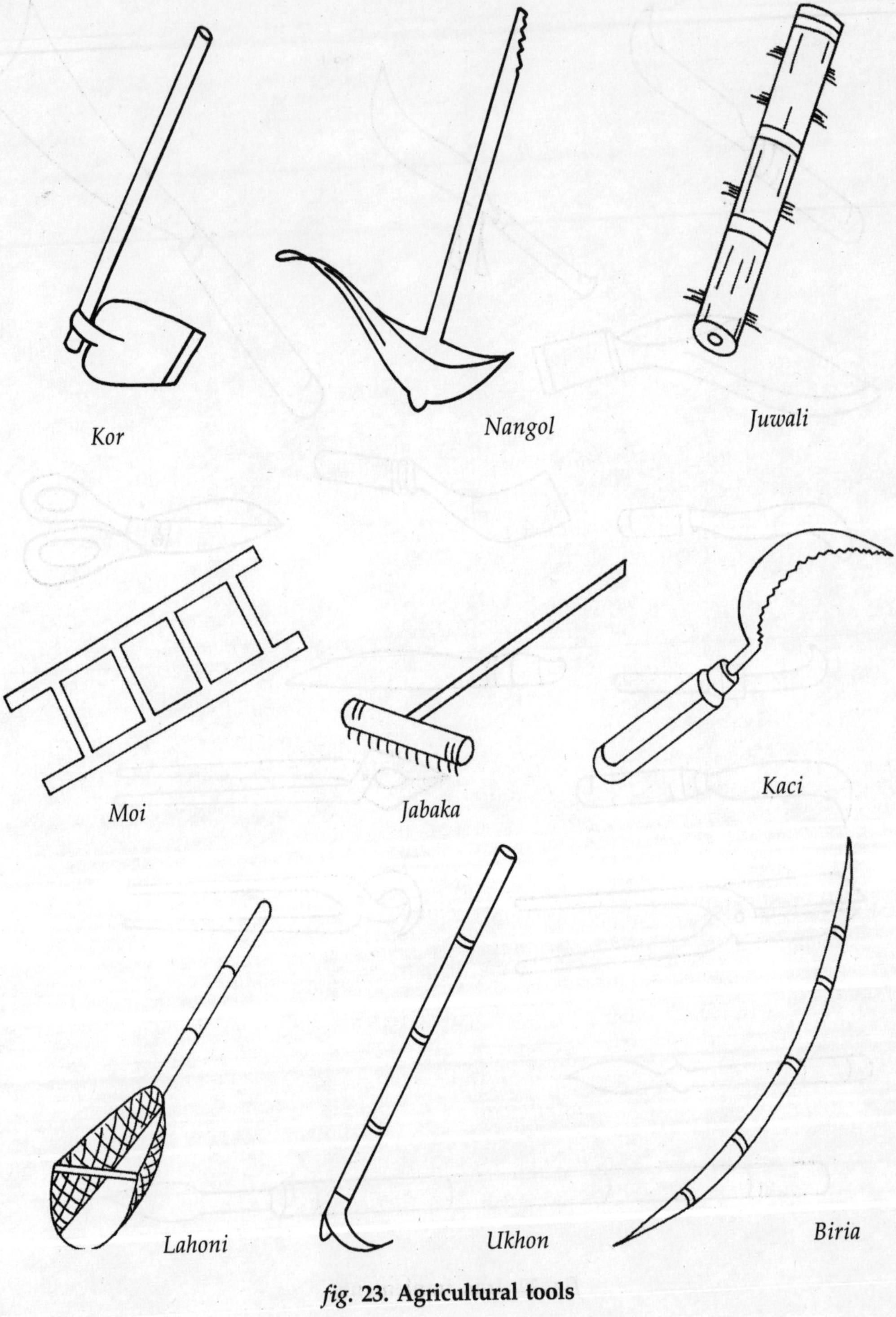

fig. **23. Agricultural tools**

it is then taken out by the tongs and hammered to get the required shape.

They use two tongs, one in each hand. The left hand tong held the red-hot-iron in position, while a blunt chisel is held by the right hand. The helper then takes the heaviest hammer and slow and heavy strokes are given on the head of the chisel. After each stroke the blacksmith change the position of the chisel.

Then the iron is put back into the fire for re-heating and such process is repeated for required shape of the device.

The Misings of Assam know the art of making *dao*s and knives and manufacturing traditional ornaments of cast bronze and silver. It is mentioned earlier that *dao*s are the main tools for basket making, home construction and such other works. The whole range of *dao*s found among them can be classified into three groups depending upon the size and shape. These are (i) long blade with short wooden haft, (ii) short flat blade with long wooden haft.

SOME IRON IMPLEMENTS OF THE MISINGS

The yokse

A *yokse* is a type of sword, it is made of steel generally 2 to 4 ft in length. It is used for ceremonial wear and the priest used it while dancing. It is a straight blade with a cutting edge. It is narrow towards the end and broad towards the handle.

The oyak

It is a dagger similar to a *dao* made of iron and its size varying from 1 to 1.5 ft in length. *Oyak* is kept in a scabbard made of flat bamboo sticks.

The *oyak* is used for cutting meat, felling trees, cutting wood, etc. It is also called *matsig*.

Axe (kuthar)

It is an iron blade having a wooden or bamboo handle used to cut the logs.

Arrowhead

Bow and arrow are used while hunting. Making of arrow tips from iron is common.

Besides these iron implements the Mising artisans utilized other tools which are mentioned in wood carving unit of his chapter. The importance of these iron implements in the socio-economic life of the people has not diminished even in modern age. Kitchen apparatus are made of metal. The dishes for eating called *bankahi* are beautiful brass dish.

A copper made three-legged stand to keep a simple dish at a higher level from the floor is used. It is called *baria*. It is also made of brass-metal. Bel-metel bowls called *bati* are common for serving *apong* and for serving curry while eating rice. Such *bati* has a volume of half litre capacity.

Weapons of offence and defence are very few. As the people are peaceful and there are no hostile activities of the neighbouring people, these artefacts are out of use and are met with in very few houses.

The Mising folk are now not found to be engaged in any metal craft like blacksmithy, goldsmithy or brass works. There-fore detail discussion of these crafts is avoided.

Jute Products

Jute is one of the most important commercial crops of India. Historical records show that jute fibre was used for cloth manufacturing in sixteenth century AD.

In Assam, jute is called as *morapat*. Here the fibre yielding part of the jute plant is utilized for making ropes of different dimensions. These ropes are utilized in wearing implements, agricultural tools and keeping domestic animals. Besides bags carrying nets and sacks are made out of jute. No jute made dress is observed in my field study.

CARRYING NETS OR JOLOYA

The Misings ordinarily carry things in baskets. The women-folk carry these baskets at their backs while the men-folk carry in poles and *dangpasi*. Besides these, they also use a kind of jute-made rope device or net to carry their goods. One such pair of nets with goods can be carried by placing over the shoulder by means of a bar.

Mat Weaving

Matting is similar to basket weaving where bamboo, reeds, cane, sungrass, *patidoi* and such other marshoi plants and weeds are used as material for product. Like in basket weaving twill, check, diagonal weaving techniques are adopted. Moreover the craftsman weaves mat from *patidoi* (*Finium dichotoma*) which is a water-grown plant about 6 to 7 ft tall and of about 1.5 to 2.5 cm body diameters. The barks of the plant are split away and dried under sunlight. Such mats are

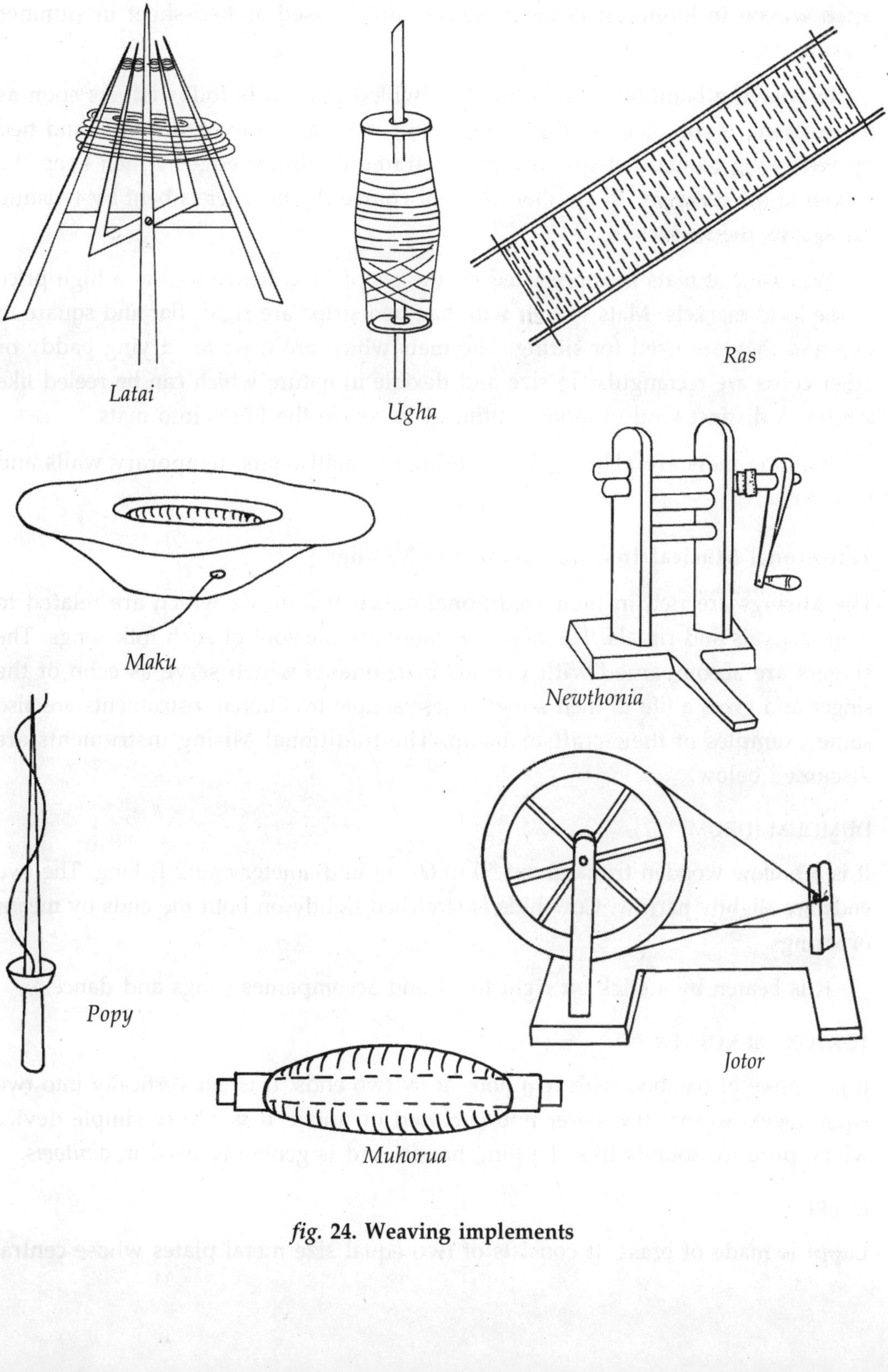

fig. **24. Weaving implements**

often woven in looms. It is very smooth and is used as bed-sheet in summer season.

In weaving bamboo mats, generally twilled pattern is followed. As soon as the weaving is complete all the four sides of the mat are twisted a little and tied up with long bamboo strips in order to frame the outer edges which keep the woven strips compact. In another form, of course the boarder is bent by twisting the splints themselves.

This kind of mats is appreciated by the people and hence sold at a high price in the local markets. Mats woven with bamboo strips are rigid, flat and square in size and they are used for sitting. The mats which are used for drying paddy or other corns are rectangular in size and flexible in nature which can be reeled like a tube. A distinct kind of loom is utilized to weave the fibres into mats.

Bamboo mats are also used in roofing of small boats, temporary walls and floor mats.

Traditional Musical Instruments of the Misings

The Misings are rich in their traditional dance and music which are related to their festivals and rituals. The notes of music are the soul of such folk songs. The singers are accompanied with various instruments which serve as echo of the singer and gives a life to their songs. These simple traditional instruments are also some examples of their craftsmanship. The traditional Mising instruments are discussed below.

DUMDUM (DRUM)

It is a hollow wooden trunk about 50 to 60 cm in diameter and 2 ft long. The two ends are slightly narrow. Cow hide is stretched tightly on both the ends by means of strings.

It is beaten by a stick on right hand and accompanies songs and dance.

TOKTOK OR KOKTER

It is a piece of bamboo with two nobs at its two ends. It is cut vertically into two equal levels so that the lower nob is closed or uncut. It is a very simple device which produce sounds like clapping hands, and is generally used in *oinitoms*.

LUPPI

Luppi is made of brass. It consists of two equal size metal plates whose central portion is bulged and conical having a small hole through which a jute made rope is inserted to facilitate it with the hand. The operator takes two *luppies* on his two hands and hit them smoothly. This produce the musical notes. *Luppi* is accompanied with the *dumdum*.

GUNGA

It is a mouth organ made of a small bamboo which produces sweet musical sound.

PAMPA (HORN)

It is also a mouth organ made from buffalow's horn and reeds. The operator blows air by his mouth and the fingers gradually open and close the holes of the pipe. Two different varieties of pampa's are observed: one is *tulu pampa* and the other is *aguk-tapong*.

DANDUN

It is a string instruments similar to a violin.

DUMPAK

It is a simple musical device made from bamboo shoot.

KAKTOG

It is a chatter type string instrument made from very simple meterials.

LAWNONG AND BARBANG (BELL)

It is a circular metal plate of brass about 3 to 5 mm thickness. It is hung by a string and sound is produced by beating it. The lawnong is rung at a time when someone dies in the village, at the urgent call of the *kgbang* and in *gumrug* dance of *Ali-ai-Ligang* festivals. In all these occasions the ringing bell informs the villagers.

KURULIPULI (FLUTE)

It is a flute made from bamboo, it has two varieties — *Kotopong* and *Futuk*.

YAKSSA (SWORD)

While the priest dances in connection with some rituals he used the sword called *yakssa*. Some metal plates are arranged on it which produce sound by their movements.

Chapter 6

Folk Architecture of the Misings

Introduction to Folk Architecture

A SETTLEMENT is an organized colony of human beings including the buildings in which they live or work and the track or streets over which their movement takes place. People settle in places where basic needs are easily fulfilled. For instance, the supply of drinking water is one of the most important considerations for settlement. Villages are located in the neighbourhood of an agricultural field in the areas where water is available for both drinking and irrigational purposes.

Compact pattern of settlement is found among the Mising tribes and there exists a tendency to shift the site of settlement along the sides of the rivers. Settlements are mostly unplanned. Generally the families of the same clan live together and hence the name of the village comes according to the surname of the clan.

The houses of the Misings are not arranged in rows or in any other definite order. Every village has its meeting place called *murong ghor*, cremation ground and place for religious performance (*namghar*).

Village Structure

The general arrangement of an average Mising village of Assam is very much similar to that of a non-tribal village.

Villages are generally surrounded by paddy fields and often by low lying areas. In their house compounds (*bari*), trees like cocount, arecanut, banana, mango, jackfruit and bamboo are grown. In public lands big or small trees are easily seen.

Most Mising villages had no P.W.D. roads. The roads financed by *ancholik-panchayat* or *gaon panchayats* are common. Roads are not well maintained. Roads became dusty in sunny days and muddy during rain. Each village is usually divided into several locations called *subas*.

The *murong* and *namghar* are integral parts of a Mising village. These are generally situated in the middle of the village. The factors influencing the compact pattern are given below:

(1) People depend on cultivation and animal husbandry. Hence there is a tendency to live close to streams or rivulets and cultivated fields.

(2) The form of settlement is also influenced by caste which forms the compact settlement pattern. Another reason of compact settlement is security and protection of lives and crops from wild animals and enemies.

(3) The settlement is often named after the clan, which signifies the caste of the families of the villages. The house types are the same. All the livestock is enclosed for protection against wild animals and thieves. As the favourable locations are extremely limited, the Mising people are compelled to form compact settlement.

(4) Formerly, the Misings were isolated from the non-Mising, but they gradually selected road-side places and chose to live among the non-Mising populations. Formerly many factors led the tribes to choose the river banks as their dwelling-places.

The lands of the river banks were unused by the plainsmen of Assam. Different kinds of reeds like *nal-khagori, ikara,* thatching woods, sungrass grow in abundance on the river banks. The land is fertile and unused grazing land offer grass to their cattle.

In the beginning of the twentieth century the Misings were more or less a migratory tribe. In Mill's report we find:

> They are very migratory in their habits. Cultivating the *chor* lands and changing every third, fourth or fifth years and because of this nature they don't construct house of long durable nature.[1]

But nowadays they have almost given up their migratory nature.

---

1. *Mill's Report on the Province of Assam*, p. 670.

Classification of Architecture

Depending upon the nature of functions the folk architecture of the Misings can be studied under three heads.

1. Domestic architecture.
2. Religious architecture.
3. Recreational architecture.

Domestic architecture is a rectangular platform house build for the social unit, the individual family, human beings and animals. It provides shelter and security for basic physical functions of life. It includes courtyard, roads, fences, field and store house, etc. To store their paddy and corn a granary (*kumsang*) and a cattleshed for cows are constructed sepa-rately.

The Housing Process

SELECTION OF SITE

There are a number of factors that are taken into consideration before a site is selected for settlement. The first and most important factor taken into consideration is the availability of plain lands for constructing houses. It is generally away from deep forest. The second factor is the availability of water. Houses are generally built near water bodies. Settlement is almost compact. Prominent among other factors which determine the location of the house are the link path to the house and reasonable separation from the neighbouring houses.

A plot may be abandoned even after the house has been constructed. In most cases the reasons for abandoning the houses are premature deaths among the family members or a general belief that the plot will bring ill luck to the family. Mising villages are always established on the bank of a river despite facing too many troubles every year due to natural calamities like flood and storm. The distribution of villages is seen along the river Brahmaputra and its tributaries. A typical Mising village consists of 20 to 50 houses constructed in a haphazard manner without proper planning. Compact settlement is adopted for economic reasons of paddy cultivation and other *rabi* cultivation. These two types of agriculture require large labour force for trasplanation and harvesting. Hence they reside in compact settlement patterns. Moreover the Mising people have other non-agricultural activities and cottage industries which are also located in the same settlement.

In the past years, the need of defence from external lawless elements was important. This also led to compact settlement. Some social customs and traditions are also significant factors for house constructions. The houses are often constructed facing the river. Whenever a plot is to be selected for the construction of a house, some religious texts are to be performed. This ritual is called *panam*. Before the construction begins a *mibo* is invited to pronounce whether the selected site is free from evil influences or not. When the holes are dugg in the ground for the posts of the house, *mibu* the priest of the village examines the spot by observing magico-religious test. He puts some rice grains bound by a leaf into the holes. Each bundle contains as many rice grains as there are family members. On the next day the bundle is to be taken out and examined. It is believed that if any insects are found inside the bundle, then the members of the family will suffer skin diseases if they still utilize the foundation. If the grains are found separated to each other there is probability of quarrels among the family members. And if any of these grains is lost, this plot is abandoned. Sometimes three or four plots are rejected due to unfavourable *panams*.

While fixing the bamboo posts the owner recites the following:

tata-taya nulu, tat-long-ka oag-akum bertee, dekpe omna medang oyadek praman chil, lengkan-nangks ommna petam peki dung.[2]

O ancestors! I intend to build a house on this land. Show me the signs of your approval. Swearing in the name of ancestors, I declare that I expect the signs of your approval.

In starting the works of a house construction the Mising considered Monday, Wednesday and Thursday of the week good days. The days on which parents have died are consi-dered good.

Whenever a new house is to construct the owner starts collecting bamboos and logs. In bye-gone days there was no question of purchases or sale as the bamboos and logs were collected from the forests. The villagers, friends and relatives help in house construction. In this customary assistance, the male relatives and neighbours take part in actual construction work.

They are served with *apong* or tea off and on, and at noon they are given food; no payment is made.

---

2. R.P. Srivastava, *Impact of Community Development and Cultural Change Among the Misings of Assam*, Dibrugarh University, Dept. of Anthopology, 1972, p. 95.

First, the central post is created. At the same time holes are dug at some distance from one another, on which supporters of the platform of the house are placed. The day on which the members first start to use the newly constructed house is observed as *Akum Gisa* on which occasion they arrange a feast and invite the villagers and relatives.

MATERIALS USED FOR CONSTRUCTION

From the earliest time of building to the time of industrial revolution, timber, bamboo, reeds, cane, straw, stone and iron rods are the raw materials used for architecture. These are locally available in the hills and plains of Assam. Various species of bamboo and cane are found in this area which are suitable for basket making, mat-weaving and constructing houses. Woods are used in the forms of logs and planks. Logs are used for the structural framework of the house and provide foundation support. Logs are also used to make the floor of the house. Strong logs are used to give support to the fire places. Logs are also used to make the ladders. Planks are used to make doors. Bamboo wall or matting is tied to the logs or planks with cane or thin bamboo strips.

A TYPICAL HOUSE

The dwelling house of the Misings varies in construction according to the family. The better built houses, though rather few, are comfortable and multipurpose. The ground plane of their ordinary dwelling house is rectangular and of about 15 to 25 ft in length and 8 to 12 ft in breadth. The plinth of the floor of the house is gradually raised by platform of bamboo or wood. The wall posts are about 7 to 10 ft in height. The wall posts and the platform supporting posts or long are planted vertically on either side of the house.

The main ridge-pole (D) is placed across the two main posts (A) and held in position within the holes made on the top of the post or fastened with ropes made of cane. Two more tie-beams or purlins (E) are placed paralled to the ridge pole over the wall posts (C) on either side (*fig*. 27).

The remaining five to seven pairs of rafters (R) are placed in similar position over the purlins (E) and the ridge poles. The ends of the rafters are fixed and fastened with the tie-beam with the rope of cane, or iron nails. Free-ends of the rafters are projected about 1 to 2 feet from the purlins.

The bamboo frame of roof with square holes is placed over the rafters. The thatching grass is laid 2 to 3 inches in thickness over the framework of the roof in several layers. Every layer is fastened with the roof frame with a bamboo strip.

The finishing touch to the roof is given by placing two other thatching purlins over the roofs, parallel to the ridge pole.

To make a strong support to the roof some additional poles called *eayings* are given lengthwise under the rafters. The part of roof that is placed outside the walls is known as *dula* and the rain water falls on the outside of the house which is known as *panipota*. In the opinion of the Misings, the house contains ten layers, five at the roof portion and other five at the platform of the house. In the Mising language it is called

Tatoto rumongok kow o: gobo rumongok.[3]

THE FOUNDATION AND PLATFORM

All house rest on foundation of wooden logs. The floor is raised about 5 or 6 ft high from the ground. The floor of the house is in the form of a platform supported by lateral logs tied to the vertical logs which are planted in the earth. The wooden beams placed breadth-wise above the posts of the platform are called *ertog* (*karka*). The bamboo or wooden beams placed lengthwise upon the *ertog* are called *jopong*. The small size bamboo placed and tied with the *jopong* is known as *binor*. Some thicker flat logs or planks are used below the bamboo floor matting to make it stronger. Long pieces of split bamboo form the smooth platform (*pisso*) which they use to sit, sleep, take meals and to perform all household works. Bamboo is crushed and then knitted finally to make the floor matting.

As the floor of the house is raised from the ground level, the area below the platform is used by the pigs, dogs and such other pet animals. This space is also used to store wood, log and such other material which may be required for maintaining and repairing houses.

POSTS AND CROSSBARS (LINTEL)

The posts and crossbars function doubly as load bearer and supporter in construction.

The job of the cross beam or bars is to bear loads that rest on it without deforming or breaking. The job of the post is to support the crossbars and the rafters without crushing.

FRONT PORTION

Most of the houses have a front verandah called *lotta* which is covered by the

---

3. G. Pegu, *Dohtoropia Mising Ghar in MSA*, p. 305.

extended part of the roofs of the main houses but this portion has no side wall and platform. It is an open space generally used for husking paddy, weaving, performing other crafts and storing domestic and agricultural articles. It is sometimes use as shelter of goat, cow, etc. Next to the *lotta* portion, it is followed by *tungong* part of the house which can be reached by climbing the ladder (*kobung*) with the help of the side handle rod called *lakgun*. *Tungong* is an open space at the front portion of the main house having platform but no side wall. It is 4 of 5 ft high from the ground. The ladder may be of different designs. A wooden log tied at the top and dug in the ground is cut at different places to facilitate the placing of steps while climbing. The *tungong* is used to sit during daytime. Formerly the unmarried boys slept on it. It is observed that in some houses the *tungong*s are big enough to accomodate 10 to 15 people.

ENTRANCE TO THE MAIN HOUSE — THE "YAPOG"

Immediately after the *tungong* portion of the house the door *yapog* of main house is fixed. A typical Mising house contains two doors for entrance and exit and no window. The front door is called *tungong-ko-yapog* and the back door is termed as *eyapo-kurku-yapog*. The front door or *tungong-ko-yapog* is generally fixed on the right side of the front wall.

The door may be hinged on the top or side of the walls to open and shut. Doors may be revolved about the vertical axis in the centre of the opening. A large variety of materials are used for door construction. Wood, bamboo metal or a combination of these materials are commonly used. Doors are made of wooden planks and supported by wooden frames. The doors made of bamboo strips with strong bars have no frame, but they are tied suitably with the wall posts. Doors made of bamboo strips are most common in the villages.

No windows, ventilators and chimneys are provided in a traditional house. But some families today provide these things and have almost modernized their houses. There are several reasons for not providing windows and more doors and ventilators. During winter cold breeze enters the house and makes it colder. Secondly the rain water may enter the inside of the house. Thirdly windows and ventilators may harm the side walls.

L — Lotta; *K* — Ladder (*kubang*); *T* — Varanda (*tungaon*);

E — Main entrance (*tungon-ki-yopog*); *S* — Room for sleep (*soyer*);

M — Fire place (*moiram* or *mcram*); *P* — Side for foul (*kokdung*);

F — Backdoor (*eyapo-kuroku-yapog*); X — Side for storing water (*panisang*).

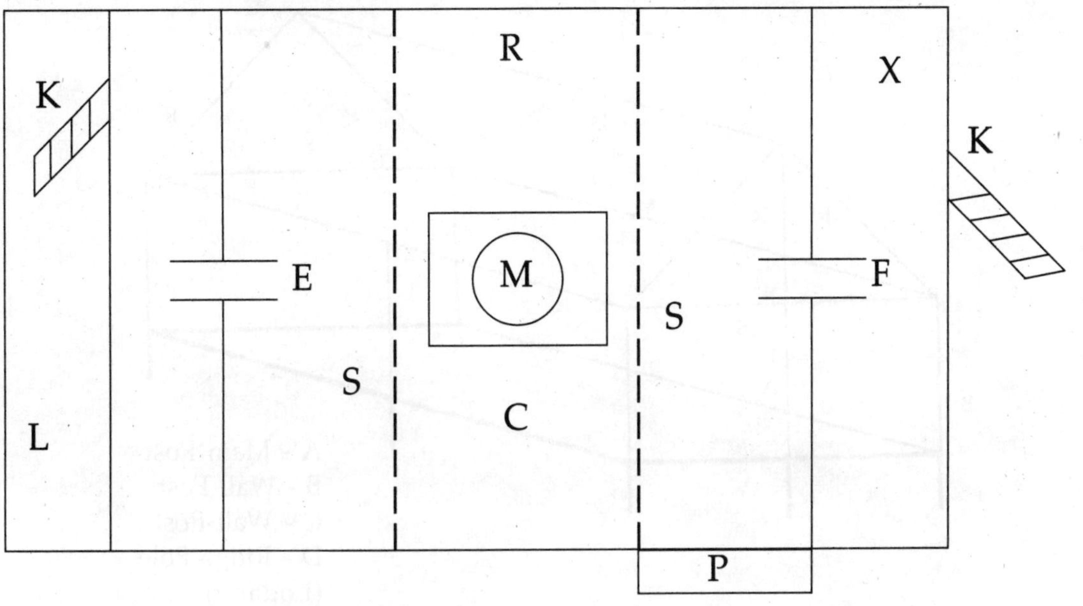

fig. **25. Inside layout of a Mising house**

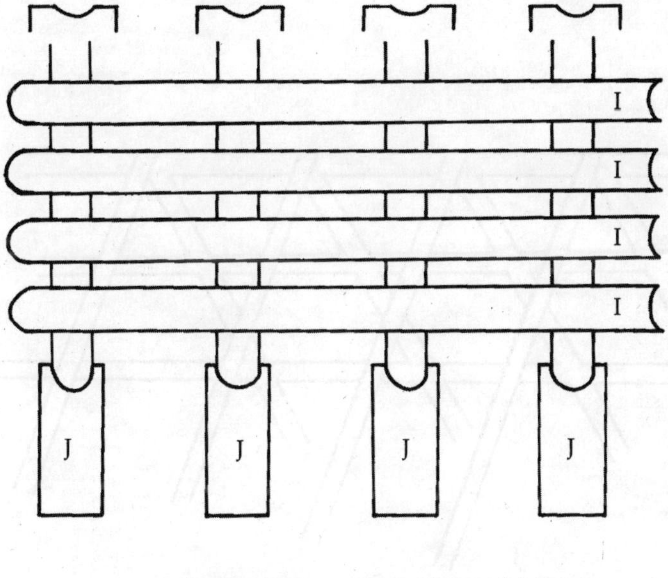

fig. **26. Construction of the platform**

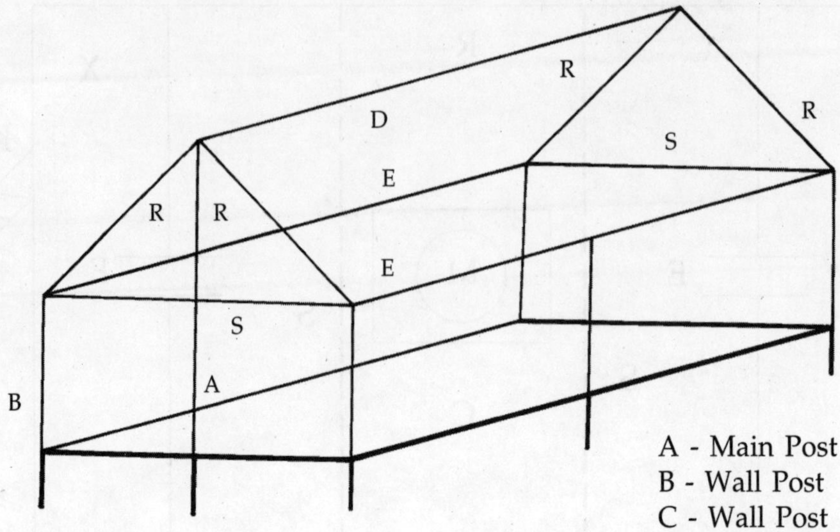

A - Main Post
B - Wall Post
C - Wall Post
D - Ridge Pole (Lodang)
E - Purline (Dugoing)
R - Refter (Sayang)
S - (Bangkung)

fig. **27. A typical house structure**

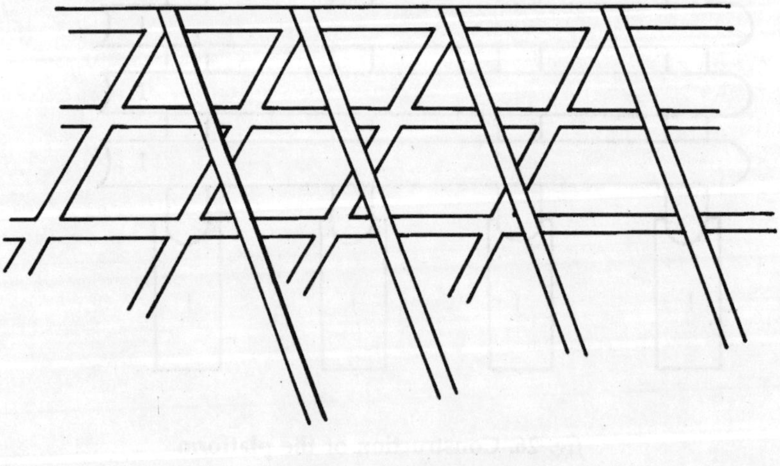

fig. **28. Frame of a roof**

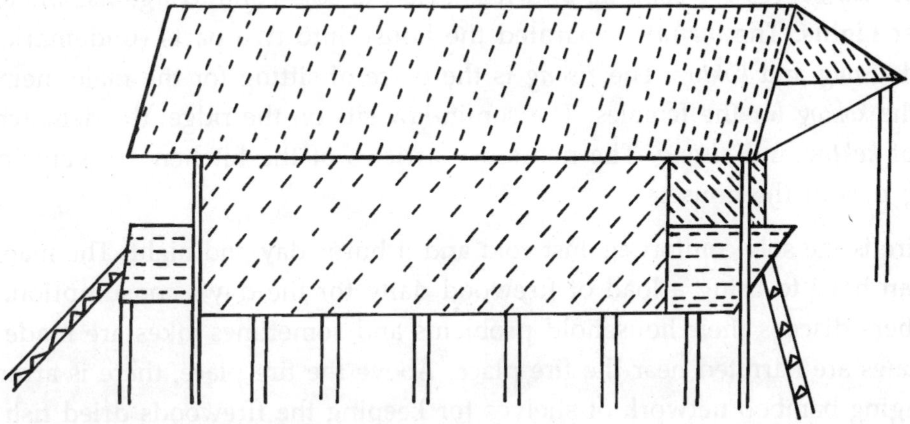

fig. **29. Side view of a Mising house**

DIVISION OF THE HOUSE

There is no partition in a traditional style of house, but different portions of the house have different names and uses. The system of the partition with bamboo made wall is not found it their traditional residential house.

The first half of the house is known as *soyer* or room. This portion is generally used by the married couple of the family. They sleep here and keep their articles.

At the middle of the house the fire place *moiram* or *mcram* is established. The fire place separated the room into two halves *risong* and *koktog*. Next to the *moiram* again the *soyers* start. The last *soyers* are utilized by the old persons. The *koktog* portion is considered sacred and the female members during their menstruation period are not permitted to come to this portion of the house. The ladies do not use the articles of sitting and eating of their elders.

The last part is the *panichang* or *kare*. In some houses this is a lane leading to the backdoor. The flooring is also the same material as that of the main house. It is used to store drinking water and for washing utensils. There is an extended shed on one side of the main house to keep the fowls. This shed is called *kok-dung*.

FIRE PLACE OR MOIRAM OR MCRAM

The fire place or *moiram* is the most important place in a Mising house. It is placed in the centre of the house. In case of bigger family there may be two or even more *moirams* inside the house. In such cases the sites of the hearths are selected in such a way that each hearth covers an equal floor area.

Moiram serves for cooking and it is also the sole comfort against the chilly winter nights. The *moiram* separated the house into two parts (undemarkable) called *risong* and *koktog*. The *risong* is the place of sitting for the male members and the *koktog* for the females. The son-in-law sits on the ridge, the demarcation line of *koktog* and *risong*. The necessary articles of the kitchen are kept in the *koktog* part of the house.

Fire is the sole comfort against cold and it burns day and night. The man and woman have to bring a load of firewood daily for the day's consumption. The members discuss their household problems and sometimes jokes are made and folk tales are narrated near the fire place. Above the fire place, there is arranged a hanging bamboo network of shelves for keeping the firewoods dried fish and meat for preservations. This device has three parts or tiers known as *poiraboo*, *rangbo* and *kumba*. These are suspended one above the other about 2 m above the fire place.

THE CONSTRUCTION OF THE FIRE PLACE

At the time of construction of the platform of a house, the place of the *moiram* is required to be decided first of all. The portion on which the *moiram* is to be constructed is left open. No floor matting is knitted on that portion. If bamboo matting has been knitted it is cut out. The size of the fire place is 3 ft × 3 ft. The *moriam* is supported on four logs which are planted in the ground and join at the top. The junction of the top of the log posts are kept a little below the floor matting Wooden planks (*gulung*) equal to the size of the opening of the floor matting are place on it and a heavy layer of mud is plastered on the plank pieces. This is done to prevent the plank from fire. Three pieces of stones are placed on the mud. The warming pot and pans rest on these stones. Sometimes three iron bolts are fixed in equal distance circularly so that the pan rests on them.

It is a custom to clean the fire place with mud every morning. Putting one's foot on the hearth is restricted. Food and drink are served to the guest near the hearth. Low wooden seats (*pira*) for sitting are laid around the fire place.

Size of the House

The length of the house depends on the size of the family. Depending upon the length and breadth of the house the Mising house can be divided into three types — a small house for a small family having one fire place. Secondly, a big house which is extraodinarily bigger than the general category of houses. Such houses are possessed by the joint families having three or four fire places.

Finally, a medium or general type of house having two fire places. The majority of the Mising houses come under this category.

Decoration of the House

In olden days the heads of the wild animals killed by the members of the family were displayed on the wall. These heads are reminders of the hunting expedition of the family. Some families decorated the walls with the skins of wild animals like deer, tiger, monkey and goat. These skins are used as mattresses. These are of course not used regularly.

Some families plastered the wells with mud and cowdung. But in most cases the traditional house walls are not plastered. If there are no widows or vantilators the plastering of the walls prevent light into the house.

Granary (Kumsang)

A store house for grains to consume throughout the year is built by these families whose product of rice is well and can surpass their need. The granary is usually constructed at a considerable distance from the dwelling house so that fire can't reach and damage it. It is also a platform house whose floor is made of bamboo matting woven thickly and plastered with mud mixed with cowdung. Walls are also plastered half each. One small size door equal to a window is fixed in the house. The size of the granary also depends upon the needs of the family.

The type of granary made by the Mising folk is quite suited to protecting corn from floods, dampness as well as from insects.

Cowshed

Cowsheds are erected and fenced around keeping gateway for entrance. No walls are made in the cowshed. Sunlight is taken into consideration in this case also. It is cleaned every morning. Smoking arrangement at night is made in the cowshed to protect the cows from mosquitoes.

Latrine

There is no provision of latrine in the house and the people relieve themselves in the neighbouring jungles and riversides. A few houses have constructed urinals at one corner of their compound. As for sanitaion, there is hardly any regular arrangement in most of the villages. The domestic animals clean their natural toilet.

Variations

Though the construction of a typical hut is same as described above variation in respect of construction and the material used in the same was observed in a few cases. Some families build a platform room only for Kitchen and rest of the house is either L-shaped or U-shaped having no platform.

Recreational Architecture

For communal participation in athletic events, dramatic and musical performance for private luxuries, baths, museum, etc., every folk society construct recreational house in different names. In most cultures, recreational institutions have their origin in religious rites, but they easily gain independence.

The recreational building, tradionally built by the Misings is called *murong*. It is a big platform oriented house made of wood, bamboo, thatch and cane in the middle of the village. The house lacks walls and doors and its platform is covered with sufficiently polished mates.

The main function of the *murong* in the past was to guard the village at night form the enemies. It acted as a training institute. The adolescent and unmarried young men used to sleep in the *murong* and keep the village guarded. If unfortunately enemy attacked the village they would immediately inform the villagers so that they could manage to run away from the village. Today however, the dormitory has been replaced by a public hall. No longer the youth guard the village in the present context. The youths and the other villagers gather in the *murong* during the festival to chalk out the programmes. The pillars of these *murong*s are generally wooden logs on which the folk carpenters curve out decorative motifs.

Religious Architecture

Namghor is the religious institution in a Mising village. It has two separate sections namely *monikut* and *kīrtan ghar*. The *monikut* is a two roofed house built in north-south direction. The *kīrtan ghar* is built perpendicular to the *monikut* in east-west direction having a *tup* at the front. The *monikut* part is smaller in size having a door in the middle of the western wall. *Thapana*, the place of the divine image is at the middle of the *monikut*. It is also known as *singhason*. The *kīrtan ghar* on the other hand is an open hall where the people pray god, perform *bhawana*, etc.

The villagers build their *namghar* by communial labour and collecting the materials by contribution from each family. In some *namghar*s a *batsora* and *so-ghor* are also built in their respective positions.

Some Case Studies Relating to House Constructing Traditions and Settlement Pattern

With the help of a few case studies we shall be able to explain the nature of settlement pattern, house types, material used in construction and impact of modern styles of housing among the Misings.

CASE STUDY 1

A case study of the pattern of settlement of the village Gandhia Mising Gaon under Nakachari police station and Nakachari mouza was undertaken during the year 1997-98. The following type of settlement occupied the village at that time. The village contained 130 families of the which 34 families migrated to Mil Gaon which is situated in the east of the present village. The villagers of the Gandhia Mising Gaon belong to the clans *pow, mipun, panging, rangon, tie, mili* and *pasar*. The villagers followed some rules in arrangement of their huts and the front doors. According to the oral tradition, the villagers had came from the hilly areas of present Nagaland and settled at the plains of Namti Pathar area. Later they migrated to the present settlement area. The area was a thick forest which they converted to cultivable land and settlement area. It is heard that one man who first led the team to the present village and encouraged people was named Gandhia. The name of the village derived from his name. It is situated between two rivers, the Teok river in the north-east and the Puthi river in the southern border of the village. At present the village contains 98 families. A map of settlement structure of the village is attached herewith. It is observed that the availability of building material is of primary importance in considering the house type of the region. The chief among them are bamboo, reeds, timber, etc. Bamboo is the material for the construction of walls. The second important material for wall is reed. In modern types of buildings bricks, iron rods and galvanized roofs are used.

Out of 98 family only 9 family have their houses on ground floors and all others possess platform houses. The well-to-do family builds the platforms with RCC piles and beams. All the families follow Hindu religious fold having a *namghar* in the midst of the settlement area. A club and a theatre hall (*natghorh*) and one primary school are established in the village. The recreational and religious buildings are now permanently built. The drinking water was obtain from the two rivers — the Puthi and the Teok river. Now the villagers have constructed ring wells and a reservoir inside the village.

It is found that 40 families have their front doors towards the east, 21 families towards the south, 12 families towards the north direction and the rest have them in either north-west or north-east directions.

Almost all the families construct the platform with bamboo matting and one family covered it with planks. No RCC style of platform is found. The huts are arranged on both sides of the village path with entrances through the courtyard. No non-Mising people have settled inside the village except four Bengali families on the outside of the village who came and settled later than the Misings. There are four shops inside the village. The main road runs between Amguri town and Morioni. Two other shops are also found on the side of the main road. Except these shops all other houses are used for residence. No factory or industry exists inside the village.

Type of Settlement of the Village

The houses are closely huddled together. The compact settlement with streets of irregular width are observed. The houses are almost in variably street-fronted. There are separate bedrooms, kitchen and store rooms in almost all families. All the villagers possess a house with more than one room.

Material for Wall

Vegetable material like reeds, bamboo and timber constituted the important building material for walls. In modern types of houses, bricks constitute the important material in wall making. Traditional *chang-ghor*s are not plastered with mud. No venti-lation or chimney is arranged.

Material for Roofs

The roofs are constructed with bamboo lattice covered with thatch. Two roof houses are most common.

Settlement Pattern

The area of settlement is almost rectangular and permanent.

CASE STUDY 2

In order to study the settlement pattern and house designs I visited the village Bahphala of Porbottia mouza under Pulibar police station in 1998. The village is situated on the bank of river Amguri and the Dishoi. The river Brahmaputra is at a distance of 1.5 km and Jorhat town is at 18 km from the village. The year witnessed great flood all over Assam. Floods did great damage to the village Bahphala. During my visit to the village I saw several road and bridge damages.

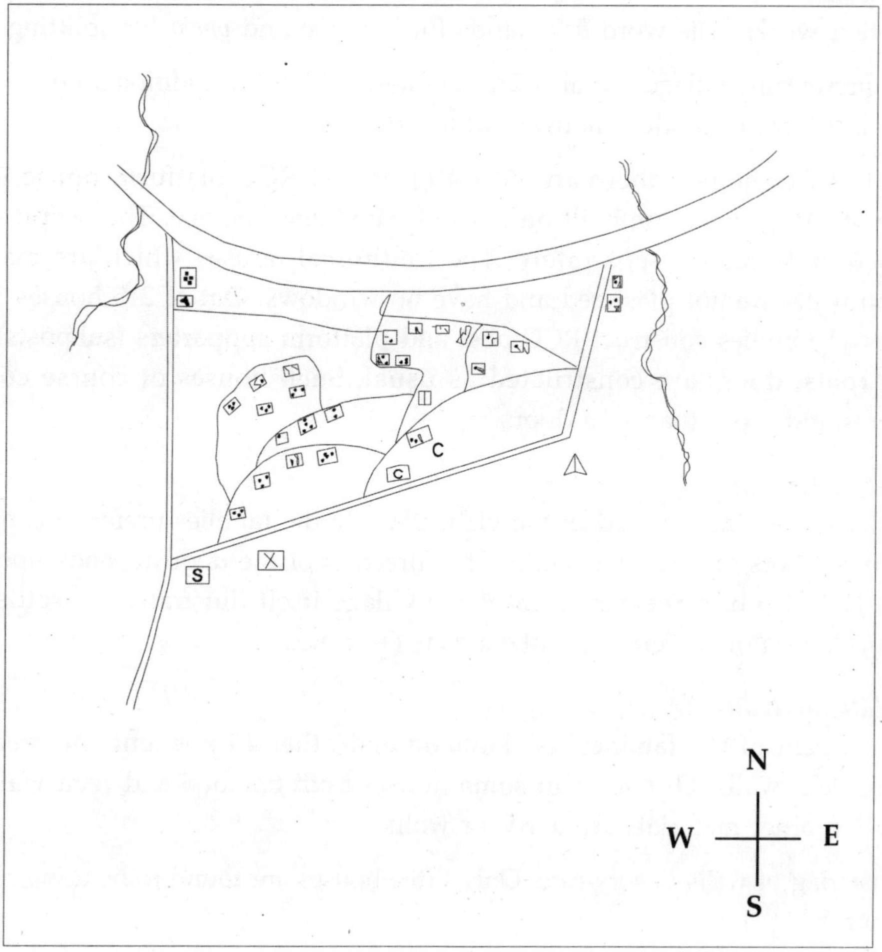

═ Link Road
— Sub Road
☐ Huts
[S] School
[C] Club/ Murong
[X] Play Ground
△ Temple
☐ Shop
⊕ Tank
≈ River

***Map.* 2. Settlement patterns of Gandhia Mising Gaon**

According to Sri Shawana Pagu (76) the name of the village originated from a strong man of olden times who could split a bamboo easily for making house or such other works. The word *bah* stands for bamboo and *phala* for splitting.

At present the village contains 215 families residing in traditional houses with a little influence of modern housing designs.

Out of 215 houses there are no *matighor* and RCC platform house in the village. All the houses are built on piles of wood and bamboo. The people made cowshed and granary sepa-rately. The traditional houses which are made of bamboo walls are not plastered and have no windows. Out of 215 houses in the villages 11 families construct RCC post and platform supporters (subposts). The walls, roofs, doors are constructed as usual. Such houses of course contain windows and more than two doors.

Type of Settlement

Compact settlement is found in the village where the families prefer to construct their front doors towards the south. The direction of the door depends upon the roads. The map of settlement area of the village itself illustrates the settlement pattern. Pattern of settlement is like a plus (+) mark.

Materials for Walls

Sixty per cent of the families use bamboo and other 40 per cent use reeds for making their walls. Of course in some houses both bamboo and reed walls are found. No other materials are used for walls.

Plastering of walls is very rare. Only three houses are found to be using regular whitewash.

Roofing Materials

Thatch dominates as the roofing material but tin (galvanized roof) is also not uncommon in the village.

Every family has its homestead and courtyard but most of the families have their agriculture farms away from the house. Only betel nut trees, and other fruit trees are planted in their respective *barries*. There is an old saying about the position of the kitchen, cowshed and planting trees which goes thus — *uttare saur-dokhine garu* — means kitchen in the north and cowshed in the south.

This traditional rule is not strictly followed in the village.

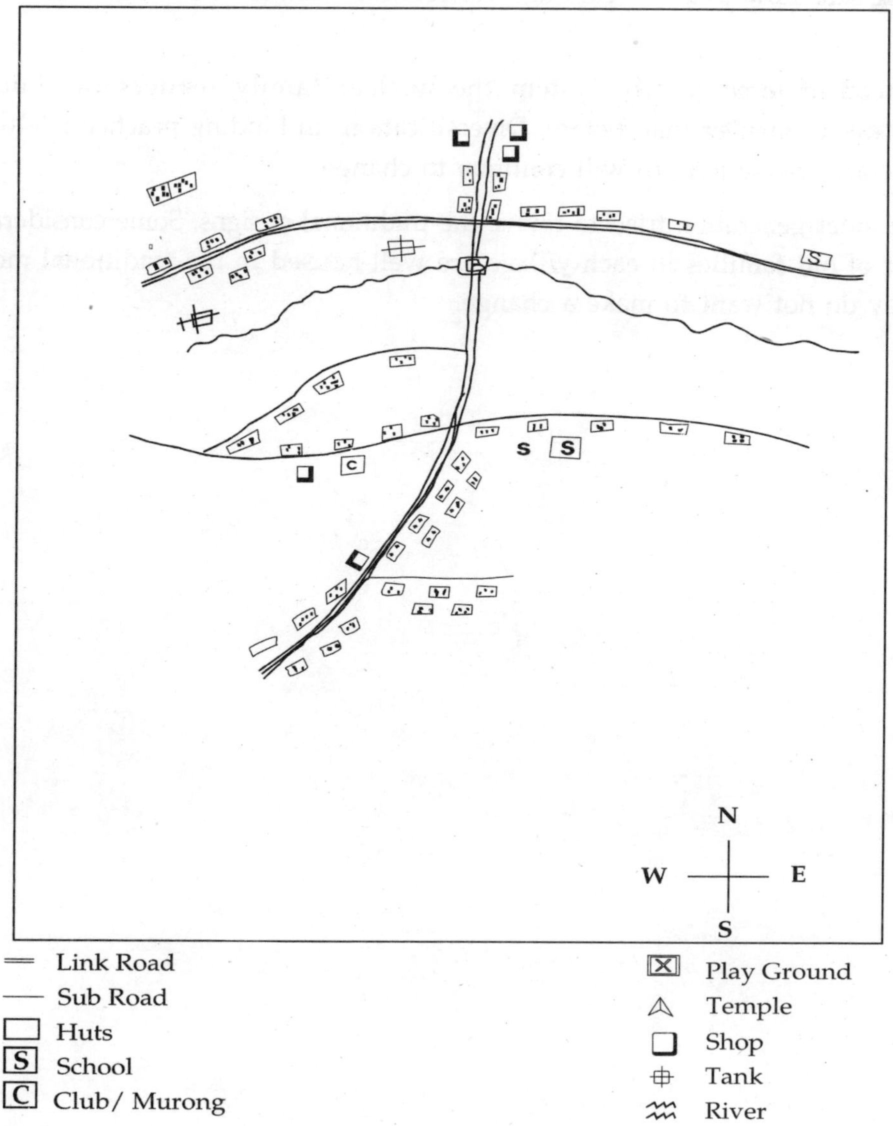

Map. 3. Settlement pattern of Bahphala Gaon

Result of Changes in Family Size

Housing requirements have got to differ with change in family size and composition. Housing patterns tend to mirror the existing condition. The average dwelling size now and 50 years ago reflects the change in average size of the family.

Instead of joint family system the nuclear family renders the houses comparatively smaller than before. Diversification in binding practice is always possible and house pattern will continue to change.

The older generation tried to revive the traditional designs. Some considerable number of old families in each village are well-housed in the traditional mode, and they do not want to make a change.

Chapter 7

Folk Cookery of the Misings

THE study of folk cookery is a part of folk culture which covers the whole subject of food production, preparation and preservation along with the actual cooking methods and consumption of food. Foods should be both tasty and look good, for which basic cooking knowledge is essential.

Dietary factors maintain the health and protect the body from diseases. The rule of diet in health and diseases is more evident in the life of the tribal folk. In this chapter, I shall try to analyse how locally available food products have been used by the Mising folk for maximum nutritional benefits. For a successful discussion and analysis this chapter is divided into following units, e.g. :

1. Food production.
2. Rice — The staple food.
3. Curry — *Bhaja, pora, pitika, khar, tenga, tita, jalla.*
4. The vegetable fruit groups.
5. The pulse group of curry.
6. The meat group.
7. The fish group.
8. The egg group.
9. Food during festivals.
10. Prepartion of *apong.*
11. Role of *apong* in life.
12. Food preservation process.
13. Traditional process of salt preparation.

14. Food for sick persons.
15. Food prohibition — *Gannas*.

Food Production

Anthropologists and archaeologists have tried their best to give an idea regarding the origin of agriculture. They have excavated various places where people lived long ago to learn how the earliest men lived and obtained their food. From these findings and historical records we have come to know about three great revolutions in production of food of the world.

In this respect Dermott says

> The first great food revolution took place when men began to grow food crops and to domesticate animals. From the study of the tools found in many sites, researchers believe that agriculture began in the east and then spread to Europe about 12000 years ago.[1]

The second food revolution occurred in Europe and America during the later part of the 1700s and continued to 1900s. During this time farmers used simple hand-made tools for planting and reaping.

The third food revolution started when man started his urban life and agriculture itself become a big industry.

Although modern equipments have brought a tremendous change in the field of agriculture yet the folk technique of cultivation and folk cookery still exist in rural India. Thus traditional methods of food production are still a living art among the Misings and other people of Assam.

The method of cultivation and nature of crops production determined the character of agriculture. The Mising cultivators produced various species of rice like *ahu, lahi, shali* and *baou* etc. But *ahu* and *baou* paddy are principal food crops. They sow *ahu* and *baou* seeds in the same plot of land, and start harvesting *ahu* crops in May and June. The *baou* crops take longer time for growth and cannot be easily damaged by flood. The *sali* paddy cultivation is not popular among the Misings living in flood affected areas. They also produce various *rabi* crops during the winter season. Vegetables, *dal*, eatable roots, mustard oil seeds are produced in this season.

---

1. I.E.Mc. Dermott, *Food for Modern Living*, New York p. 7.

***fig.* 30. Domestic utensils**

The economic condition of the Mising depends on the agricultural products. Land is a private property to each family. Apart from the private cultivation, group cultivation also exists in their society.

Rice cultivation is carried out in an extensive scale. Most of the families are self-sufficient in rice and very little is imported from outside. Other chief products are ginger, mustard seeds, turmeric, pepper, betel leaves, *arecanuts*, onion, chillies and so on. Fruits like pineapples, jack fruits, mangoes, lemons, bananas of various species are available in each Mising village. Wild vegetables generally grown in the fields along with cultivated crops contain nutritional and medicinal values. Such wild vegetables are common food items of the Misings in general.

The cultivated vegetables are melon pumpkin, tomato, cabbage, cauliflower, nolkhol, carrot, beat, turnip, pea, brinjal, cucumber, bean, etc. The principal crops produced by the Misings may be shown in the following ways, e.g.:

Food Crops	Period of Sowing	Period of harvesting
1. *Ahu* paddy	Feb. and March	May and June
2. *Baou* paddy	Feb. and March	Nov. and Dec.
3. *Sali* paddy (*amdang*)	July and August	Nov. and Dec.
4. *Lahi* paddy (*amro*)	Sep. and October	Nov. and Dec.
5. Mustard seeds	Sep. and Oct.	Nov. and Dec.

The Misings are non-vegetarians and as such both fish and meat are their favourite food items. They collect meat from their own livestock and fish from nearby rivers. They eat almost all kinds of animals except beef.

The Mising menu, however, consists of

(a) plenty of rice (normally the large red-round variety),
(b) a meat curry prepared with herbs, chilli, potato and so on,
(c) fish fried or boiled with herbs or dried fish called *namcing*,
(d) omlettes, fried in plenty of oil/fats, and
(e) *apong* and *chai apong* — the rice beer.

Rice (apin) — The Staple Food

Rice is the world's most versatile crop. Rice is the staple diet of more than two billion people in Asia and many million more in Africa and Latin America.

Observes R. Dutta Sarma:

> More than 90 per cent of the world's rice is grown and consumed in Asia alone. About 15000 to 16000 years ago, wild rice grew on the northern and southern slopes of the Himalaya. This variety of rice is known as indica, could withstand variations in temperature and even drought. It spread to northern and eastern India, to northern South-East Asia, and to southern China. The species of rice grown in India is known as "Oryza Indica." In Sanskrit paddy is called Vrihi.[2]
>
> Rice forms the cheapest source of food energy and provides large portion of the caloric and protein requirement of the human body. Rice is predominantly a starchy cereal and provides energy but to a large extend it also furnishes protein and vitamin for a large section of population.[3]

The rice is the staple food of the Misings and Assamese people throughout the year. As mentioned earlier, the four types of paddy *ahu, sali, lahi* and *baou* are cultivated by the farmers of Assam. The corn of the *lahi* are smaller in size whereas the *ahu, baou* and *sali* are of big size. The *ahu* and *baou* are of course red in colour.

After harvesting the crops are sun dried on locally made mats called *asup*, made of bamboo strips and then hulled by means of the husking device called *ural*. *Ural* is a wooden mortar and it is operated by a wooden pestle called *kiper*. It is then fanned with a winnowing fan called *apoo* and the husks are separated with a sieve.

There is nothing remarkable in the methods of preparation of boiled rice called *apin*, The husked rice is washed with water before preparation. The rice cooking pan known as *danking* is placed on the hearth and water is poured on it. When the water gets warm, rice is put into it and boiled for about half an hour. They do not separate the gruel from rice.

> In some families the husked rice is put unwashed into a big brass vessel (*botuwa*), and set them boiling on the fire of the hearth. When boiled into the half, the mouth of the vessel is covered with a banana leaf and is taken off the fire, but placed very close to the hearth, the gruel is not

2. R. Sarma, *The story of Rice*, p. 10.
3. N.R. Devi, *Effect of cooking on Physicochemical Properties of Few Rice Varieties of Assam*, unpublished MSc. thesis submitted to Home Science Dept. of Agriculture, University of Assam, 1990.

extracted but allowed to be soaked into the cooked rice. When ready, it is served along with a curry of leafy vegetables.[4]

Rice (*bhat* or *apin*) is very often served also as breakfast item in many families. A large amount of rice in Mising villages is used to prepare rice beer called *apong*. Besides, *apin* items like *chira* (flattened rice), *muri* (puffed rice), *pithaguri* (powdered rice) and *akhoi* (popped rice) are also prepared out of rice. Various types of popular cakes (*pithas*) are also made of rice. The snacks prepared from uncooked rice are known as *ambug* by the Mising.

Boiled rice can be divided into many kinds. These are *poita bhat, karkara bhat, jaubhat* or *nisoniabhat, khud choul bhat, khisiri, bora bhat, sunga choul.*

ASI POMNAN ADIN OR (POUTA BHAT)

Rice soaked in water overnight is called *asi pomnam adin* and is a very popular item of food in hot seasons. Many Misings take it as breakfast with salt, chillies and dry fish. Raw onions are also taken with it.

PINKA APIN OR (KARKARA BHAT)

The rice cooked on the previous night but not soaked in water is called *pinka apin. pinka apin* is actually the remains of the previous night's meal. It is eaten with hot curries and fried items.

MAR APIN OR (NISONIA BHAT)

It is also called *jau bhat* which is to some extent a liquid type of soft preparation of rice. It contains more water than the normal boiled rice. People eat such *bhat* as breakfast or tiffin at afternoon.

AMUN AYING (KHISIRI)

It is a dish composed of rice, pulse, mustard oil and various other species cooked together.

Bora Bhat

Bora is a species of rice group having a paste like property and a distinctive taste. The rice is boiled in steam. The procedure for its preparation is somewhat different from that of ordinary *bhat*.

4. A.K. Dutta, *Sociology of the Mising community of Assam, p. 106, an unpublished Ph. D. thesis submitted to Guwahati University.*

Sunga Choul

It is a prepared by pouring rice and water into bamboo tubes and are burnt on fire. It is taken mainly with salt or molasses.

Purang Bora

In festival like *Ali-aye-Legang* the Mising folk arrange communal feast in which the rice is boiled in some small packets of green leafs of *tora* grass. The bundles are boiled in a big pot called *bor karahi* and are served with the leafy packets.

Normally rice is taken with various kinds of seasonings called *anja* or *tarkari* or *bynzon* which means curry. It is also called *sak*. The Mising term for curry is *oying*. The people take three meals a day. The first in the morning, a second at noon and the third in the evening.

There is no variation in the menu at these meals. The gaps between these meals are filled in by sips of *apong*.

Curry (Oying)

Folk cookery is in a way connected with culinary objects, skills, food habits and on the other hand with beliefs, taboos, rituals and symbolic system of a culture. Different methods of preparation of different curries can give an idea regarding the food ways of a community or a group.

The common name of the curries depends on its taste like *tenga* or *kudak; tita* or *kona; dignum* or *jalla* and *khar*.

Moreover, depending upon the cooking processes the food items are commonly identified as — *pora* or *baranum; pamnum* or *patatdiya, bhatat diya, pitika, sijua* or *ranam khori-kinam* or *kharikat diya, vapatdiya, kholatdiya* and so forth.

DIVISION ON THE BASIS OF TASTE

Kuno Owing or Tenga Sak (Sour Curry)

The vegetable curry mixed with lemon juice (sour) is called *tenga sak* or *kudak oying*. Instead of lemon juice some vegetables like *tengamora, nakung* (*noltenga*) and fruits like *owetenga* (*chempa*) tomato, *thakara* are added as ingredients to the curry. It seems to go popular with fish in summer days.

Kona Oying or Tita Anga Sak (Bitter Taste Curry)

The curries made for bitter taste is called *tita sak* or *tita anja* or simply *tita* which means bitter. Wild vegetables like, *dorun, sokota* (dry leafs of jute), *bahok, tita phul, kona bunko* (*bhacury*) and fruits like *kerela*, are added in required suitable quantity to the curry. Belief has it that such curry can increase the digestive capacity of a man and can remove round worm which is a parasite of the stomach.

Khar (Alkali)

Khar is also called *seka* which is an alkaline preparation popular all over Assam. The Misings along with other neighbours prepared *khar* by an indigenous process. Nowadays, the practice of preparation of alkali at home is seen to be declining and sodium bicarbonate powder purchased from the market replace the home-made *khar*.

Khar

Khar is also widely believed to have medicinal properties. The pregnant woman is not advised to take *khar* in any form.

Jella (Dignum)

The taste of capsicum or pepper is favourable to most of the people. A separate curry of pungent taste is always present with the meals. In absence of such curry chilli or black pepper is consumed in raw with the meal to get the pungent taste. Depending upon the cooking methods the food items may be divided into following sub-groups, e.g.:

(i) *Pora or burnum* : It is nothing but a roasted item. Roasted potato is called *alu-pora*, roasted brinjal is called *bengana pora* and so on. Such *pora* items are commonly eaten with *asi pomnum apin*, i.e., previously boiled rice containing sufficient water.

(ii) *Pitika or eyonum* : Generally vegetable fruits boiled with rice or separately in water or mashed and made into lumps after adding salt, oil, onion, and chillies. Such soft pulpy mixture is called as *pitika*.

(iii) *Bhanja/bhaji* : A *bhanja* or *bhaji* is a fried item. The green leafy vegetables, fruits and fish, etc., are fried in mustard oil without adding water in it. Vegetable fry is called *sak bhanji*, fish fry is called *mac bhanji* and so on.

(iv) *Panam/patat diya* : This is a dish prepared by a special process of roasting or boiling. For example, fish, or vegetable which is to be cooked in this process should be cleaned first and then seasoning like salts, onion, garlics, mustard oil and chillies should be added to it. All things are placed with a layer of banana leaf very carefully.

This is then inserted into an oven when the first few layers of leaves of the bundle are scarred, the preparation is removed from the oven. The substance is then taken out of the leafy bundle and is ready to serve.

Ratto/boiling: All cooked food items are called *ratto* which means boiling.

The Vegetable Fruits Group

Vegetables are excellent sources of vitamines A and C and have an important place in daily meal. Vegetables are served in raw as salads (*satoni*) and cooked also. Salads consist of vegetables and fruits. Tomatoes, cucumbers, raddishes, carrots, cauliflowers, green beans, peas, etc., are used for making salads. They prepare a sort of curry by boiling green vegetables and pulses with which salt, powdered turmeric, onion and peppers are mixed. These boiled or fried vegetable leaves are eaten as side dishes with boiled rice.

The oil generally used for preparing food items is extracted from mustard seeds. The vegetables when fried without water constitute the item called *kor*. Vegetable fruits like brinjals, lady's finger, cucumber are cut into slices, dried and either fried in oil or roasted. Cucumber is also eaten as raw with salt. Brinjals are often roasted.

The seeds of jackfruit are boiled with other vegetable fruits and consumed as curry with the main meals. Similarly tomatoes, raddishes, sweet potatoes, pumpkins, beans are kitchen vegetables favourite to them.

The pumpkin is boiled and eaten. Mustard leaf is prominent among leafy vegetables. During off cultivation seasons the edible leaves of various herbs are boiled and consumed in abundance.

The use of salt, chillies, ginger and garlic is known to the Misings. Chillies are grown in abundance. The Misings have a great liking for chillies.

Vegetable groups: Various wild grown vegetables (plants) are favourite diet with the main meals. Names of some popular vegetables are given below:

Tazik takpang, takuk, notka, dermy, ombe, kirpottali, dorun, futkola, brihlogoni, ebtab, adolia kosu, donkodoksi, ringpung, III-kasu, matikaduri, *ranku* (banana flower), *onger, pakkam, ashut, kalmou, bangu, vhakuri* (*knona-banco*), *didum, chirombo* (ends of cane), *morsong, champa, pipoly, jeyeng* (lilly), *mejanga, nolmora, namkung* (not tenga), *vavty, changmora, gangya, kuduk* (liman), *kaki* (mango), *mebo* (*ciral*), *mirsi* (cilly), *potu* (mustard seed), *tappa, balang* (jackfruit), *mekkong* (cucumber), *ori* (coriander), *tuloi* (*laisak*).

The people collect varieties of leaves, tubers, etc., from the jungles to supplements their food resources. Mustard oil, is a cooking medium. They also use oil from pig's fat. Such oil can be separated while the meat is boiling in water. The oil that floats over the pan is removed with a ladle.

The cooking technique used by the Mising women-folk are given below which are based on some case studies.

Case Stydy 1

Srimoti Putoli Paow (56) and Alibi Regon (60), of Sham Mising Gaon, Teok, under Jorhat sub-division told me the following methods of making curry with wild-grown vegetables which are favourite to them.

(i) **Curry no. 1: *Amba* with meat curry:** *Amba* is a wild vegetable and its younger leaves are collected and they are ground smoothly or cut very smoothly. It is then mixed with boiling meat curry. This makes the curry more tasteful and produces a light golden colour. It is more effective if the juice of the leaves is added to the curry.

(ii) **Curry no. 2: *Kirpotoli* with *singi* fish:** *Kirpotoli* is a wild born vegetable. It is collected locally and washed properly and cut into small sections (2 mm in size). The fish specially the *singi* variety, is fried and the vegetables mentioned above are then added to it. Salt, tamarind, chillies are added to the curry as needed. It is served hot with meals.

(iii) **Curry no. 3: *Bihlogoni* with *kusia* (*egu*) or Hagfish:** *Bihlongoni* — a wild-grown vegetable. *Kusia* — a kind of water-living worm.

(iv) **Curry no. 4: *Champa oying* or *Padub oying*:** *Champa* or *owetenga*, a fruit having acidic taste. In prematured stage of the fruit, is cut into small sections and a curry with fish is prepared.

(v) **Curry no. 5: *Eco oying*:** It is a curry of tender bamboo shoots commonly called *khorisa* in Assamese.

(vi) **Curry no. 6: *Organg oying*:** The wild grown vegetable called *kasu* and its tubes are boiled with salt tamarind and chillies. If the tubes are used for preparing curry then it is called *orang oying* and if the tender leaves are used in the curry then it is called *ungocin oying*.

(vii) **Curry no. 7: *Kolpasala*:** The young shoot of banana plant is called *kalpasala* in Assamese. Like other section of the people of this region the Misings are also fond of eating *kalpasala* and *kaldil* (banana flower).

(viii) **Curry no. 8: *Brihlogoni* with chicken.**

(ix) **Curry no. 9: *Bihlogoni* with pork.**

(x) **Curry no. 10: *Futukala* with *singi* fish.**

(xi) **Curry no. 11: *Doron* with *kusia*.**

(xii) **Curry no. 12: *Ibtab* with pork.**

The procedures of cooking all these curries are almost same as described in **curry no. 2.** Vegetables are always cut into thin sections and fruits are cut into slices.

KHAR OR ALKALI

Kalkhar is prepared by an indegenous process from roots and barks of bannana tree. The dried roots or barks are burnt in fire. The ashes are treated in an open pot. The pot has a little hole in the bottom. Water is poured very slowly on the ashes are allowed to deposit in another pot.

KHAR OR ALKALINE CURRY OF SOKOTA

Sokota is an Assamese word used to mean the dried leaves of jute plant (*olap*) when the jute plants are cut at their maturity, the young branches are kept together and dried in sunlight. Such dried leaves are ground into powder and preserved in bamboo tubes or baskets.

PROCEDURE FOR MAKING CURRY

In a hot pan, some quantities of mustard oil, onion, chillies and turmeric are added. *Sokota* powder of required quantity is poured into the pan and alkaline solution is added to it. After proper boiling in required water the curry becomes suitable to eat. Salt should be added as required.

This curry is popular among the Misings and other non-tribal Assamese people the curry gives a slightly bitter taste. Similar types of curry can be made with dried *sewali* (night jasmine) and *bahak*, a kind of flowering plant.

ALKALINE CURRY OF PACHALA

Pachala means are offshoot of banana. It is cut into thin sections and fried with *kalakhar* salt, chillies etc. It is also mixed with a meat curry.

KHOROLI

What the Assamese called *Khoroli* is prepared from various vegetables without having acidic or alkaline taste.

Different vegetables like *lai, lofa, paleng* and other wild vegetables having young leaves are cut together and are cut together and are washed properly other necessary ingredients are (1) onion, (2) small fragmented rice grains, and (3) edible oil.

By heating the pan, a little quantity of mustard oil, oil seeds are poured and the chopped leaves of vegetables with salt, turmeric are added. The small fragmented rice grains are ground into powder and are added to the vegetables in the pan. It is then heated to a certain extent. After proper boiling the pan is removed from heat and it becomes ready to serve with the main meals.

NEEM LEAF FRIED

Neem is a tall tree which have certain medicinal values. Several modern medicine are also extracted from the leaves of *neem* tree. The leaves of *neem* tree are fried (dried) and are eaten with meals. In the same way, *narasinha* leaves, *sewali* leaves, *doron* leaves can be fried.

Bhebeli Patat Dya

Bhebeli is the name of a wild-grown vegetable on the river banks of Assam. The tender leaves of the plant are bound in a soft banana leaf and put in the hearth. After a few minutes it is roasted and is removed from the hearth. Then the roasted leaves are separared onto a pan in which onion, salt, chilli and others are added and all these are blended, and then the stuff is served along with the main dish.

Another similar item called *nalmora patatdia*. It has an acidic taste and is prepared from a climber.

Balong Oying (Curry Prepared From Jackfruits)

Jackfruit (*balang*) is a common fruit of Assam which is favourite to every household. It ripens in the months of June, July and August. Curry prepared with green jackfruit is popular among the Misings.

The small pieces of jackfruit are boiled with potatoes or with meat.

MEDICINAL HERBS

The Misings take various curries prepared out of some medicinal plants or herbs which have medicinal quality. Of those *booking papu, argina manimuni, bhadailata, padina, macandari* are worth mentioning. Those are prepared after they are mixed with salt, chilli, onion and others.

Pokom and *dermi* are two other such varieties of wild grown vegetables which are favourite to people. The *pokom* is eaten only in the month of March and April. It is said that in other months the taste of the vegetable species is bitter. These two varieties of herbs are also celebrated in the folk songs of the Misings.

The Pulse Group of Curry

Among the pulses, the *mati* or *pered aie* is eaten after being boiled, *magu* both in raw and after boiling in water is taken as a side dish with rice. Besides these two varieties other pulses like *rahar* (*Cajanus indicas*), *mosur* (*Phaseohms roxburshii*) are also taken after being boiled in sufficient water. But the *mati, magu* and *khasari* or *kola mah* are cultivated by the Misings and are stored for the whole year. Other pulses are imported from outside. The favourite pulse curry among the Misings as found in the Jonai areas of Dhemaji district is the *pered aie*. It is the curry of a black pulse commonly called *mati dal* in Assamese. *Pered* or *mati* variety of pulse is common cultivation along with the *lahi* paddy. The cultivation of these varieties of pulse is found in river sides. To prepare the curry of any variety of the pulses, one should keep the pulse grains under water in a pot for at least an hour. This softens the chaff which can be removed by washing properly. The pulse is then boiled in water in which potatoes or other vegetables or fruits like papaya are added. After proper boiling some families consume it without adding any oil or that sort of substance. Some others add mustard oil and fried onion to it. In another form *champa* (a fruit containing acidic taste) is added to it while boiling goes on. A vegetable like *coriander* locally known as *ori* is added with a view to getting a sweet smell.

Khesari mah or kola mah is now banned by the medical department of Assam. It is a delicious dish for all the inhabitants of upper Assam including the Misings.

Mosur, rohor and *mugu* are not cultivated locally but are imported from outside Assam. The cooking process of these pulses found among the Mising societies is more or less similar.

Some amount of pulses are boiled in water as required and salt and turmeric are added to it. After being boiled for sometime the liquid mixture of pulses and water is poured in hot mustard oil mixed with cumin, chilli, etc.

The *rahar* pulse was uncommon among the aged Mising people. They use only *matimah* in their day-to-day life. In some special ocassion they prepare a curry with *magumah*.

Meat Group of Curry (Ading Oying)

Mamsa or flesh is not a regular food items for the Mising folk. Meat with *apong* is essential for entertainment of a distinguished guest. Meat groups of curries are known as *ading oying*. *Ading* means meat and *oying* stands for boiling.

The traditional method of cooking of the *ading oying* is to follow certain steps. At first the meat is cut into slices and washed properly. Salt and turmeric are mixed with it and put into the boiling water. Vegetable fruits like potatoes, papaya, onion and vegetables like *dermy, ombey* are cut into small sections and are added to the boiling curry. The boiling pan is covered with a metal disc and allowed to heat properly. Fats like mustard oil is used for frying the slice of meat in the preparation of *vajinam ading*. In fact, preparation of meat dish does not involve any elaborate cooking. The meat slabs are boiled in water and when it becomes soft it is eaten with salt, chilli and *apong*.

Some other processes of meat preparation are given below:

KHORI KINUM

To prepare this type of item the Mising families have several iron spocks of 0.5 mm diameter and of at least 2 ft of length. The meat pieces are stitched on it like a garland in different spokes and are placed on the fire. The pieces of meat on spokes are frequently readjusted so that each of them gets sufficient heat from the hearth. *Eogo tago* is such a delicious meat item which is about 2" thick. The Assamese term for such items are *khorikat dia*.

Dried Under Sunlight or Smoke

The dried meat is called *dinsan*.

Fish Group

Fish provides an excellent source of protein for human diet. Besides protein fish flesh also provides minerals, iodine, vitamins and fats. Assam is blessed with the water resources offered by the river Brahmaputra and its large numbers of tributaries, streams, and swamps which provide the occurrence of a large variety of fresh water fish resources. The fish varieties are *rahu* (*Labeo rohita*), *mirigel* (*Cirhinus mrigala*), *chital* (*Noctopterus chitela*), *kandhuli* (*Notopterus*), *ari* (*Mystus seenghala*), *pabha* (*Ompokpobo*), *barali* (*Wallagoattu*), *puathi* (*Wallattu*), *kawai* (*Anadus testudes*), *magur* (*Clasias batrachuses*), *singhi* (*Heteropnes fossilis*), *sal* (*Channa*), *sol* (*Channa marulies*), *goroi* (*Channa panctaus*), etc.

All kinds of fishes are used as fried item but different processes are followed to prepare curry with different fishes.

ROU AND BAHU FISH

Generally rohu and other fishes are prepared as a salted curry together with potato, salt, chilli, turmeric, cassia leaf, etc. Instead of acidic taste people like to prepare curry of pungent taste with such kinds of big fishes.

BORALI FISH

It is generally prepared as a sour curry with tamarind or lemon and some vegetable fruits. Generally vegetable fruits like bottlegour and tomato are preferred with such sour tasting curry.

MAGUR FISH

It is generally prepared with bamboo shoots as salted curry. Some herbs are also used to prepare curry of *magur* fish.

THE PROCEDURE FOR FISH CURRY

Frying of fish in oil or fat is not done by the Misings. They generally cut the fish into slice and boil them in water. Some tender leaves of vegetables are added to it while boiling. Besides making of curry with fish there are some other traditional processes of fish prepartion and consumption.

(i) ***Pora mas* or *barnam ongo*** : The fish is put into a burning fire to roasting. After proper roasting it is washed in water and fins an grills removed.

(ii) ***Khorikat dia mas* or *ranam ongo*** : The fish is burned with a metal stick.

(iii) ***Kholat dia mas* or *sunna ongo.***

(iv) ***Dried fish* or *namcing.***

(v) ***Patu vaji* or *akai vaji*** : The bile of fish is cooked with rice in a good proportion.

(vi) ***Amion oying*** : It is a curry of fish with fragmented rice.

(vii) ***Eco oying*** : It is fish curry with bamboo shoot.

(viii) ***Unga san oying*** : The dried fishes are ground into powder and preserved. It is taken with potato, pumpkin and some other vegetables.

Egg Group

Eggs (*appes*) are supplied by the domestic fouls like the hen and the duck. All the houses of the Mising village have their own fowls for supply of eggs and meat. Eggs are taken as omlettee or are boiled. Boiled eggs are later added to curry by following certain process. Half boiled eggs called *apperanam* are eaten with salt and chilli as a side item of the main meals.

PREPARATION OF OMLETTEE

The liquid portion of an egg is mixed with salt, turmeric, onion sections and fried in the hot oil on a pan. As one side of the substance is fried it is carefully turned over with a spoon so that both the sides get fried well.

Food During Festival

On festival occasions the Mising people prepared special kind of food items from rice.

CHIRA OR FLATTENED RICE

It is prepared from *sali dhan* (*sali* paddy). First the rice is soaked in water for a night and it is fried and then husked quickly.

SANDAHA OR *KORAI*

It can be prepared from any variety of paddy. The *ukhua chaul* is fried and ground into powdered form.

KOMUL CHAUL OR *BHONJA CHAUL*

It is uncooked rice made to sock in water until it becomes soft.

PITHA OR CAKE

Pitha is prepared from powdered rice. In festivals like *Bohag Bihu* the people of Assam prepare *til pitha, ghila pitha* etc.

Preparation of Apong

Like other Mongoloid groups, the Misings also consume rice beer prepared by their own process. The rice beers used by them are known as *apong* and *sai apong*. A new born baby is welcomed with a drop of rice beer and similarly a deadman is given farewell with a drop of rice beer. The rice beer is used both in ritual and social conte. No worship is complete unless and until the offering of rice beer is made. From the cradle of life till the burial of the man rice beer plays an important role. A guest is welcomed with a cup of rice beer. Even many social problems can be solved with the help of rice beer. In some areas *apong* is known as *nagin apong* and similarly *sai apong* is called *paro apong* in some areas. The *nagin apong* is creamy white while the *paro apong* appears to be of dark greenish colour. The process of preparation of *apong* by the Mising people is given below.

BOILING PROCESS

The responsibility for rice beer preparation is confined only to the women-folk of the Misings. Rice grains are first made to soak cold water for 45 to 72 hours. It is then boiled in a large pot up to a certain level. The expert women know the appropriate steps to be taken during the boiling process. Boiling should be stopped in such a stage that it is neither half-boiled nor over-boiled. The water is then drained out of the boiled grains which are then spread out to dry.

The rice so prepared in the above method for making beer is called *ponek* which is quite dry and cold. Thc grains are mixed with *epop* (a cake of medicine) in right proportion and rubbed between the hands. This *epop* contains intoxicating properties.

This mixture of rice grains and *epop* are then put into an earthen jar (*kiling*) filled with water. The mouth of the *kiling* is to be closed by straw. It takes a period of four to five days for fermentation. The first drop is offered to God.

MAKING OF DRY CAKE (EPOP)

A kind of cake like medicine is to be prepared from the plants and herbs which accelerate the fermentation process. The essential herbs and plants are available in the jungles of Assam and some are grown with the cultivated crops. The women-folk can distinguish them very easily. Although there are 15 to 20 different varieties of herbs and plants, all are not necessary in the process of preparation of *apong*. Generally 5 to 6 different varieties are sufficient.

A case study may substantiate our hypothesis. I was told by an informant Srimoti Putali Paw of Sham Mising Gaon, Teok, that she and her family used 7 different plants for making *epop*. Her grandmother had taught her about some other vegetables also. These ingredients are young and tender leaves, roots and flowers of different plants.

The large conical basket (wicker) used for straining rice beer is called *pobor*. The small-sized wicker for filtering *poroapang* is called *taisuk*. The first extract of brew has higher percentage of alcohol. It is called *po:yi*. The residue of the *apong* called *arung* is a good food for the domestic animals.

Role of Apong in Life

From birth of funeral, sowing to harvesting, friendship to revenge, argument to settlement, in abduction and murder and from happiness to sorrow there is no occasion which can be completed without serving of *apong*.

Apong is in fact a part of the diet among the Misings. There is no household where *apong* is not made and there is no age group which refrains from drinking it.

Apong is a part and parcel and an inseparable necessity of all medications, rituals and celebrations. All festivals like birth and marriage need *apong* for welcoming the guests. Whenever negotiations take place to regularize abduction, elopements, murders, etc., the people that assemble together are served *apong*. It serves as an item of dowry whenever the bride-groom's party goes to propose to a girl, they carry a load of *apong* with them.

Apong preparation is a serious drain on the economy of the Misings. All the year they run short of cereals because a huge amount of rice is spent for *apong*. There is no fixed time to drink *apong*. Drinking becomes heavier during the winter season due to cold.

Food Preservation Process

From prehistoric time, man has been using some processes to prevent the spoiling of foods. They knew a number of ways to preserve food. The chemical changes taking place in foods are caused by bacterial action, oxidation and enzymatic action. Due to those actions the vitamins and colours are spoiled. The folk may not know about those reasons but fortunately they knew some processes to prevent those actions. The process of preservation learned thousands of years ago and still maintained today are (i) fermenting, (ii) salting, (iii) smoking, and (iv) drying.

FERMENTATION PROCESS

By using bacteria into the foodgrains they allow them to ferment which help in preserving food items for long time. They use different fermenting agents. In preparing the alcoholic liquid (*apong*) this process is used.

SALTING

Foods packed with salt do not spoil because becteria cannot live in a very salty environment. Salting has been used as a means of preserving food especially fish and meat and fruits like lemon.

SMOKING

In the smoking process, the food items are hung over fire. smoking preserve food partly by drying it and partly by forming a protective coating.

DRYING

Some food items which are available in certain seasons are put under direct sunshine to dry which evaporate the water molecules. Bacteria, which destroy the food cannot grow without water. The Misings traditionally used this method to preserve their surplus food items like fish, meat and certain vegetable fruits.

FOOD ADDITIVES

Folk medicines (chemicals) which are added to foods to improve or preserve their flavour, texture, colour and quality are turmeric, salt, tamarind, and juice of certain vegetables. The use of turmeric powder gives long life to the food substance. Use of dry leafs (oscimumsanctum) show some effect on the control of the growth of fungi.

DRYING OF FISH

Fish is in abandoned quantitites in the rivers, damps and low lying paddy fields. In Assam the fish is sufficiently caught in the winter season. The Mising tribes like dried fish and hence they preserve it by sun-drying.

Certain processes are adopted for drying of fishes. Big fishes are cut into slice before drying. Salt is rubbed in the gills, mouth and scales of the fishes. It is kept in sunshine for 3 to 5 days. During the drying period salt solution penetrates into the fish and they grow firm and hard.

It is finally kept in earthen pots with tight covers.

PRESERVATION OF "EKUNG" (FROM BAMBOO SHOOT)

The villagers collect young and soft bamboo shoots from the woods and they are then washed and cut into small pieces. These pieces are then ground in *ural* and made very soft. It is then kept in bamboo containers. Such prepartion is ready to eat with salt and is mixed with fish and vegetables.

PREPARATION OF SOKOTA

It is the dired young leaves of jute plant. The young branches of jute plants are dried and then the dried leaves are grounded and preserved in bamboo baskets or containers. It is used to prepare curry and has some medicinal use too.

Traditional Methods of Salt Preparation

It is worth mentioning here that salt was once prepared in Assam by some indigenous process.

(i) Salt was prepared from *borpuni*. *Borpuni* is a water-born plant which is dried and burnt and ashes are collected. Such ashes are boiled and its residues are used as salt.

(ii) The leaves of *tazik* or *dimoru* plant are dried and its ashes are used as salt.[5]

Food for a Sick Person

The Misings know that an ailing person must take special food to regain his or her health. They offer special food to a woman after the birth of a child. Curries of plantain flower, *karum* stems, *cacas* with black pepper, leaves of *bahadaileta* (*Hupestis-monnieria*), etc., are given to a woman in post-natal period.

They believe that if the curry of *ottle grurd* is given to a woman in post-natal period, the flow of breast milk becomes sufficient. Like other sections of people there are some food taboos in pre- and post-natal periods of a woman. Thus a man suffering from pox has to take vegetarian diets. Spicy food is not given to a patient of dysentery. Such a patient is given loosely-cooked rice along with a curry of papaya, *kaschal* (*Mussanguinea*) etc.

During the summer season, bitter dishes are prepared from the flowers of *bakka* (*Adhatada, vigica*) or night jasmine, leaves of *neem* (*Media azard rachta*) *dorum* (*Lacus linifolia*) or dry leafs of jute to help people get red of worms. Almost all

5. J. Khonikar, *Chutia Jatir Itihas Aru Loka Samskriti*, p. 419.

their daily activities are directed towards the solution of the food problem. The daily life of the Mising folk is mainly devoted to the primary task of food collection.

In my field visit to the Godhia Mising Gaon of Jorhat district one aged informer Sri Priya Rampow (70) remembering his early days, said that oil was not commonly used in his early days while making curries. They get the taste of oily foods in festivals only.

Although the curries were cooked without adding oil it was very tasty due to the use of tender leaves of vegetables and matured roots in sufficent quantities and perhaps proper combination of items.

Food Prohibition : Gennas

There exist some traditional rules of prohibition relating to food items in the Mising community. It rests on faith held from generation to generation. They refrain from the use of chillies for one meal on the occasion of any rituals function. The people of village observe *genna*s for two to five days by abstaining from certain kinds of food in *Dobur, Ali-eye-Ligang* and *Porag.*

In their individual rites they have to eat all the meat on the same day cooked for the occasion and no part of it is to be preserved. All the food offered to God is prepared (cooked) by the left hand and no chilly is used in it.

Milk is generally not taken as their food item. A pregnant woman is not allowed to eat eggs.

An improvement of diets can be seen in recent years. Some vegetable fruits like *kopo, bangoc,* brinjal, *pakom, marsang, tayo, otosad* are prohibited at night in the month *Puh* and *Māgh*. Similarly *lou, urohi,* brinjal are prohibited in the month of *Puh, Jeṭh* and *Bhāda* of the Assamese calendar.

Chapter 8

Folk Costumes of the Misings

COSTUMES is a marked characteristic of any culture. Fashion in dress is as interesting to observe as any other fact of human self-expression.

Assam and the north-eastern States, which can be called home of various tribes have their distinct costume33s by which they can easily be identified.

The Mising women are fond of colours and they weave their own dresses at their own looms. Clothing of the Mising folk is generally sparse and made of thin cotton. In the winter season, they use woollen and *eri*-silk clothes for their clothing. Man usually wear white cotton or silk dress while women wear colourful embroidered dresses.

By way of systematic analysis, the various dresses of the Misings may rightly be divided into the following units:

(a) Male's dress.
(b) Female's dress.
(c) Ornaments.
(d) Headgear and hair style.
(e) Tattooing and body painting.
(f) Cosmetics.
(g) Utility articles worn with dress..

Since the Misings were once hillsmen, they used minimum clothes as necessitate. But the innate sense of beauty made them gradually use fine clothes and ornaments and many other things.

In early days they used *kaping*, which is a strip of cloth worn between the legs and warped in the belt of the waist. It is woven with coarse hand-made spun threads. This *kaping* in course of time underwent a change into *ganro-urgan.*[1] It was stated by old informants that about eighty years ago men used to wear a short piece of cloth like *ugon* called *matak.* Turban was a common headgear. Female dress consists of *gara* and *gapa. Gara* was an unsewn cloth like a *lungi* worn to cover the lower part of the body. It is now called *ega.* The *gapa* on the other hand is worn to cover the upper part (from waist) of the body which is now called *ribi-gasang.*

Male Dress

In case of male costume it is almost similar to the non-Mising population of Assam. The cut-and-sewn forms of garments are less used than the plain woven ones.

Some of their hilly prototyped costumes had modified and they adopted the present ones.

Mibo-galuk is a shirt with open front and short sleeve, with strips of coloured designs over the back and waist. The shirt hangs from the shoulder and cover half of the body. It is woven with home-spun cotton threads.

Gadu-galuk is another form of shirt made of cotton. Thick cotton threads are used for weaving this type of shirts which are suitable for winter. Red and blue strips are stitched together alternatively to give it a colour pattern and design. *Gadu-galuk* is dyed in blue, black or chocolat colour, but often cream-coloured *galuks* are favourite. These coats cover the body from neck to waist and are half sleeve and open in the front. It is used on ceremonial occasions, marriages, etc.

Damur is a piece of hand woven cloth generally 5 ft long and 3 ft wide which is used for headgear. Its two ends are decorated with coloured threads. The turban of characteristic shape is arranged visible on the top, above the forehead.

Ugon, is a lower garment and it is a long piece of white cotton cloth used like Hindustani *dhotī* to cover the lower part of the body from waist downward. It is wrapped round the waist, the longer end then plaited and tucked in at the front by making a loop and the shorter end is passed between the legs and tucked in the waist at the back.

The *ugon* (*dhotī*) is thin and traslucent. It has charmingly arranged foldes in

1. S. Gogoi, *A Study on the Cultural Life of the Misings of Lakhimpur District,* Unpublished Ph.D. Thesis Submitted to Dibrugarh University, 1996, p. 14.

rhythmic patterns. The *tangali* or *jinrak* (waistband) is a piece of cloth like that of a *damur* which is wrapped around the waist over the *galuk*.

> A Mising man wearing his *damur, galuk, ugon, tanglai* and a *dao* with its scabbard (*sobuk*) hanging across his chest is an imposing figure.[2]

Male persons use neutral colours, plain cloth and specific forms of dress. In the winter season, they use *eri-chador* (*tapungasor*), woollen shawl, coat and cap. Young boys wear the *dhotī* of *damur* like a *luṅgī* while in work and long pant and shirt while going outside of the village. The young boys also wear undergarments but the old have no such use. Similarly the young Misings use shoes and rubber sandals while the old generation do not use footwear. The aged men wear a cotton self-tied turban of white cloth. In byegone days men carried a curved knife (*dao*) in his belt. The scabbard is covered with dyed leather tape or ribbon.

Children up to 6 years remain naked in summer as seen in the villages. Half pant and *gangi* are used by them. Sometimes a piece of loin-cloth is worn round the waist. During winter woollen and warm clothes are wrapped on their bodies. From about 5 or 6 years of age upwards girls wear a "frock" and a piece of cloth imitating her mother or elder sister.

Female Dress

The dresses worn by girls and ladies differ from one another. The girls of one to three years hardly wear any dress. The dress of an unmarried girl is different from that of a married woman. An unmarried girl use an *aga* (a kind of *luṅgī*) to cover the lower part of her body from chest downwards. It is tucked in about the breast in thick folds and falls down up to the neel. In some places it is called *matak*.[3] It is generally blue or red coloured unsewn cloth. A blouse or *bodice* is used to cover her upper part of the body. A piece of cloth called *kupop* is used to cover the chest and back of her body. Slowly and gradually *kupop* is going out of use. The *kupop* is thinner and finer in texture than an *aga*. Another form of clothes having a beautiful motif at the middle which is called *rumbu* or *pothali* is worn over the body.

WINTER DRESS

The women use beautiful shawls woven out of imported wool or from *eri* silk and

2. N. Pegu, *The Miris of the Brahmaputra Valley*, p. 13.
3. Informer, Priyaram Pow, Bahphala, Jorhat.

from cotton yarn which they wear on their bodies to protect themselves from cold.

No socks for feet or gloves for hands are used tradi-tionally. Winter is beaten by warm of the fireside.

During the time of child birth the mother of the child wear a special dress called *para-rumbey*.

TABOO IN DRESS

Wearing a black *gara* (*mekhela*) in her period of menstruation is tabooed.

An unmarried girl does not wear *pathali* or *sagrog*. A married woman ought to use *sagrog* instead of *sagbung*.

DRESS OF THE DEAD BODY

A male dead body is to be dressed in new white woven clothes called *tongani* or *dumer* having no coloured borders.

HEADGEAR AND HAIR STYLE FOR THE WOMEN-FOLK

Mising women keep long hair. The girls generally do not wear any headgear. Women back brush the hair and bind it in the shape of a ball called *khopa*. This simple hair style is made by parting the hair at the centre and wound to form the *khopa* which can be seen on the back side of their head. Different kinds of hair balls (*khopa*) are made by the women to beautify themselves. Some are round and some others are of the shape of a spadix of banana tree. In Assamese language *negheri khopa* and *koldiliya khopa* are frequently mentioned in the folk songs. In Assamese proverbs *khopa* has an important role. In one such proverb the words run thus —

aor siga suli tar siga suli
mari jao negheri khopa

The one who has no sufficient hair to make a big knot (*khopa*) can collects the thrown away hair loops of others and thus can make a big knot with false hair.

To perform a *negheri khopa* type of hair style, the female folk use loops of black yarn or false hairs which are rounded together with their real hair, tightly knotted at the nape and are fastened with black ribbons. Hair pins, hair clips and brooch are used to keep the hair in proper position. Black thread and strings made of their own fallen hair are also used to bind the loop.

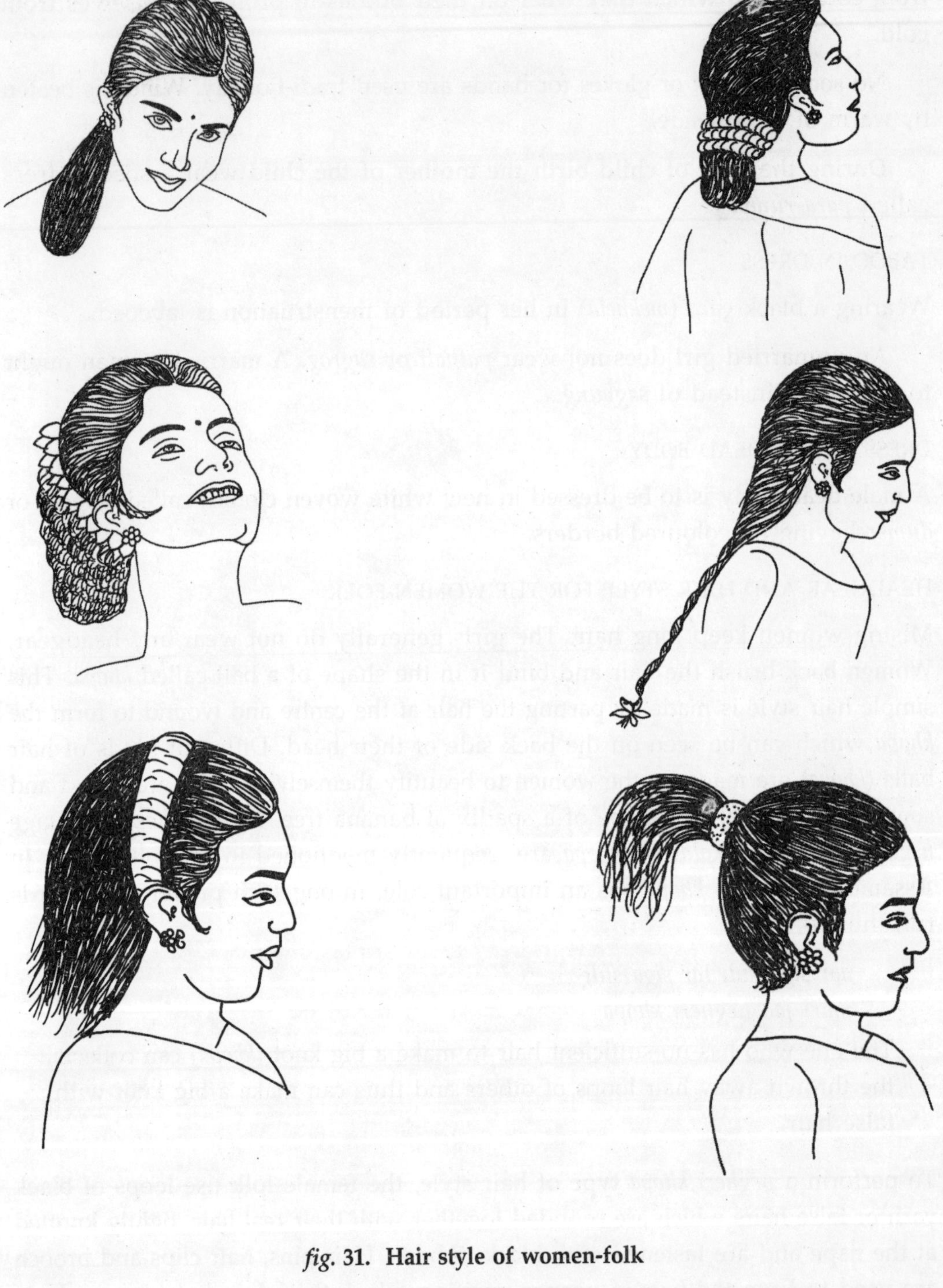

***fig*. 31. Hair style of women-folk**

fig. 32. **Female headdress**

To form a *koldiliya khopa* on the other hand a woman does not take help of any other ingredients then her own hair. Her hand combs the long hair smoothly and forms the desired complex knot (*khopa*). A comb is essentially used in styling one's hair. A wooden comb with decorated motifs in it was used as hair ornament in byegone days. They used flowers in their hair knot to decorate the hair. Chaplets of leaves and flowers are frequently seen around the high top knot of hair especially in the festivals and public celebrations.

The use of veil (*oroni*) is also seen among the married Mising women-folk like among other sections of Assamese society. Like the Hindustani women the Assamese women also cover their hair and even mouth with the ends of the *chador* that is worn by her. The Mising perhaps adopted this style or custom to take veil only in front of elderly people from the Assamese society. A simple type of turban unlike the male turban is also seem in the working field or during journey. Such turbans are similar to a veil having beautiful borders.

The hair style of an unmarried girl has something different. The young girl instead of making the knots (*khopa*) allows her hair to hang in a loop at the right shoulder. Clip, ribbon and brooch pins are used for perfection in looks. Hair pins purchased from the market are used to keep the hair in proper position.

COIFFEUR OF THE MEN-FOLK

At present the hair style of a man young or old is simple. He cuts the hair 3 cm to 5 cm long and parts into two unequal parts. Some people back brush their hair also. Partition of hair in the middle like a female does is uncommon.

*fig.*33. **Hair style of man-folk**

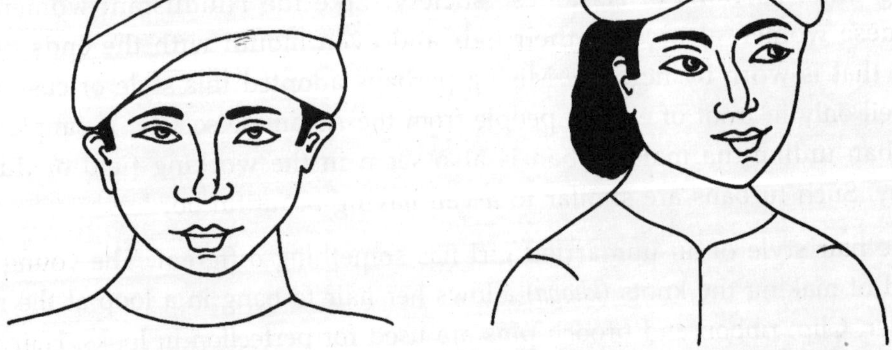

fig. 34. **Male headdress**

It is known from my aged informer that in early days the man-folk also kept their hairs like a woman and constructed a hair knot (*khopa*) at the back which contained a comb also. Of course, the side hairs were cut short and only the central portion remained uncut which helped to make the knot. A man without such *khopa* was not honoured in other Mising villages and not even allowed to enter the house. Artificial colouring of hair was not known. Now the people keep their hair up to the nape, like other people of the villages.

HAIR CARE

Both male and female wash their hairs regularly. Ingredients used in olden days was either *kalkhar* or *monichal* (a kind of fruits having highly alkaline poperties).

At present also this two things are not outdated among the village folk. People now prefer to use soap buying from the market for their bathing.

Mustard oil and *til tal* are used both the sex as cosmetic. No other traditional cosmetic items are found in my field study. Hair cutting at regular intervals is done with help of scissors and a comb. There is no professional barbar in the Mising villages. Some who are experts in this job help others. No payment is made. Shaving is done wih razors.

Ornaments

The elegance and refinement of the costume is reflected in the ornaments also. From ancient time gold, silver and copper are used to design ornaments. Gold is known as *hiraṇya* and *svarṇa;* silver as *rūpa* and copper as *tāmra*. These are continued to be used in ornaments often crusted with *ratna* or jewels. The traditional forms of jewellery of India are more or less in the same kind, slightly modified in certain respects though they may be known by different names.

The Mising man-folk once used ornaments of ear, fingers and neck which are obsolete today. The women-folk are fond of various kinds of ornaments and in modern age also they prefer their traditional ornaments. Those traditional ornaments are mentioned below.

EAR ORNAMENTS

The earrings worn by the ladies are called *kentu*. These are made of gold or silver or other precious stones. Four kinds of *kentus* are observed — (i) *birbir,* (ii) *takar,* (iii) *jangphai,* (iv) *thuria* or *turi.*

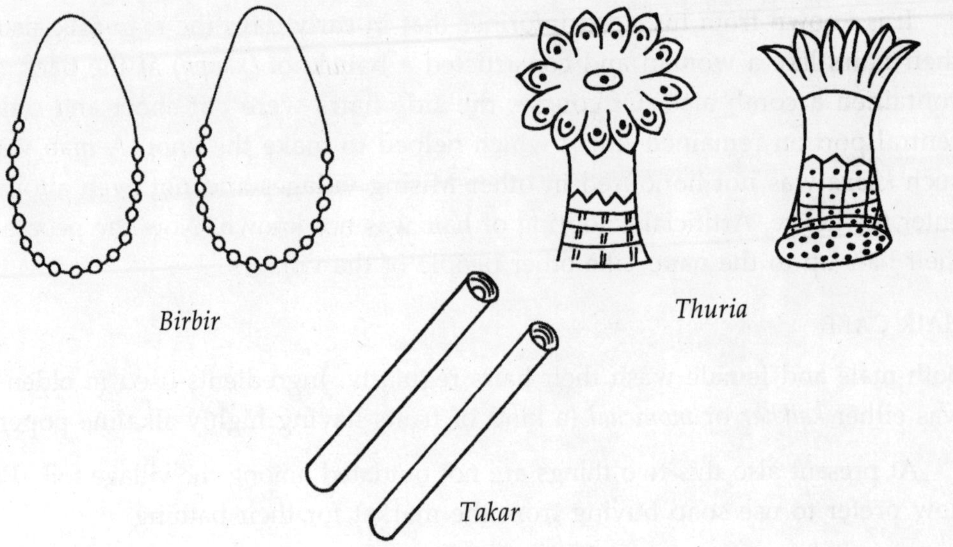

fig. **35. Ear ornaments**

Birbir is an ear ornament of white bead like the seed of a small plant, like the seed of a rice plant. Such seeds are braided together with a yarn and are used as earrings.

Jakar is the earring made of *pira* (a kind of reed).

Jangphai is an ornament made of amber and is coated with gold or silver at the ends. Small precious stones are set on both front and back.

Thuria is an ear ornament like the shape of a lotus with a heavy steam. It is made of gold and red coloured stones are studded on it. Silver made *thuria* is also popular.

The earlobe on the lower part of the ear is perforated with a single hole. After perforation a cotton thread is passed through the hole and is kept there for about two weeks is healed. Then the thread is removed and a fine bamboo strip or a fowl's feather is passed through the earlobe. For healing the wound the juice of turmeric mixed with mustard oil is applied. The perforation is done for wearing ornaments. In olden days men also used to puncture their earlobes for wearing earrings.

NECK ORNAMENTS (DOKSARI)

The neck ornaments of the Mising ladies are called *doksari*. Several kinds of *Doksaris* are used by the Mising women-folk. Those are as follows: (i) *tapi*, (ii) *galpata*, (iii) tampilamg, (iv) *sumyalaksin*, (v) *bartop*, (vi) *jonbiri*, (vii) *gajara*, (viii) *maduli*, (ix) *polomaduli*.

Tapi

It is a necklace made of white beads. The bead necklace is beautified by silver rings and metal pieces. *Tapi* is generally not used daily. It is worn only on ceremonial occasions. It is a symbol of wealth also. The beads are round and large and are hollow inside. The wearer hangs it round the neck.

Galpata

It is a metal ornament generally made of gold or silver. The ornament is more or less like a belt around the neck as it is attached close to the neck. The word *galpata* is of Assamese origin where *gal* means neck and *pata* means belt or strip. On the top and bottom of *galpata* two rows of white beads or red rubies are arranged on lines. In the middle portion several gold or silver stars like flower motifs are arranged. Fine coloured stones are studded on these flower motifs. Two ribbons are provided on both the ends to provide for a tie on the back of the neck.

Tapilang

It is a chain made of silver coins. It is used as a necklace.

Sumyalaksin

Tiger's claws are collected while hunting in the past. Those claws or nails were arranged in some order and worn like a necklace. It is now rare in use.

Bortep or Dogne

It is a necklace used by the *mibu* (the priest). This ornament is made of beads. It is believed that there are living and dead beads and the *mibu* uses the laying one for his religious performance.

Jonbiri

It is a golden neck ornament which seems like a new moon or like a bow. Some golden balls are hungs at the bottom. At its top a hole is made from which a ribbon hangs. Motifs of flowers, leaves, butterflies are carved on it.

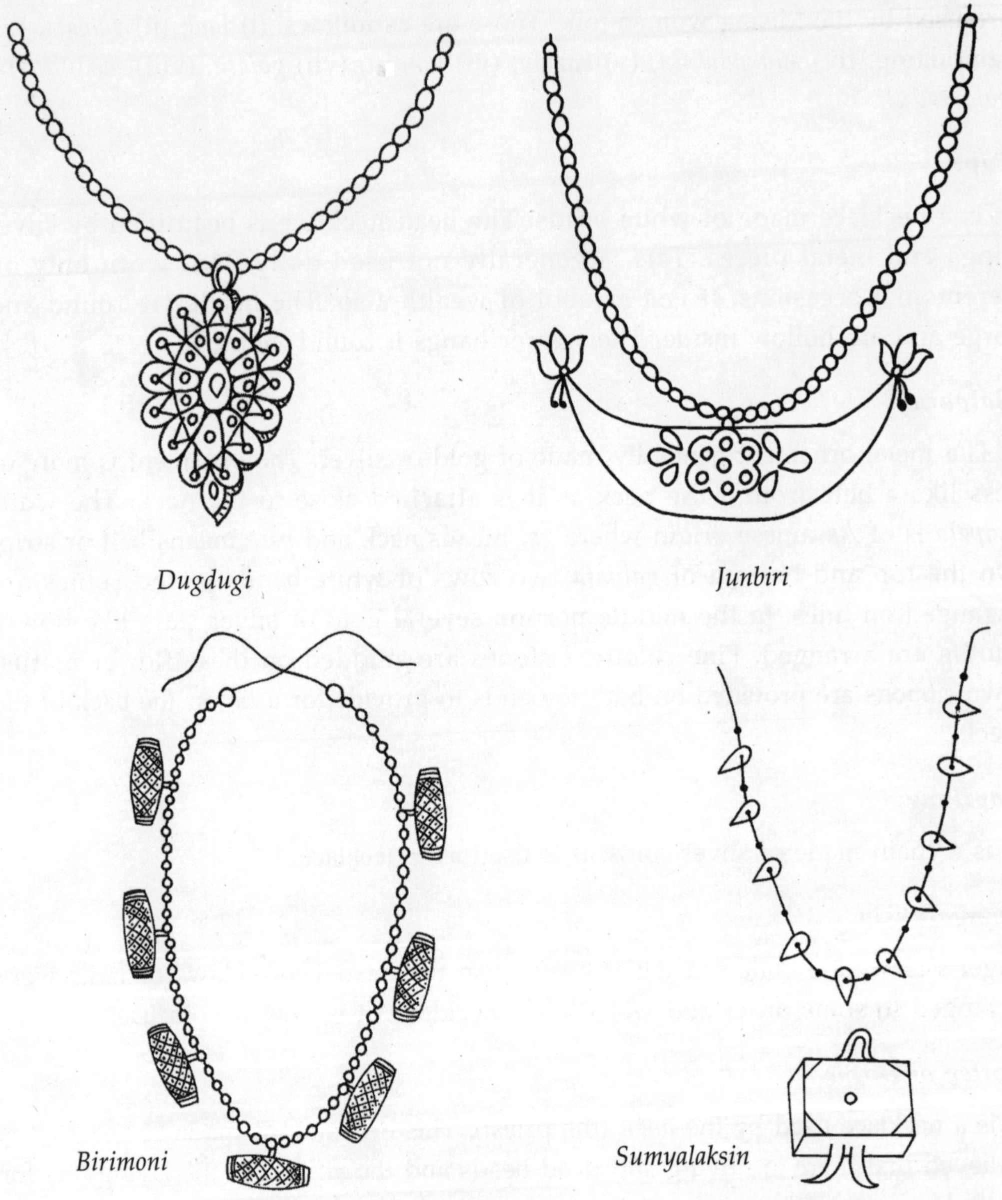

fig. 36. **Neck ornaments (Doksari)**

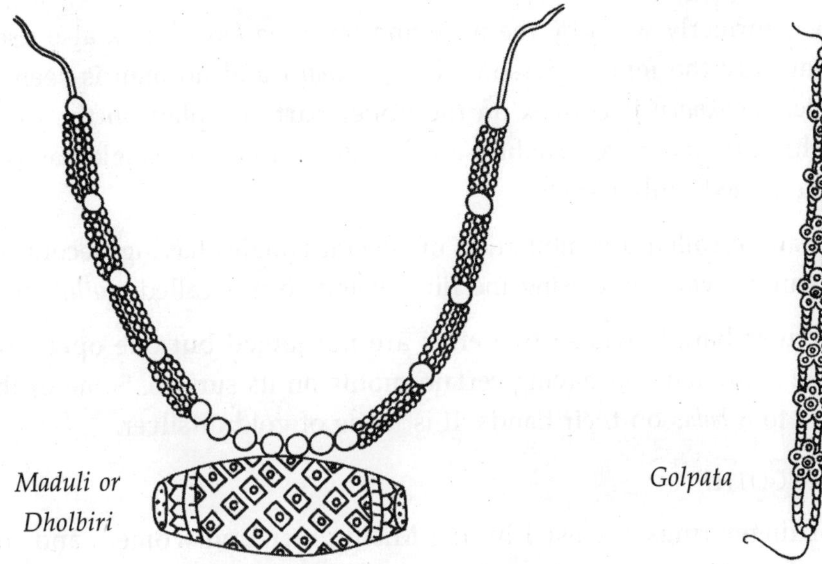

fig. 37. **Neck ornaments (Doksari)**

Gajara

Gajara is similar to a *jonbiri* but bigger in size. The middle part of *gajara* is of course more convex than that of a *jonbiri.*

Maduli

Maduli is a drum-shaped ornament made of either gold or silver. Red or blue stones called *bakhar* are studded on it. The inner portion is filled with resin or lac. *Maduli* is often called *dholbiri* because of it shape like a drum. *Maduli* is often fixed with a garland of red or white *moni*s (bead). The *moni*s are of different types, e.g., *pwalmoni, mottormoni, silikhamoni,* etc.

Dugdugi

It is a heart-shaped gold or silver ornaments on which red *bakhors*, i.e., tiny precious stones are studded. It is fixed in the middle of a garland consisting of red of white *monis*. A blue stone *moni* called *dogna* is also arranged with all the above-mentioned neck ornaments.

BANGLE (KONGO)

Kongo is a metallic ring worn on both the hands. Metals like brass, gold, silver, aluminium are used to make different kinds of *kongo*s or bangles. The types of *kongos* used by the Misings are — (i) *gumkharu,* (ii) *muthikharu,* (iii) *bala.*

Gamkharu was formerly worn by the male and later the female folk also used it and at present only the female persons use *gamkharu* and no man is seen to wear any bangle. *Gamkharu* is convex on the upper part and plain in the inner side. Like on other ornaments red rubbies are studded on it. The bangle has two halves which are joined with a stick.

Muthikharu can be called a combination of several bangles having decorative motifs on it. It can be worn by closing the fingers and so it is called *muthikharu.*

Bala is a circular bangle whose two ends are not joined but one open and pointed. It is like a circular rod having certain motifs on its surface. Some of the old ladies used 4 to 6 *bala*s on their hands. It is made of gold or silver.

FINGER RING (ANGOTHI)

A few forms of finger rings are used by the Mising men and women, and the rings are made of gold, copper or silver.

NOSE ORNAMENTS

Ornaments for nose are not popular. Today some girls use small rings on their noses. Ornaments for teeth, head and forehead are also not popular among the Mising folk. Similarly foot ornaments are unknown to them. The young girls in olden days used a smooth rope as a foot ornament. It was a cotton rope often red in colour known as *lagin*. In byegone days man also used certain ornaments of which mention may be made of the following.

(i) *Ludurai* was a metal made heavy garland whose upper part was covered with gold layers and shaped like a car wheel. It was worn as neck ornament with a black ribbon. Generally well to do family members used this ornament.

(ii) *Long karu* was a gold or silver made nail like nose ornaments worn by the young and aged man of the Misings.

Tattooing and Body Painting

Tattooing of different parts of the body was prevalent among the Misings in olden days. Nowadays tattooing is of limited use among the Misings. No tatto mark is drawn on arms, chest, neck or foot. The female persons always wear on their forehead a red spot or a black carbon spot (in the case of unmarried girl) and the married women were the same with *sindur*. Unmarried girls often seem

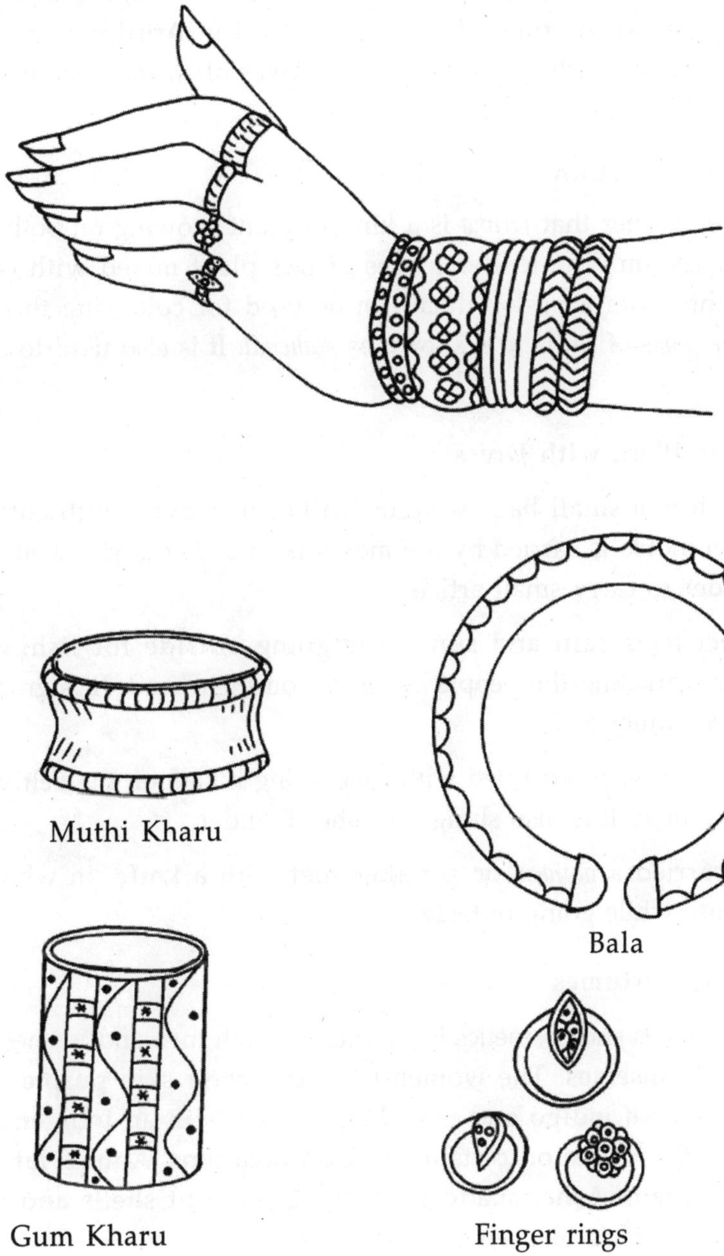

fig. **38. Ornament for hand**

to take a vertical line on their forehead instead of a round spot. The eyebrows are also painted with carbon black. An ommision to do so is regarded as a social and religious offence. At the time of the *Bihu* festival in April both boys and girls coloured their hands with *jatuka* by giving a layer of *jatuka* paste made from the leaves of a kind of tree.

PREPARATION OF JATUKA

It is mentioned earlier that *jatuka* is a kind of plant growing on both hills and in the plains of Assam. The tender leaves of this plant mixed with certain other leaves of plants from a paste which can be used for colouring the fingers and nails. In other parts of India it is known as *mahendī*. It is also used to colour in the hairs.

Utility Article Worn with Dress

A *sogon* which is a small bag made of leather or woven with cotton or wool having certain motifs is carried by the men-folk. It is tied with a belt or is carried on the shoulder to carry small article.

To protect from rain and sun while going outside for fishing, hunting, cultivating or marketing the people use a *japi* on their head. It is gradually being replaced by the umbrella.

A *dao* inside a scabbard fitted with cane string is tied on the belt by the males as a protective item. It is also slung over the shoulder.

Women carried a *payago* or handkerchief with a knife, in which they put betlenut for use while going outside.

Cosmetics and Perfumes

The use of perfumes and cosmetics is adopted by both men and women to decorate and beautify themselves. The women-folk stain their skin purple with henna, their hair blue with indigo and pencil their eyelids in an indigenous fashion. They decorate their faces on certain specified occasions. Animal fat is generally used as cold cream. Ashes made by burning coconut shells and mixed with mustard oil are used to blacken the eyebrows.

The old items of cosmetics are now obsolete and the younger generation use various creams purchased from the market. They use nail polish of red, purple and blue colours to decorate their nails of hands and feet. Talc powder and creams are used to smooth their face. The women in some houses rub the body with oil. The oil keeps the skin supple and the unguents give the skin its necessary elasticity in the heat of the sun. Vegetable oil and animal fat are the main items of the traditional cosmetics. Mustard oil, *til tal* are commonly used before bathing and are also used as hair oil. The use of perfumes in old days was unknown. Only in the recent years it is being used by the young generation especially on the marriage or festival occasions.

Chapter 9

Tradition and Change of the Material Culture of the Misings

Tradition and Change

THE term "tradition" has been derived from the Latin word *tradio* which means handing over something. Thus the term "tradition" in English means handing over and handing down being or delivered and so on.

Tradition may be written or oral. The oral practices or opinions which are transmitted to us from generation to generation are familiar to us and can be called tradition. It is the heritage of human society.

Traditional society displays significant social, cultural and linguistic variations, in which they constitute a historic pattern of society. Such traditional society has traits like simple techniques, domestication of animals, use of local raw materials and bartar system, etc.

> Everyone learns the culture into which he is born, the human environment and life experience of no two people are absolutely identical. Consequently, although a culture or society produce similar products these products are not absolutely uniform. No two people act and react in exactly the same way. Each person has unique personality.[1]

Social change occurs in all societies and in all periods of time, but the rate of social change differs from society to society.

---

1. G.M. Froster, *Traditional Societies and Technological Change*, p. 12.

No society has ever been static and socio-cultural change is a relative concept. Socially, economically, technologically and demographically, the tribal societies have passed a number of phases. Various factors determine those directions and also the rate of social change. It is observed that "culture is learn rather transmitted biologically." Men adopt new things and behaviours and also forget some parts of their tradition.

Traditionalism is an emphasis on past values and activities. It also implies a present time orientation.

> The Indian society has now changing itself from an agricultural to an industrial society from a colonial society with emperors and monarches to a republican society. From society based on caste and class to a society aimed to be casteless and with equal opportunities to every citizen guaranted by Indian Constitution adopted in 1950.[2]

After Independence, new policies were initiated to bring about the desire of socio-economic upliftment of the vast majority of population mostly in rural areas. The new constitution of India lays down the principle of equality of all citizens which opens a new chapter for the backward classes in economical, educational and social positions.

The beginning of nineteenth century initiated the process of change and transformation among all the tribes over the entire north-eastern part of the country.

Historically, the changes among the Misings are seen in their traditional cultivation and habitat. Until the early eighteenth century they lived in the hilly areas of Arunachal Pradesh. After migration to the plains of Assam, considerable changes have taken place in their habitat, art of agriculture and horticulture and in other fields of material culture.

They practised *jhum* cultivation or shifting cultivation in hilly areas and under such conditions individual ownership of land was not necessary. But after coming down to the plains of Assam they adjusted themselves with the flood prone areas of the Brahmaputra valley. Now they adopted the wet cultivation like other farmers of the state. Due to considerable influence of Assamese culture, their parent culture seemed to weaken gradually.

---

2. B. Kuppuswamy, *Social Change in India*, p. 6.

With the degradation of the environment and the depreciation of forest there has been a sharp decline in many of the traditional economic activities such as hunting, trapping of birds and animals.

The younger generation are involved in modern occu-pations like horticulture, settled cultivation, terrace cultivation and activities like business, trade and small-scale industries.

There has been a perceptible decline of crafts like dyeing, metal works, basketry in traditional ways.

The process of changes is visible in the forms of Sanskritisation, Westernization, modernization and development among the tribe.

They are not culturally poor and they have some better dresses, houses and furniture and household utensils, weapons and better food which are same among other settled agricultural tribes or non-tribes of Assam.

Social scientist M.N. Srinibash points out that lower caste adopt the customs, food habits, dress and rituals form the upper cast for higher position in the society, which is termed by Srinibash as "Sanskritization."[3]

This include the process of Hinduization of the tribal people. The same is applicable in respect of material culture also. The long-term British rule in India brought a change in Indian Society in almost every nook and corner. This is termed as "Westernization."

The tribal societies of different parts of the country, particularly Assam and the North-Eastern region are undergoing a process of transformation in the sphere of social, cultural, political and economic fields. In the past days, contract of the tribal with the outside world was limited and the changes in their traditional mode of life were generally slow but with the passing of time it is seen that the conservative nature of the tribal is giving away to some extent in the sphere of their traditional life and culture. The improved communication, easy accessibility to markets and free contact with outside people have led them to import many manufactured articles.

People are going for modern housing and non-traditional mode of living. Modern furniture, utensils are becoming part and parcel of the housing equipments. However, the poor and the rural families are still adhering to their traditional housing system and the mode of living.

3. Y. Sing, *Modernization of Indian Tradition*, p. 5.

In the field of traditional society, it is observed that the younger generation support nuclear family system. Most of the young educated persons are found to have their own individual families immediately after their marriage.

Any change due to cultural contact is usually accompanied by the process of cultural reinterpretation of the new and the old. The native and the foreign, may therefore co-exist and be combined and yet they may not appear as in congruent or self-contradictory. This process is called syncretization.

Modernization is the process of change by which individuals change from a traditional way of life to a more complex, technologically advanced, rapidly changing style of life.

D. Roy observed that:

> The impect of industrialization is something different which acts in a much faster way than any other agent of social change specially upon tribals. The impact of industrialization not only often forces the tribals to adopt many industrial cultural traits, it also often makes them bound to re-orient their socio-cultural life with significant structural and organizational change: giving up of many traditional beliefs, values and customs of their own adoption of many situation socio-cultural elements not only bring some change in their cultural totality. It often affects the tribal identity too.[4]

In this chapter I shall deal with these social changes in the Mising society that have made rural life remarkably different today from that of a decade ago. These changes and trends will make rural life in the future distinct from the rural life as we know it today. Twenty years ago they lived without the benefits of automobiles, electricity, electronic communication, chemical fertilizers and public education. The commercial advertisement on radio and television programmes promote a desire for new household goods.

These facts of changing profile are observed in the field study during this research work and the data can be divided under the following heads:

(1) Change in folk art and craft.

(2) Change in architecture.

---

4. D. Roy, *Man in India*, vol. 176, no. 4, p. 339 (The Munde — A Tribe in Agro-Indian Miliea).

(3) Changes in costumes.

(4) Changes in folk cookery and kitchen arrangement.

The impact of Hinduism is the main source of acculturation which influences all aspects of their life. Gradually, the old hily religious activities are either diminishing or vanishing.

CHANGE BROUGHT IN ART AND CRAFT

Folk art is bound to change with the change of time when the basic factors of the society are shaken. The Misings people who are holding a government or semi-government service or accept other business to earn money are no longer dependent upon their craft skills. They have in most cases moved out of their traditional villages to sub-urban or urban location and frequently deal with the modern way of life. Nowadays we find a few basket makers in a Mising village. Generally they fulfil the needs of the villagers. Plastic made containers take the place of the bamboo basket.

The crafts of blacksmithy and pottery have declined.

The artisans are commonly referred to as *bahoi*. They remain slow in service and only in the occasional festivals or marriage they create or construct some decorative art forms with the request of the host. As the Misings are coming in contact with the outside world their artistic vision is also influenced by the outsiders. But because of their conservatism towards traditional designs which have special significance and meaning the new innovations too are slow and gradual. The changes in the art of their traditional dress items are very slow. But we observed that many motifs are borrowed from the non-Mising Assamese designs. Some motifs also seem to be borrowed from the Bodo people of Assam, and these motifs are gradually becoming popular.

The local market provides the craftsmen opportunity to sell their products. In recent years some businessmen especially the shopkeepers collect these products from the villages and sell them in their road-side shops and in towns at great profit. Weaving is going on as usual, but the act of spinning has vanished. The weavers utilize yarns from the market. The raw material, viz., the yarn is now not widely manufactured in Assam. It is brought all the way from places like Mumbai and Chennai. Similarly rearing of silk worm is also decreasing gradually. It is observed that the Misings have not hesitated to adopt the improved technique but they are not willing to change their own motifs and patterns of weaving.

CHANGE IN FOLK ARCHITECTURE OF THE MISINGS

Most villagers like to have modern houses in place of traditional one. The economically sound families build their houses in new styles. Some people build their houses like other sections of non-tribal Assamese people do. In their opinion the ground floor houses are more comfortable than the traditional *chang ghor*.

It is observed in some villages that the families who build R.C.C. or modern "Assam type" houses also build another platform house by the side of the main house or at its back which is smaller in size and is used to perform the traditional practices. This certainly proves that the emotional attraction of traditional lore and respect to the traditions has not been totally lost yet.

It is discussed earlier that the same house is used for all purposes in the villages, but it is also observed that some families build saparate kitchen which is certainly the effect of the influence of the non-tribal Assamese of the State. Likewise they now construct separate rooms for sitting and entertaining guest which is often called "drawing room."

The following table illustrates the trends of modernity in five different Mising villages of the state.

Table 9.1 : Change in house construction

Name of the vill., dist., sub-division	*Numbers of traditional houses Chang ghor*	*Numbers of modern house*	*Matighar*	*Total*
Sundorpur vill., Jorhat Panchayat: Holongapara	14	2	4	19
Sham Mising Gaon Teok, Jorhat	20	Nil	7	27
Gondhia Mising Gaon Morioni	54	36	6	96
Ratanpur Majuli	95	40	72	207
Bohikhowa vill., Bokakhat	52	2	18	72

The above indicates that the numbers of traditional *chang ghor*s are greater in number but the number of modern types and *mati ghor*s are not negligible either.

Two influences have been working great change in home construction among the people. One is the trend towards modern building method and its popularity and the other is less durability of the traditional types of houses. Both trends change the structure of the Mising housing nowadays. Since a house is the most expensive single item which is essential for shelter of the family, it should be durable and adequate for living.

The non-Mising Assamese people in the neighbouring villages trend to construct their houses with bricks and irons which inspires the Mising folk too in that direction.

Trends of Settlement

The rural settlement of Assam specially on the river banks have certain problems of their own which differ from those in other parts of the country. The havoc of flood and soil erosion is the major problem which destroys life, property and cultivation. This certainly affects the rate of development of settlement in the region and contributes to economic backwardness of the people. Due to the soil eroison and heavy flood of the Majuli sub-division in 1997, many Mising people lost their houses and temporarily resided on the embankment or road sides. A few such families are resettled in grazing lands granted by the state government under rehabilitation programmes.

CHANGE IN FOLK COSTUMES OF THE MISINGS

People of the younger generation are adopting some new style but the older generation does not favour the idea of borrowing fashion of innovation on the traditional design and colours. Women's dresses are almost unchanged in villages but it is natural that instead of the traditional attire they have accepted *mekhela chadar* like other Assamese ladies. Women sometimes wear the same cloth in different ways to suit different occasions. The college going girls use *surridder*, the Punjabi fashions of attire and the "Indian Sari." Women in villages of course do not need to cover the shoulders.

In case of male costumes, it is easier to trace the influence of the Western dresses. The traditional *galuk* and *ugon* are gradually replaced by long pant and shirt. Among the educated and upper income groups, the machine made clothes seem to be popular both in rural and urban areas.

Footwears, like sandals and shoes of various styles have become popular. Foot ornaments like *marpong* and cane made bangles are now obsolete.

The hair style of man-folk has undergone complete change. Once they kept long hair and made a knob called *dumgog* like the *nisi* groups of people. Now they keep short hair like other plains peoples of Assam. The headgear is going out of use. The old style of *paguri* covering a part of the ears is almost gone. The young people wear woollen caps or clothes in winter instead of the turbans. The women-folk in byegone days used a silver ornaments called *murkuongappun* in their hair knobs. They also used silver hair pins (*murkongvggap*), bamboo hair pins (*ko:ti*) and the thorns of hispid deer which are now replaced by plastic pins and hair clips.

Similarly, although the old style of ornaments has not lost the popularity, yet the women seem to wear new style of jewellery or other modern fashionable ornaments which they are in fact, able to buy at low cost. Once men-folk used ornaments on nose and ears, which is obsolete among the new generations. Men today use only rings on the fingers as ornaments. Some of the traditional ornaments like *takpor*, *dognc* (neck ornaments), *nogorang* (nose ornaments) are now obsolete. Modern trend among the girls is to discard the earrings and the *thuria*. However the old ladies are not influenced in respect of their ornaments and dresses. One still sees some of the ladies without upper garments.

Terrylene shirts and nylon sarees are common. Preparation of indigenous dye is not essential because colouring materials are easily available in the market. The indigenous colouring process is no more in vogue and chemical dying is popular among the weavers. The easily available coloured threads in the local market do not encourage the production of old dyes.

The city jewellers copied the folk designs and by using morc malleable metal and they re-design the ornaments which seem to be popular among all levels of people. One of the items for which there is tremendous and continuous demand is glass bangles. Other glasswares are also popular.

Similarly plastic made ornaments are growing popular. Gems enjoyed great popularity with the people. It is therefore not surprising that the Mising also now utilize precious stones, corals and shells in their modern ornaments. Inter-State trade in the remotest corner encourages people showing interest in special designs of the other areas.

The women of Assam have hardly ever adopted purely foreign fashions. The Mising women nowadays use undergarments like *chemise* on the upper part of the body covering the breasts. It is either sewn at home or bought from the market. It was unknown to the old ladies. Similarly a lower garment called petticoat is used today by the ladies.

Aesthetically hand woven clothes are more superior to the machine-made clothes and their durability is four times more than that of mill-made ones.

People realized this difference and hence the weaving craft has been revived. Handicraft products can now compete with mill-made ones in the market.

As it is mentioned earlier, some ornaments called *dogna* (a blue stone *moni*) and *ludrai* are worn by the women-folk as necklace but it is gradually growing uncommon among the youths. A group of Abar people from eastern hills came and exchanged these ornaments for rupees. This proves that the *dogni* has its great value in the hills today.

CHANGE IN FOLK COOKERY OF THE MISINGS

Rice is the prime food in the past and present. *Āṭṭā, maidā, sūjī* are not used by the villagers but the town and city dewellers use these food products. Guadually these food habits are extended to the villages also.

For entertaining their guests, the Mising usually offer *apong*, but it is seen that they also accept the tradition of offering tea and betelnut like other sections of Assamese people.

Nowadays egg (*api*), milk (*gakhir*), oil (*tulang*) are also parts of the food list but there were unknown formerly. The readymade food items (packet foods) have also entered into the villages although these are used very occasionally. This is the impact of the shopping centres set-up in the tribal areas. Some well-to-do families accept the modern methods of cooking and gradually such processes are growing popular amongst all. The cooking media like *ghī*, mustard oil and various edible oils (hydrogenated oils) are used by both rural and urban people and the frequent visits to the urban hotels give the people new taste which they also introduce to their daily life at home.

The impact of Hinduism prohibits them from eating beef. Formerly milk was not taken by the Misings. Now milk and tea gradually replace *apong* among the followers of Vaiṣṇava faiths.

For the purpose of cooking and eating all the rural tribes and non-tribes utilize the age old metal pots and dishes and wooden vessels.

Some families use liquified petrolium gas (LPG) stoves and electric equipments heater, pressure cookers, etc. The pots, cups and dishes of Chinese clay and steel have also entered into the kitchen along with the plastic bottles, containers, jars, buckets, mugs and water containing drums. These articles are gradually replacing the brass metal dish, pots (*kahi-bati*), water containers (*lota, kalah*) and bamboo vessels and even the earthen-wares.

The kitchen arrangements are affected by the change of family structure. The joint family system has converted into nuclear family. Hence in such cases the cooking pots, pans, etc., are changed into smaller size.

An illustation of change of kitchen arrangements with the change of family structure is provided by some case examples given below.

Aluminium utensils are frequently found in the kitchen nowadays because aluminium utensils are much cheaper and lighter in weight than the traditional brass metal utensils and pots.

In my field visits to the Gondhia Gaon under Pub Nakachari Gaon Panchayat of Jorhat District it was informed that people used some copper three-legged stands to keep the dish for food which are not found now. The families now exchange these materials for metal dishes or plastic utensils. The *bankahi*s made of brass metal are still found in some families.

In another field visit to the Bahphala village under Baligaon Gaon Panchayat, a family under the hatriarch named Sri Sowena Doley said that his family possessed many utensils of "olden types" but after separation of the family members the old properties were also divided among them which are now replaced by the owners with smaller size metal pots or they even buy china clay pots and dishes. There was no cupboard, meatshelf to keep the kitchen pots in traditional kitchen or *moiram place.* Now the families like to keep a meatshelf in their kitchen.

CHANGE BROUGHT INTO THE AGRICULTURE

Agriculture was once synonomous with rural life in every part of the world. It is still so in a less developed country like India. In developed countries, farming is considered a business and the difference between it and other businesses are rapidly diminishing.

To increase the production in the field of agriculture, the Mising farmers also adopt new mechinery and methods like tractors, chemical fertilizers, irrigation, use of high yielding seeds in their cultivation like other people of the region.

The agricultural loans and subsidies facilitated by the government schemes help and encourage the rural cultivators in their field of work.

It was mentioned earlier that while living in the hilly areas of Arunachal Pradesh they practised *jum*-cultivation and a few agricultural tools were applied. Those are *egin* (bamboo basket), *epo*, *kiyap* (axes), *dao* or *yoktung*, etc. They now practise wet cultivation methods using implements like *nagal-juwali* (plough) with the help of bulls to plough the land.

At present some farmers use tractors and power tillers along with their traditional plough.

In the flood-prone areas no fertilizer was used except cowdung or other animal fertilizers to get good hervest. But in the present picture we observe that chemical fertilizers are also used by the people for increasing production.

Similarly insecticides, pesticides, etc., are now known to the farmers.

The competition in production among the farmers may also indirectly be a factor of rural change causing a rapid adoption of modern methods in cultivation. The farmers can do their works sooner and increase their production at a high rate.

In Assam, especially in the Mising villages the farm production increases not only for new technology used in the field but for utilizing more space in agriculture. The number of workers in the field gradually decrease due to the acceptance of other professions.

People grow three types of paddy, i.e., *sali, ahu* and *bao*. *Bao* is suitable for swampy land. *Bao* was the only paddy cultivated by them prior to the Independence of India.

The major change among the agricultural communities are that they were once full-time farmers and at present are part-time farmers. But it is a recognized fact that agriculture has increased dramatically in the last 30 years. This increase of productivity is due to the suggestions of extension workers, due to hybrid seeds, fertilizers, weed sprays and proper ploughing.

Another factor that always hamper the paddy production is the heavy flood of the river Brahmaputra and its tributaries which can be solved in some places by protective measures. In the areas which are still affected by flood the farmers cultivate *rabi* crops which are profitable to them.

After adopting other business, trade and official services their working time-table in the agricultural field has change.

CHANGES IN COMMUNICATION MEDIUM AND TRANSPORT

The traditional communication system within the neighbouring villages is beating of drums and bells (*lelong*) sending of messengers while certain communal problems like death of a man, attack by foreigners, etc., arise.

Such processes are still existing in rural villages. People now utilize the postal and telegraphic ways of communication. Radio and television (almost one in each villages) are found in each villages through which modern ways of communication enter into the life of the folk. Telephone and fax are mediums in only available in towns.

Likewise the transportation medium is also undergoing a tremendous charge. The traditional transporting system like elephants, horses, boats are now replaced by scooter, public bus and motor boats.

The farmers carry their local products to the market in bamboo baskets, bycycles and small carriages. The job of carrying is done by men-folk. Hand boats are the important conveyance for export and import in Majuli, Dhakuakhana, Bodoti and Dhemaji areas. Now motor boats are used for such purposes but the traditional hand boats are functioning as well.

Chapter 10

Summary and Conclusion

IN the foregoing chapters I have analysed some aspects of material culture of the Mising community living in the Brahmaputra Valley of Assam. A brief survey was carried out in 12 villages where the Mising people are living.

Dividing into a number of clans, the Misings, formerly known as the Miri belonging to the Mongoloid stock of the Tibeto-Burman group and before coming down to the Brahmaputra Valley, the lofty hills of Arunachal Pradesh were their traditional home. Their way of life, closely adopted to their surroundings persisted for thousands of years. There has always been socio-cultural as well as biological interaction among the tribes and non-tribes and as a result they are now living at different levels of modernization.

In the pre-British society, they were structurally fabricated by a chief called *gum* as its head. He, with the help of his council of elders solved the disputes of the villagers. After Independence the power of the *gum* has been transferred to a government official called *gambuha*.

In the villages, all the Mising houses look more or less alike. There is a small front room (*lotta*) at the ground level, followed by a varanda and large rooms (*soyer*) on piles. At the back there is an open platform.

In the front room, the ladies carry on husking of grains, storing of fuel-wood and weaving in looms. Each entrance can be approached by a ladder made of logs of wood bearing several notches. The floor of the main house is made of interlaced split bamboos and is supported on poles. The flooring of the platform is done either by planks or by bamboo matting. In case of bamboo matting it is woven either in hexagonal forms or in twill design. The hearth (*moiram*) is at the centre of the main house.

Certain rules are still observed in building a new house. In olden days, while selecting the site, usually a magician or priest was consulted, regarding whether construction of the house in the site would bring goodluck or badluck. Now the people are more concerned whether the site is dry and sunny or not.

In settlement patterns, following characteristics are noticeable:

(i) Settlements are generally located along the river sides near the agricultural fields. The settlements have assumed a more compact form.

(ii) The influence of traditional caste, clan, kinship and language has led to the development of compact form.

(iii) Each village has its own common place for meetings and discussions. The traditional design of *chang ghar* dominates the villages.

(iv) The distribution depends upon soil fertility agricultural production, natural water supply, grazing ground, etc. Most villages are unplanned, smaller in size and closely set-up and are best with poor transport facilities. For this reason they are often close to the river courses. They use building materials available locally. Climate and vegetation have profound effects on their house type. Bamboo, reed, straw, grass or leaves are the dominant building materials used in the construction of houses.

The salient features of distribution and density of rural settlement and their pattern of houses and modern impact have been examined in detail.

Craft traditions are slowly vanishing along with their skills and folk technologies. With the coming of the British rule in India, the crafts of this land were thrown off and industrial capitalism was projected into India. It came into conflict with the age-old economy of the country. The rich classes preferred articles of foreign make to native products.

The breaking up of joint family system also affected many crafts. Under the old system, the family was the heart of economic production. Collective labour on their traditional craft is impossible under new nuclear family system. Hence their traditional income sources are stopped and new ways of earnings are found.

For the economic development and employment opportunities of the people, the craft should be revived and developed. The problem of the crafts and craftsmen should be solved by revival and reorientation of craft traditions. This can be done by suitable schemes of self-employment for the youth by improvement of designs, promotion of exports and internal marketing.

Weaving is one of the great folk industry that supports the economy of the Misings. It has not declined although the industry made clothes occupy the market in every nock and corner of the state. Observing the working spirit of the young weavers it can be expected that this handicraft industry will remain in its proud position in future. Every Mising house has a loom and this enables the women, both young and old, to give full vent to their love for this craft. The craftsmen of other parts of India have improved their techniques while the Mising craftsmen have failed to keep pace with them.

The weaving of *gadu* or *mirgim* declined in the villages due to the poor supply of cotton. Once the hilly tribes come down with load of cotton from the hills of Arunachal Pradesh and Nagaland and exchanged it for dried fish and old ornaments — a tradition which is now stopped. In recent years, mill-made yarn has become more popular and production of cotton has sharply declined. Yarn is bought from miller, though a small quantity is spun in the village also.

The Misings of Assam have developed their primitive culture by inventing and adopting traditions from others. Their material culture comprised the use of iron and wood for making their tools, silver, gold, copper, for fashioning their ornaments, cotton and silk for spinning and weaving, horn and ivory for making comb and musical organs, the utilization of leaves, barks and gourds for food vessels, etc. Use of wild grass and bamboo for weaving basketry, mats and for building their houses, jungle creepers and jute fibres for making of ropes and strings required for many purposes and so forth.

The Mising folk art on various forms of costumes are fully appreciated by society at large. It has not undergone any decline but has been modified up to some extent which is accepted by other sections of Assamese society. Their textile designs with distinctive motifs and varieties of colour are associated with some meanings which have sociological significance and mystic ideology knitted with religious belief.

The motifs on their clothes also indicate the high degree of craftsman ship and artistic excellence.

At present the interest in folk arts and crafts are growing. Modern artists often find inspiration in old art, and a lot of people execute old skill as a hobby.

Majority of the cultivators still use indigenous implements manufactured by village carpenters. A number of improved tools and implements are gradually being adopted by the cultivators, artisans and craftsmen. Factory produced implements influenced the carpenters. The implements made of iron are not indigenously made but are purchased from the urban markets.

The Misings normally take two meals a day, lunch in the midday and dinner in the evening. There is no variation in the menu at these meals. Every family brews its own *apong* and serves it as a drink and food throughout the day to everybody irrespective of age. It is essential in any traditional religious festival. The gap between the meas are filled up by sips of *apong*.

Meat and fish are occasional delicacies; fish when a catch is organized and is successful and meat when there is a sacrifice or festival in the village. Boiled food with salt and chilli are most common. Frying has been recently adopted. Although they cultivate mustard seed, mustard oil is sparingly used as foodstuff. They generally mixed the pulse with vegetables. Women and children folk collect wild edible greens from the forest and fields.

The Misings were familiar with the general method of boiling, baking and frying food. Modern baking ovens have not replaced the traditional fire place (*moiram*) and methods like baking in hot ashes.

Social scientists, however accepted acculturation as an important element of social change which denotes the transformation of culture or social elements from one another.

Though the Misings have their own language and tribal religion, they have now accepted the Assamese language and the Hindu fold of religion.

Due to the advancement of the communication system to the rural areas in different ways, the isolation is being broken up among the people. Social changes are taking place in their societies in tremendous space. It is noticeable in their cultural activities. In an independent and rapidly developing India, all the people come forward into the stream of modern life. But this can be perfect only if it flourishes without harming the fine qualities of our age-old culture which can contribute to the rich Indian aggregate culture.

A movement for preservation and re-practices of folklore material has been launched today in almost all parts of Assam. The Misings of Assam also show their attention to preservation of their racial, religious and tribal identities. Their art and craft hidden the old heritage. Their costumes and ornaments reflect their aesthetic values.

As we know every person spontaneously learns the culture into which he is born and the life experiences of no two persons living in two ends of the country are absolutely identical. So the heritage of every small nationality is felt important by the social scientist.

The young blood always seeks change. The traditional Mising culture is in a transitional phase and is passing through the process of acculturation in many aspects. There is a change in family structure, social institutions and the caste system. Though the rate of change is quite slow, the fact remains that the Misings are gradually adopting the habits of the outsiders. Marriage customs are changing gradually. Marriage with non-Misings has been started. The set of old laws seems to be threatened. The people are also becoming aware of social evils and the unhealthy traditions.

Now the people in remote villages also perfer household articles like hurricane lamp, gas light, etc., instead of burning fire, wood for light at night, torches for a night journey, etc. Radio and TV for information and entertainment, cycle or scooter for transport, umbrella for rains: razors, scissors for hair cutting, sawing machine for log cutting and machine for sewing clothes, hand pumps for water supply, etc., have grown popular.

In the field of education, politics, business and journalism the tribe contributes a lot to strengthening the state. They select their representatives for panchayat, assembly and parliament.

Suggestions for Upliftment

On the basis of this study following suggestions are forwarded for uplift, welfare and progress of the tribe.

(1) The customs and practices which are felt essential should be preserved.

(2) The folk craftsmen should be encouraged both by the public and the government that they can earn more and more for progress in economic life.

(3) Modern technology, hybrid seeds should be introduced in the field of agriculture for good harvest.

(4) Landless farmers should be allotted land for cultivation.

(5) Weavers, carpenters, bamboo workers (basket makers) should be given loans in subsidiary basis for their establishment.

(6) The Misings of Assam have been harassed by flood every year. It is the duty of the government to try to save their life and property from flood with the help of modern engineering and technology.

(7) All India Radio, regional T.V. stations should feature special programmes relating to the folk culture of the Misings and the folk artists should get chances in realizing their creative potential through these mass media.

(8) The government should open craft centres with a view to promoting the local products, making them available to the local people, reducing their dependency on outside products and thus popularizing them in state and national level.

(9) The craftsmen should be enable to revive their works in the light of modern requirements and taste.

From a specific standpoint, and from findings based on observational and interview evidence I conclude with the following lines.

Cultural interchange and assimilation brings the Mising tribe to the present position. Everyone is borrowing something from another culture in order to complement or replace his own. All the cultures are not fully assimilated. Some of them maintain distinct identity and yet pave the way to peaceful co-existence.

Examining all, it can be concluded that the Mising people are still maintaining their traditional identity, and can be considered a chief component of the Assamese culture.

Informants

The selection of informants for intensive study was made on the following basic

Name and address of the infomant	*Age*
Smt. Minashori Kutun 2No. Dah-ghoria Bodoti, Lakhimpur	28
Smt. Muruli Chinta Kamalabari Ghat, Majuli	47
Smt. Royna Gum Dhopak Goan South Kamola Bari, Majuli	35
Sri Bhupen Pegu P.O. Bahphala Jorhat	35
Sri Sowana Pegu Bahphala, Goan Jorhat	60
Sree Rajen Pow Gandhia Mising Goan Jorhat	32
Sree Priya Ram Pow Gondhia Mising Goan Jorhat	70
Sree Manik Yein Dikhowmukh Jen Mising Goan, Sibsagar	65
Mr. Amulya Mili	35
Mrs. Rupa Mili Dichangmukh, Sibsagar	30

Pl. 1. Border (*Pari*) of a *Ribi-gasang* (Motifs : Diamond and zig-zag lines along with cross marks).

Pl. 2. Border (*Pari*) of a *Ribi-gasang* (Motifs : Diamond inside diamond on green grounds. For *Gasang* diamond motifs are incomplete).

Pl. 3. Border (*Pari*) of a *Ribi-gasang* (Motifs : Floral motifs. Eight lines for the *Ribi* and three lines for the *Gasang*).

Pl. 4. Border (Pari) for a *Ribi* (Motifs : Dotted lines with alternate colours. The *Ghai* consisted of diamond and paharia design. Above the main *pari* triangles are connected with five dots each).

Pl. 5. A *Ribi* and a *Gasang*. (Motifs : The main motif consists of unequal squares of different sides. The *Ghai* is consisted of cross marks and diamonds. Alternate '+' marks of red, white, yellow and blue are occure for the ribi and both '+' and '-' marks occur for the *Gasang*.

Pl. 6. A *Ribi* containing flower motifs with multicoloured bands.

Pl. 7. A *Ribi* containing dotted lines.

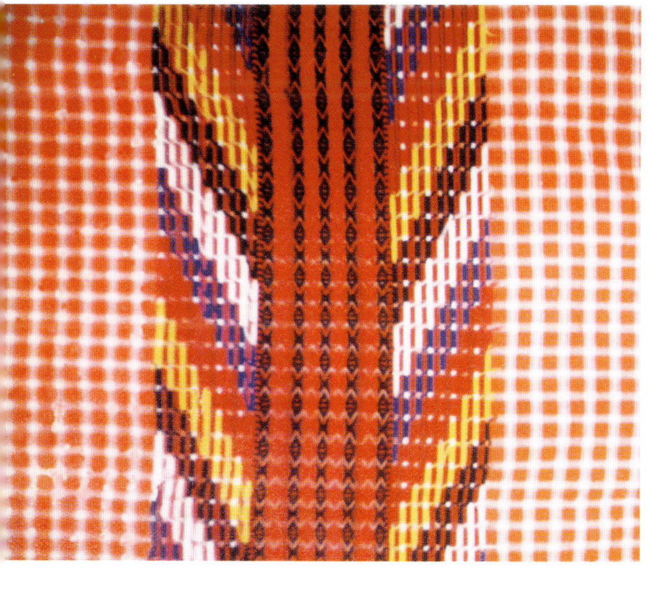

Pl. 9. *Pathali* (Female dress) (Motifs of a butterfly is depicted in the middle).

Pl. 10. *Pathali.*

Pl. 11. Embroidery (Needle works)

Pl. 12. Table cover, a Mising girl is performing frame embroidery.

Pl. 13. *Ribi Gasang*. Orange, blue, violate and white coloured diamond motifs are drawn on red ground.

Pl. 14. Needle work (embroidery). Animal and floral motifs.

Pl. 15. Decorative works on *Chaloni* on which a lotus and two birds are drawn.

Pl. 16. *Ribi Gasang* (multi coloured).

Pl. 17. Frame work of embroidery (woolen works).

Pl. 18. A red coloured *Ribi* containing motifs of butterflies.

Pl. 19. Shawls and *Ribi.*

Pl. 20. *Gamosa* or *Damur.*

Pl. 21. *Gamosa* or *Damur.*

Pl. 22. *Gamosa* or *Damur.*

Pl. 23. *Ribi Gasang.*

Pl. 24. A *Chanaki* (Draft for loom embroidery).

Pl. 25. A *Gasang* carrying ornamental designs.

Pl. 26. Shawls.

Pl. 27. Border (*Pari*) of a *Gasang*.

Pl. 28. An artistic arrangement of a bath place for marriage occasion.

Pl. 29. *Ribi Gasang* (Bottle green).

Pl. 30. Woolen shawl (Red).
White, red and black stifs are occured alternately.

Pl. 31. Different styles of motifs in *Ribi*s.

Pl. 32. *Ribi Gasang* — white base (Motifs of butterflies occur).

Pl. 33. Shawl. Flowers of different colours occured on a black ground.

Pl. 34. Storing baskets (bamboo uses).

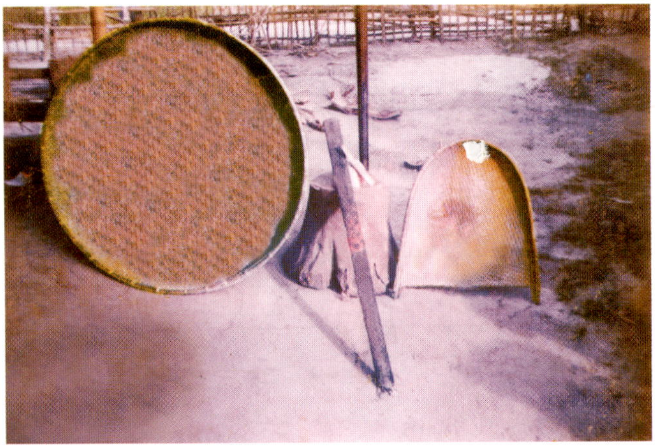

Pl. 35. Husking device and winowing fans.

Pl. 36. Storing basket (cane work) for cloth (*Japa*)

Pl. 37. Cane made sits (*Mura*)

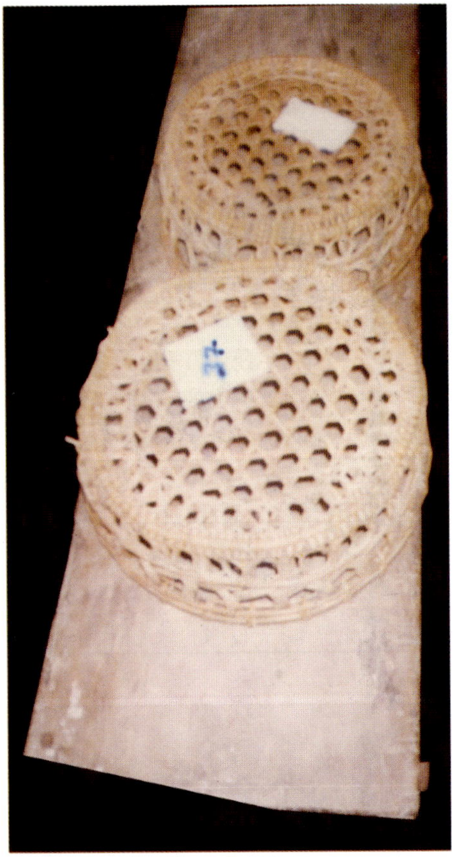

Pl. 38. Bamboo made *Japa* and fans.

Pl. 39. A hat made of sun grass.

Pl. 40. A long bamboo bridge on the way to Jangrai Mukh (Majuli).

Pl. 41. Wood cut for furniture.

Pl. 42. Transitional musical instruments.

Pl. 43. Mats made from a kind of grass.

Pl. 44. A bullock cart. bamboo baskets and metal pots.

Pl. 45. Baskets and fishing traps.

Pl. 46. Spining from cotton for weaving *Gadu*.

Pl. 47. A four post loom.

Pl. 48. Preparation of *Boo*. (before looming).

Pl. 49. A women in her loom.

Pl. 50. A *Gadu* (*Mirjim*).

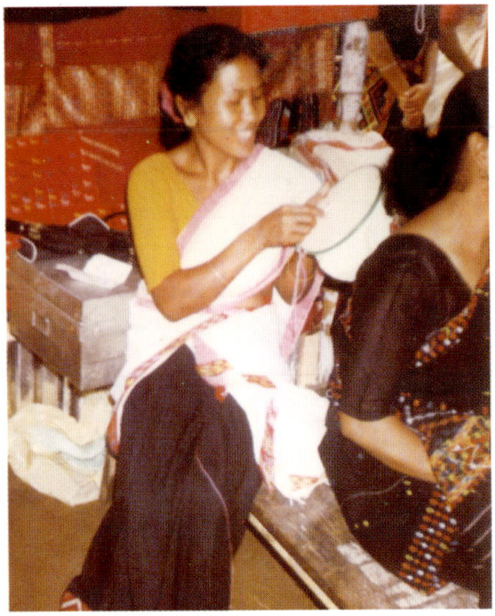

Pl. 51. A Mising girl is busy in embroidery.

Pl. 52. A typical house in Bahpholla village Bamboo, threads, wood are the material used for construction.

Pl. 53. A Modern house in Bahpholla village. Roofing materials used in this construction are galvanised sheets (tin). The walls are plastered with mud. It contains eight windows and four doors. The posts are made of cement and iron rods (RCC). Coconut and Battlenut trees are seen in the house shed.

Pl. 54. A house under construction

*Pl.*55. A small house.

Pl. 56. A modern type of house under construction.

Pl. 57. Granary.

Pl. 58. Buffalo cart carrying paddy from the field.

Pl. 59. Cultivation of mustard seed.

Pl. 60. Fishing nets arranged in the Janji river.

Pl. 61. Fishing arrangement in a narrow cannel.

Pl. 62. Fire Place (*moirum*) inside a house.

Pl. 63. Drying of fishes.

Pl. 64. Making of *pop* for apong.

Pl. 65. Brass utensils (*Ban Kahi* and *Ban Bati*).

Pl. 66. Working time dress of a woman.

Pl. 67. Cultural procession of the girls in the mising Agom Kabang.

Pl. 68. Four Mising girls in their traditional dress.

Pl. 69. Girls in their traditional dress.

Pl. 70. Back view of two girls wearing traditional dress and head gear.

Pl. 71. Hair style of four girls.

Pl. 72. Three girls in colourful costumes.

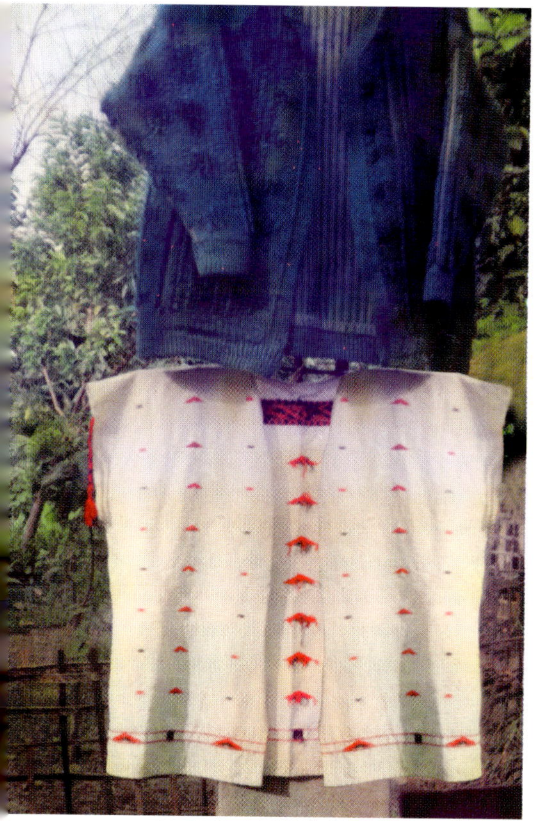

Pl. 73. *Mibu galuks.*

Pl. 74. An aged couple.

Pl. 75. Working time dress of two women.

Pl. 76. Traditional ornaments.

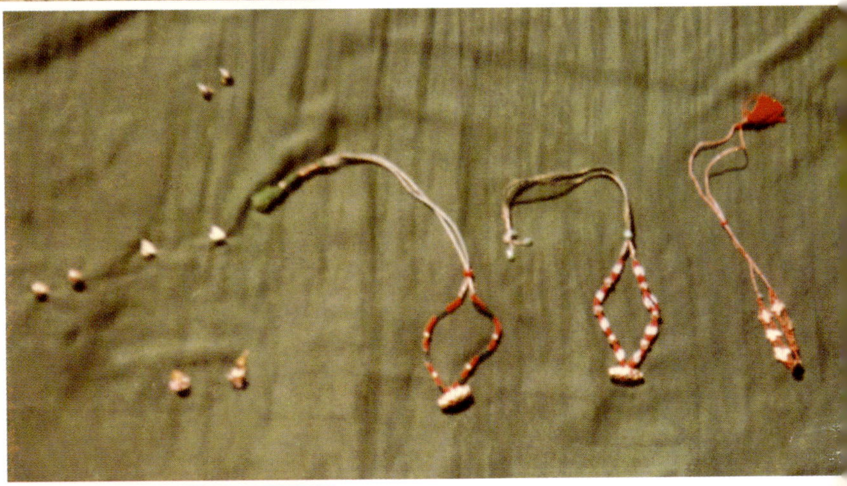

Pl. 77. Hand ornaments.

Glossary

Abu : father

Adi : mountain, a tribe of Arunachal Pradesh

Ading : meat

Aga : female dress

Ago : grave

Ago-gulang : place of burial

Aie-sakam : ritual for goddess of pox

Akai vaji : fried bile of fishes

Akhai : puffed rice

Ali-aye-ligang : a festival of the Misings

Alig :bride Price

Ambug : fried rice

Amdung : a kind of paddy

Ami : man

Amion oying : a curry of rice

Amo : elder brother

Amro : a variety of paddy

Anga : A kind of arum

Angothi : finger ring

Annoi : mother's/father's younger brother

Anyi : father's sister

Aong-bang : songs of worship

Apin : cooked rice

Apong : rice beer of the Misings

Appe/Apv : egg

Apperanam : boiled egg

Ara-adum : bride price

Argina-matinuni : a vegetable

Arooakum : gift

Arun : pocket

Arung : residue of rice beer

Asi : water

Asup : bamboo mat

Avn-attar : gold ornament

Baau : border of a basket

Bahak : a plant

Bala : a kind of hand ornament

Balang : jackfruit

Bango-kabang : councils

Bana-kabang : several village councils

Bari : house compound

Baria : three-legged stand

Barnam : fried

Baro : a variety of bamboo

Baro-gum : a section of the Misings

Basar : a clan of the Misings

Bat : cane

Bati : bowl

Be:ra : a stand for keeping dish

Beyonibhat : feast among the marriage party

Bhadailata : a climber

Bhebeli : wild vegetable

Bhonja-chaul : snacks of rice

Bihlogoni : a plant

Bir bir : a kind of ear ornament

Bonia : a group of Assam

Boo : loop of yarn

Book papu : a vegetable

Bori : a clan of the Misings

Borpuwari : an official of the voluntary organization made for *po:rag*

Bortep : a necklace

Buta : flower motifs on a cloth

Cbong : umbrella like device made of plam-leaf

Cdum : storage basket

Chadar-mekhela : women's dress

Chanaky : a draft copy

Chang-bihu : a festival of the Misings

Chang-ghor : platform house

Chapa : a fishing basket

Chor : unused land near a river

Cipat moni :bead

Cjugtapang : a kind of musical instrument

Cpo : winnowing fan

Cpob : a cake of herbs made for preparation of *apong*.

Crtog : beam placed breath-wise to support the platform

Damur : male dress

Dandun : musical instrument

Dangoria-sakam : worship of spirits

Dahgum : a section of the Mising community of Assam

Danking : a big pan

Dekabora : a leader of the youth

Dermi : a vegetable

Dholia : drum beater

Dhoti : male dress

Dobur : religious ceremonies of the Misings

Dodgang : a socio-religious rite of a deceased person

Doglik : collection of cash and kind for *po:rag*

Dognc : red bead used in necklace

Doksiri : a neck ornament

Done-bhot : harmful spirits

Donyee-polo : the sun and the moon
Doron : a vegetable
Doying : tales
Duglalanam : a form of marriage
Dula : a part of the roof outside the wall
Dumdum : drum
Dumer : napkin
Dumgag : wooden comb
Eco : bamboo shoot
Ega : a kind of petticoat used as an overgarment by the Mising women
Ego-tago : fried meat
Ekora : a kind of grass
Ekung : a kind of food male bamboo shoot
Empu : bamboo mat
Esang : starting
Futukola : a small plant
Gadhon : bride price
Gadu : blanket made of cotton
Gajara : necklace
Galpata : necklace
Galug : shirt
Gamic : draft of embroidery
Gamkharu : a bangle
Gamosa : towel
Gama : starving
Gaon burha : village headman
Gapa : a basket
Garo/gara : female dress
Ghai : border portion of a cloth
Ghat jal : fishing net
Ghilapitha : a rice cake
Ghot : earthen pitcher
Gonor-ugon : waistcloth for male
Goroka mari : paddles in a loom
Gotra : section/unit
Gudang : a clan
Gulang : wooden frame of a fire place
Gum/Gu:m : village headman
Gupid : a clan
Hira : a potter community of Assam
Homa : a ritual of the Hindus
Ikara : a kind of reed
Jatar : spinning wheel
Jati : a species of cane/bamboo
Jcingia ponam : cane and bamboo craft
Jonbiri : necklace
Jongga : A large cooking pot
Joying : cane
Jurki/Juluki : a kind of fishing trap
Kaban : ballad
Kabung : ladder
Kalakhar : Indigenous base
Kaligosunom : making of splints
Kaman : a group
Kandar : a group of the Misings
Kaping : a piece of man's garment
Kari : a group of the Misings
Khal : group
Khopa : hair style of the female

Khorikatdia : fried with a strick

Khorikinum : fried with a strick

Khorisa : item of food made from bamboo shoot

Khoroli : a curry

Kohar : brass worker

Kohinam : children song

Kol : hole of the fishing trap

Koldilia khopa : female hair style

Kolpasala : curry of banana plant

Koma : a Mising group

Komar : blacksmith

Kongo : bangle

Kordoi : a fruit

Kotari : knife

Kuli : a Mising clan

Kusia : a long fish

Kutum : a Mising clan

Lagin : a rope use as fool ornament

Laksin : railing to climb a ladder

Langi : a fishing net

Lasum : a Mising clan

Legai : a species of cane

Lenong : a metal bell

Litegsor : earthen vessel

Lodong : a clan

Lohar : a group of people of Assam

Lokosamskriti : folklore

Longkaru : nose ornament

Lotta : varanda of a house

Ludurai : a kind of garland

Lungi : male dress

Lv-sur : an earthen vessel

Lv-thung : an earthen vessel

Macandari : a vegetable

Magbo : elder sister's husband

Magob-duglum : a custom before marriage

Marsang : a kind of herb

Matak : an old style of man's shirt

Matsig : a kind of plant

Midang : marriage

Mili : a clan

Mimbir-yama : a social organization of the Misings

Mipag : man of other clan

Miri : a Mongoloid ethnic group of Assam

Mithon : an animal

Modvt-monum : craft

Mogordana : an U-shaped necklace

Moiram/Mcram : fire place

Momanonitom : game songs

Monichal : a kind of fruit

Moying : a sub-clan of the Misings

Murkong-attar : silver ornament

Murong : dormitory for boys

Muthi kharu : a kind of bangle

Mvrsi : chilli, pepper

O sap : a kind of fishing net

Ochi : purification

Oi-ni-tam : ballad

Okum : house

Olap : jute

Olum : a kind of curry

Ongo : fish

Opin : clan

Ori : corander

Oroni : veil

Otung : long-sized bamboo container

Oying/Owing : curry

Padina : a vegetable

Pagroo : a Mising clan

Paharia : hilly region

Paksung nang : treatment of unwoven yarn of a cloth

Pamegum : a clan

Panom : payer

Pararumbey : female dress

Pasum : a kind of herb

Patatdiya : boiled by packing with a leaf

Payago : handkerchief

Pegu : a clan

Pered : a variety of pulse

Pinka upin : cooked rice left over of the previous night

Piso : the floor

Pitha : cake

Po:yi : first brew of *apong*

Pobor : a large basket

Ponek : rice prepared for beer

Ponununam : a dance of the Misings

Poramas : fried fish

Porang : a kind of fishing trap

Potub : veil

Potum : a small basket

Randa : plane for wood work

Rash : a device used in a loom to beat the weft

Ratto : boiling

Resang : dormitory for the girls

Ribi-gasang : female dress

Rumbu : a shawl used by the Mising women

Sag bung : a traditional dress item of the Misings

Sagorog : a piece of cloth used as female dress

Salat : a group of the Mising

Salimari : a bamboo bar on which the loom hangs

Samoguria : a group of the Misings

Sandaha : snacks of rice

Sankar-sangha : a cult of Vaiṣṇava

Sewali : a plant

Shayangia : a group

Sokota : a bitter food item

Somuas : a group

Sonari : goldsmith

Soraidhaka : an embroidered item used to cover the *sorai*

Sumnem Panam : weaving

Sumnyok lak sin : necklace made of tiger's teeth

Takpor/Takar : ear ornament

Tamar : a group of the Misings

Tani : man

Tapi : necklace of the Misings

Thuria : a kind of neck ornament

Tilpitha : a cake of rice grains

Tiltal : oil of til seed

Ting : the two ends of a small boat

Ugon : lower garment of man

Yaga-chut lung : a visit of the newly married couple to the house of the groom

Yakchik : big knife

Yal : soul of a dead man

Yoksa : a big knife.

Bibliography

Agro-Eco Research Centre, *Rural Life in Assam Hills*, Jorhat, 1969.
Assam Institute of Res. for S.C. and S.T., *Bulletin*, vol. 1-1, 1994.
Atal, Y., *Changing Fronties of Caste*, New Delhi, 1979.
Barua, B.K., *A Cultural History of Assam*, Gauhati Bina Library, 1986.
Barua, H., *Folk Songs of India*, 1963.
Baruah, M.K., *The Idu Mishims*, Shillong, 1960.
Bered, H. (ed.), *Gazetters of India*, Nagaland, Kohima, 1970.
Bordoloi, P.K., *Family, Marriage and Social.*
Borkotoky, S., *Tribes of Assam*, National Book Trust, New Delhi, 1960.
Borthukur, B.N., Digboy S.M. (ed.), *Change on the Indian Fringe*, Cosmo Pub. New Delhi, 1980.
Chaliha, P., *The Outlook on NEFA*, Assam Sahitya Sabha, 1958.
Chandra, H., S. Mode, *Indian Folk Art.*
Charles, Fabric, *Indian Dress*, Sargam Books, New Delhi.
Chattopadhyay, K., *Handicraft of India*, New Delhi, 1975.
Chaudhary, B.N., *Arunachal through the Ages*, Shillong, 1982.
Chaudhary, B.N., *The Hill Miris of Sobansiri.*
Chaudhary, B.N., *The Khasi Cenvas*, 1978.
Choudhary, N.D., *Historical Archaeology of Central Assam*, SR Pub. Co., Delhi, 1986.
Copplestone, T., *World Architecture — An Illustrated History*, The Himālayan Pub. Group Ltd., 1971.
Cowfoot, G.M., *Taxtile, Basketry and Mats*, vol.1, 1954.
Das, A.K., *Tribal Art and Craft*, Agam Kala Prakashan, Delhi, 1979.
Das, H.C. (ed.), *Folk Music and Dances*, Vol. IV, Institute of Oriental Orissan Studies, Orissa.

Dermott, I.E., *Food for Modern Living*, New York.

Devi, L., *Ahom Tribal Relation.*

Dhamija, J., *Indian Folk Arts and Crafts*, Indian Book Trust, New Delhi, 1992.

Dhasmana, M.M., *The Romos of Arunachal*, Concept Publishing Co., New Delhi, 1979.

Dorson, R.M., *Folklore and Folklife —An Introduction*, Chicago, 1972.

Dundes, A., *Essays on Flokloristics*, Folklore Institute, Delhi, 1978.

Dutta, B.N. (ed.), *A Study of Folk Culture of the Goalpara District of Assam*, 1975, Unpublished thesis.

Dutta, D.N. (ed.), *Folk Songs of the Misings*, Gu, 1972.

Dutta, D.S. *North-east — A study of Mobility and Political Behaviour*, 1991.

Dutta, Parul, *The Noctes*, Director of Research Arunachal Pradesh, 1978.

Elwin, V., *A Philophy for NEFA*, Govt. of Arunachal Pradesh, 1957.

Encyclopodia Britanica, E.B. LTD., London, vol. 9.

Faulkner, Ray, *Art Today*, Henry Hott and Comp., New York, 1945.

Forbs, R.J., *Studies in Ancient Technology*, Vol. III, Netherlands, 1955.

Froster, G.M., *Traditional Societies and Technological Change*, Allied Publishers Pvt. Ltd., Bombay, 1973.

Ghose, B., *Traditional Art and Craft of Bengle*, Calcutta, 1981.

Gohse, B., *Profiles of Social Change*, New Delhi, 1979.

Goswami, P.D., *Folk Literature of Assam*, Gauhati, 1954.

Goswami, T., *Kuki Life and Lore*, N.C. Hills, Council Haflong, 1985.

Grait, E., *A History of Assam*, LBS Pub. Gu., 1984.

Hjorth, H., *Principles of Wood Working*, USA, 1946.

Indian Council of Social Research, *A Survey of Research in Sociology and Social Anthropology*, vol. III, New Delhi, 1972.

Institute Oriental and Orissan Studies in India, *Folk Culture*, vol. III, Folk Art and Craft.

Jain, N., *Indian Threatre, Tradition Continuity and Change*, Vikas Pub. House, New Delhi, 1997.

Kuli, J. (ed.), *The Misings — their History and Culture*, Dibrugarh, 1998.

Mahapatra, P.K., *The Folk Culture of Bengal*, Indian Pub., Calcutta, 1972.

Mann, R.S., and Mann, *Tribal Culture Change*, Mittal Publicatons, New Delhi, 1989.

Medhi, K.D., *Handloom Weaving and Designing*, Gauhati, 1914.

Mipun, J., *The Mising of Assam Development of a New Life Style*, Gian Pub., New Delhi.

Mookerjee, A., *Ritual Arts of India*, Thames and Hudson, 1985.

Naga Institute of Culture, *The Arts and Culture of Nagaland*, Kohima, 1968.

Nath, A.C., *Material Culture of Ao-Nagas with Special Reference to Basketry*, *Vanyajat*, vol. XIII, nos. 2, 6, 12.

Navajo School of Indian Basketry, *Indian Basket Weaving*, New York.

Pal, M.K., *Craft and Craftmen in Traditional India*, New Delhi, 1978.

Parmar, Shyam, *Traditional Folkmedia in India*, Geka Books, New Delhi.

Pegu, N.C., *The Miris of the Brahmaputra Valley*, Kumarbari, Majuli, 1956.

Punia, D., *Social Values in Folkore*, Rawat Pub., Jaipur, 1993.

Reed, Herbert, *The Grass Roots of Art*, Faber and Faber Limited, London.

Robins, William, *A Descriptive Accounts of Assam*, Sanskaran Prakashan, New Delhi, 1975.

Roshon, Alkozi, *Ancient Indian Costume*, National Book Trust India, 1993.

Roy Chaudhury, P.C., *Folklore of Bihar*, National Book Trust, India, 1976.

Roy, C., *Aspects of Padam Miniyong Culture*, Res. Dept., Govt. of Arunachal Pradesh, 1960.

Royal Anthopological Institute, *Notes and Queries on Anthopology*, London, 1971.

Saraswati, S., *Indian Taxtiles*, The Publication Division, 1961.

Sarma, N.C., *Essays of the Folklore of N.E. India.*

Sarma, N.C., P.C.B. Das. Dutta, *A Handbook of Folklore Material of N.E. India*, ABILAC, Gu. 1974.

Sen Gupta, S., *Folklore Research in India*, Calcutta, 1964.

Sen, S. (ed.), *Folklore of North-East India*, Om Sons Pub. Guwahati 1985.

Sharma, S.N., *A Socio-Economic and Cultural History of Medieval Assam*, Guwahati, 1989.

Sing, Y., *Modernization of Indian Tradition*, Rawat Pub., Jaipur, 1986.

Sujit Kumar Chatterji, *Indian Culture*, Universal Pub., Delhi, 1966.

Swamy, Kuppwa, B., *Social Change in India*, Vikas Pub. House, 1972.

Taid, T., *A Dictionary of the Mising Language*, TMAPK, 1995.

———, *American Folklore*, Chicago, 1970.

———, *Art and Culture of North-East India*, Publication Division, Govt. of India, 1986.

———, *Art of the North-East Frontier of India*, 1959.

———, *Ballads and Tales of Assam*, Gu., 1960.

———, *Folklore* (India), 1963.

———, *Folklore and Traditional History*, Mouton, Paris, 1973.

———, *Folklore in the Modern World*, Mounton Published, Paris, 1978.

———, *History of Assamese Literature*, New Delhi, 1978.

———, *India's North-East Frontier*, Oxford University Press, 1959.

———, *Women in Assamia Folklore.*

Vidyarthi, L.P., *Folklore*, Concept Pub., Co., New Delhi, 1985.

Assamese Section

Barua, S.C., *Sachita Kakar Silpa Parichaya*, Prakasan Parisad, 1962.

Biswas, H., *Loksangit Samikha*, Journal Emporiam, Nalbari, 1990.

Das, N., Rajbonsi, P. (ed.), *Asamiya Sanskritik Kanika*.

Datta, B., *Simphung Gungang*, Guwahati, 1986.

Doley, A., *Mising Loke Silpa Kala aru Sanskritik Dorshan*, Guwahati, 1998.

Gogoi, L., *Dimasa Sanskritir Itihas*, Nagaon, 1989.

Goswami, P.D., *Sahitya, Sanskriti, Itihash*, Guwahati.

Goswami, S., *Sahitra aru Sanskriti*, Mahik Printers, Amrup.

Karmakar, S.K., *Sansrti Aru Monon*, Loyars Book Stall, Guwahati.

Kayangu B. (ed.), *Mising Sanskritir Alekhya*, Birubari, Guwahati, 1972.

Kayangu V.M. (ed.), *Tarun Chandra Pamagumor Rosonawali*, Assam Sahitya Sabha, 1989.

Padum, N., *Mising Asamia Path*, Assam Sahitya Sabha, Jorhat, 1989.

Pamagum, T.C., *Mising Sadhu*, Ashom Sahitya Sabha, 1977.

Payang Kataki, S., *Miri Jatir Buranji*, Mornoi, Dhemaji, Assam, 1935.

Pegu, G., *Mising Jana Sahitya*, Pakali Pakasan, Dhemaji, 1996.

Sarma, H.N. (ed.), *Sanskritik Sangrah*, Vivaren Talika Purva Bharati, New Delhi, 1987.

Sarma, B.K., *Loka Samskritik Changam*, Dudhnai Session of Assam, Sahitya Sabha, 1991.

Sarma, C.D., *Asomor Lokakhel* (Article) *Sadinia Nabajug*, 3rd edn., 23, 13 April, 1966.

Sarma, N.C., *Loka Sanskriti*, Chardraprakash, Gu., 1997.

T., Taid, *Mising Bhasar Banan Padhati*, Dhemaji, 1992.

———, *A Dictionary of the Mising Language*, Dhemaji.

———, *Ballads and Tales of Assam*, Guwahati University, 1960.

———, *Loka Sanskritir Avas*, Guwahati.

Periodicals

Bulletin, Assam Institute of Research for Tribals and Schedule Caste, vol. I, IX, 1994, vol. V, 1987, vol. III, 1985.

Mising Agam Kcbang, Lusar Gogamukh, 1997.

Mising Agam Kcbang, Lusar Jonai, 1999.

Unpublished Thesis and Reports

Devi, N.R., *Effect of Cooking on Physicochemical Properties of few Rice Varieties of Assam*, M.Sc Dissertation submitted to the Home Science Dept. of Assam Agriculture University 1990.

Dutta, A.K., *Sociology of the Misings Community of Assam*, Ph.D. Thesis submitted to Guwahati University.

Gogoi, S., *A Study on the Cultural Life of the Misings of Lakhimpur District*, Ph. D. Thesis, submitted to Dibrugarh University, Dept. of Assamese, 1996.

Srivastava, R.P., *Impact of Community Development and Cultural Charge Among the Misings of Assam*, Project Report, Dibrugarh University, Dept. of Anthopology, 1972.

Index